'This is a fascinating scientific memoir of a life dedicated to uncovering the truth behind some of the most shocking crimes. And a book that will be essential reading for every aspiring crime writer. Her ability to reconstruct violent events in her mind and to see how forensic science can be used to reveal a suspect would leave even Sherlock Holmes in awe.' *Guardian*

'Offers a chilling glimpse into her life's work. The reader, too, becomes more gripped by the forensic details than the horrors of each case. Fascinating stuff.' *Sunday Times*

'If you're ever on trial for a crime you didn't commit, the woman you want in the witness box is forensic scientist Angela Gallop. If you're on trial for a crime you did commit, you'd better hope she isn't on your case … Gallop's book is compelling' *Daily Mirror*

'This book is rarely other than compelling and despite her modesty she comes across as admirable as well as likeable. She has a rare combination of qualities - a vivid imagination, a capacity for doggedly carrying out difficult and often mundane work and entrepreneurial nous. But what is even more rare is that she has deployed them in genuinely useful work for the public good' *Sunday Express*

'Gallop has compiled a casebook that reads like The Encyclopedia Of Murder.' *Daily Express*

'One of the profession's leading lights' *Woman & Home*

ANGELA GALLOP

When the Dogs Don't Bark

*A Forensic Scientist's
Search for the Truth*

With Jane Smith

HODDER

First published in Great Britain in 2019 by Hodder & Stoughton
An Hachette UK company

This paperback edition published in 2020

1

A CIP catalogue record for this title is available from the British Library

B format ISBN 9781473678859

Typeset in Plantin Light by Hewer Text UK Ltd, Edinburgh
Printed and bound in Great Britain by Clays Ltd, Elcograf S.p.A.

Hodder & Stoughton policy is to use papers that are natural, renewable
and recyclable products and made from wood grown in sustainable
forests. The logging and manufacturing processes are expected to
conform to the environmental regulations of the country of origin.

For Jeremy, Simon and Mic for their unfailing optimism and for being constant sources of inspiration. For my brothers, especially Jonathan and David, for their continual encouragement, support and bright ideas. And for David and Gina, who make everything possible.

Contents

Prologue

By the time I arrived at the wood yard in Huddersfield on a bitterly cold night in February 1978, the body of the eighteen-year-old victim had already been taken to the mortuary. I had been working at the Forensic Science Service's Harrogate laboratory for just over three years, but this was my first crime scene. And as well as wanting to impress my boss with my knowledge and insights, I was very anxious not to miss anything that might help West Yorkshire Police identify the killer.

Something else that was worrying me as I approached the wood yard was the possibility that I might, quite literally, fall flat on my face. Not having visited a crime scene before, I didn't have any of the scene gear – waterproof trousers, anorak and footwear – that my more experienced colleagues had accumulated. So I was wearing some clothes my boss just happened to have in the boot of his car. The problem was, Ron Outteridge was a huge man with size eleven feet, and I was struggling to affect an air of competent professionalism while trying to walk in a pair of his wellington boots and control the folds of his massive anorak, which were flapping around my calves.

Nothing can really prepare you for your first crime scene, particularly when it involves a violent death, as is very often the case in my line of work. But there wasn't time for more than a fleeting moment of introspection before I had to focus on trying to work out what might have happened in the icy darkness of the wood yard just a few hours earlier. Then I began the search for any trace evidence that had been left by the killer – any fragments of clothing, hairs snagged on jagged bits of wood, or marks left by shoes or car tyres, for example. What added a sense of urgency to the need to find something that could help the police identify whoever had killed Helen Rytka was their suspicion that it might have been the Yorkshire Ripper.

I

The wrong sort of job for a woman

My brother Jonathan insists that my interest in crime began when I was nine years old and my father often used to buy me, at my request, a copy of the *News of the World* or *Sunday People*. It's certainly true that I was fascinated by all the crimes I read about. But the real reason I went with my father to the newsagent every Sunday morning – or with Jonathan when I was old enough to cycle there and back with him – was more chocolate Flake than newspaper related. And it was actually purely by chance that I became a forensic scientist.

I think I knew from quite a young age that I wanted to do science of some sort. It was a vague ambition that was partly fuelled by the various experiments I used to do with a chemistry set in the cellar of our house in a village just outside Oxford. But it might never have become a reality if I hadn't managed to pass just enough O levels to scrape into the sixth form, which is where my love of botany took root.

Growing up with Jonathan and David, the two of my five brothers who are nearest to me in age, I was accustomed to, and enjoyed, the company of other people. In fact, it was the distractions of the social side of life at school that were largely responsible for my lacklustre academic performance up until the age of sixteen.

My fees at Headington School were paid by a generous great-aunt. But because I had an almost total lack of interest in what I was being taught, I rarely did much homework until I began to study for my A levels. Which is why most of my school reports included some variation of the words 'if Angela would only try a bit harder'. So if my brilliant botany teacher Mrs Thompson hadn't lit something inside me and made me actively want to learn, I might not have done anything much with my life. I certainly wouldn't have become a scientist. As it was, I passed all my A levels – in chemistry, zoology and botany (now plant science) – and went on to study botany at Sheffield University.

I was offered the chance to stay on at Sheffield and study for a PhD after I graduated. But I was getting married. So I rejected the offer and moved back down south to be with my new husband, Peter Gallop. Then, after working for a while as a lab technician at Oxford University, I converted to a DPhil, with a particular focus on sea slugs.

I became interested in sea slugs for the same reason I was fascinated by plants, which was all to do with the way they work. It's pretty impressive, when you break the processes down, the way plants absorb water and minerals from the soil through their roots, then transport them to their leaves, where they use the green bits (chloroplasts) to convert energy from the sun and carbon dioxide from air to manufacture the food that enables them to flourish and grow. The species of sea slugs I was studying use chloroplasts too, sucking them out of a particular type of seaweed to create a sort of internal sugar factory.

And it was on the rather ambitious-sounding basis that they might prove to be the key to solving the food problems of the Third World that I was given a grant for the work I was doing. For the next three years, I spent many happy days scrabbling about on a beach at Bembridge on the Isle of Wight, filling my tiny Fiat 500 car with large containers of seawater and seaweed, and collecting the fascinating little creatures to take back to Oxford to study.

Eventually, however, while I was writing up my thesis, I realised three things: the work I had been doing was unlikely to solve any of the world's food-shortage problems; I probably wasn't going to find a job with any of the six or seven people in the entire world to whom the work was of any real interest; and I actually wanted to do something more applied that would be of more immediate importance to a larger number of people.

What we were going to do with the rest of our lives was, naturally, something my friends and I talked about quite a lot at that time. And when I was in the library one day in the summer of 1974, my good friend Stuart Milligan handed me a newspaper and said, 'This looks like something you might be interested in, Angela.' The advert Stuart had circled in biro was for a job with the Home Office Forensic Science Service (FSS). Forensic science had never been on my radar at all, but it certainly fell into the category of 'applied'. So I decided it was worth looking into. First, though, I spoke to my supervisor, Professor David Smith, who was a splendid scientist as well as a great friend and advisor, and who told me, 'There are going to be a lot of applicants for a job like that. So apply for it by all means. But don't pin your hopes on getting it.'

My husband had just decided to retrain as a solicitor, and with bills to pay and few other viable options, I sent off my CV. And, rather to my surprise, I was asked to go for an interview.

I knew I was going to have my work cut out trying to convince whoever interviewed me that I could make the leap from sea slugs to crime. So I was annoyed with myself afterwards for not having thought deeply enough about the sort of questions I was likely to be asked. If I had, I might not have had to rack my brains to think of intelligent answers to questions such as, 'What sort of traces would you look for on a lorry that has been involved in moving stolen goods?' I had amassed quite a lot of scientific knowledge by that time, but none of it seemed relevant as I struggled to think of something sensible to say. Fortunately, my answers to their questions must have made them believe there was *some* hope for me, because not long after the interview, I received a letter in the post offering me a job as a Higher Scientific Officer.

I was given the choice of working at pretty much any one of the eight FSS facilities around the country. With Peter at law college, and with the prospect of being able to be fairly flexible about where he ended up once he qualified, it didn't really matter where I was based. So I chose the laboratory at Harrogate – not far from Sheffield, where I'd been so happy as an undergraduate – which is where I started work on 24 October 1974.

Anxious not to be late on my first day, I arrived embarrassingly – and uncharacteristically – early at the large, imposing house in a leafy suburb. Luckily, someone had made an even earlier start to their working day, and I was greeted warmly before being led upstairs to wait in a laboratory.

The first thing that caught my eye when I walked into the lab was a washing line strung across one corner of the empty room that was hung with various items of what appeared to be blood-stained clothing. The next thing I noticed, as I sat on a stool waiting for my new colleagues to arrive, were some rather sinister-looking reddish-brown stains on the otherwise spotlessly clean surfaces of the lab's side benches. I was just beginning to wonder what on earth took place in there when the door opened and the first day of my first job in forensic science began.

A few hours later, I'd been introduced to so many people and had so many types of tests and techniques explained to me that it felt as though my head was spinning. One of the people I met that day, and had rather a strange session with, was the lab director, Dr Ian Barclay. I can remember thinking that his instruction to 'describe evidence in terms of teaspoons full' seemed odd in a scientific context. It made more sense, however, when he explained that it made quantities of evidence 'easier for the layman to understand'. And it was to prove useful later, when I started giving evidence in court and realised that volumes expressed in millilitres aren't always easily envisaged by jurors and other people who don't necessarily have a scientific background. What I also subsequently discovered was that Dr Barclay was a very interesting man, and so dedicated to his job that he rarely took any time off. In fact, we used to say that the only way we ever knew he was supposed to be on holiday was because he would come into work wearing sandals.

It was a bit daunting that first day being bombarded with so much information. But I was reassured to find that the work looked really interesting, and that the people I was going to be working with were all very friendly. The only negative aspect was the realisation that my new boss,

Ron Outteridge, wasn't exactly thrilled to have a woman on the team.

I wasn't the only woman working there by any means. I *was*, however, the only one destined to be what was called a reporting officer (RO). Being an RO involved going out to crime scenes, conducting and directing laboratory work, writing reports for the police and prosecution lawyers, and giving evidence in court when required to do so. The fact that I would be the only woman in that particular role seems extraordinary today, both for reasons of equality and because there are now more women than men working in forensic science. But it was simply the natural order of things at that time. Even so, I was taken aback when one of the first things my new boss said to me was along the lines of, 'I know you've been brought in to become a reporter, but you should know that I don't think it's right for women to report cases. It's the wrong sort of job for a woman. Call me old-fashioned if you like, but I believe a woman's place is in the home – literally, at the kitchen sink.'

Although it wasn't the encouraging start to our working relationship I might have wished for, it was, as I say, a different era. So I don't think I said anything in response. And although Ron's attitude towards me was pretty awful for the first few months, I soon realised he was hard on everyone. Despite his almost permanently serious expression, which seemed to accentuate the cragginess of his facial features, there was usually a twinkle in his eyes, and he didn't mean everything he said. Even so, it was a relief to find that his misogynistic gruffness was counterbalanced by the camaraderie and affable support of my colleagues.

The FSS facility in Harrogate was actually a house that used to be the home of the mother of the film star Michael Rennie, who played the part of Harry Lime in a popular 1960s TV series called *The Third Man*. The main biology laboratory had been created by knocking some upstairs rooms together, and we used to conduct blood-grouping tests on the original marble basins. There was a ballroom too, where we carried out our more complex chemical techniques; a conservatory, where we grew cannabis – solely for the purpose of estimating yields, I hasten to add; and some stables that we used as a shooting range. Goodness knows what our neighbours, in what was otherwise a quiet and respectable residential area, thought about it all. Perhaps the constant presence of police cars delivering and collecting items helped to reassure them. Or possibly not.

After spending a couple of days sitting, quite literally, at the elbows of experienced forensic scientists, watching and learning, I was given my first item to examine. It was a horrible case, involving a man who had apparently killed his wife and her dog with his bare hands in an attempt to exorcise what he believed to be the evil spirits that possessed them. The evidential item I was given to look at was a blood-stained vinyl plastic handbag that had been found next to the woman's body.

Like most of the items that were submitted to us by the police for forensic examination, the handbag was in a brown-paper bag. Folded over at the top and sealed with Sellotape, the paper bag had a label attached, listing details such as what the item was, the specific reference number it had been given, who had collected it, precisely when, and where from. After I'd been at the FSS a bit longer, I was allowed to take tapings of evidential items, which involved working your way systematically over the surface with lengths of sticky tape. Then I'd examine each taping under a microscope for hairs and textile fibres, many of which are too small to be seen with the naked eye. All I was asked to do on that occasion, though, was to describe the handbag and its contents, make a note of any damage, stains or other marks, and draw sketches of it from every angle. (I can remember wishing I'd paid more attention in art classes at school!)

It was the end of October and the heating was on in the laboratory, which was rendered even warmer by the early-autumn sunlight that was streaming in through the windows. And as I opened the handbag, I was almost overwhelmed by the sickly sweet smell of hot vinyl plastic, dried blood and the apple that was rotting inside it. As an assistant to the assistant to the forensic scientist who was reporting the case, I knew I wouldn't have been given the handbag to examine on my own if it had been critical to the investigation. But I was dismayed by what I was handling, and I can remember thinking, as I turned my head away from it quickly, 'This is terrible. Is this really what I want to do with my life?'

We often didn't know the outcome of the cases we worked on, some of which might not go to trial until months, even years, after we'd done our investigation. I do know, however, that the suspect in that case was acquitted of murdering his wife by reason of insanity and committed to Broadmoor high-security psychiatric hospital.

My husband Peter was away at law college in Chester when I moved up to Harrogate to start work at the FSS. So I spent many evenings during those first few weeks sitting alone in my rented flat, completing my DPhil thesis and wondering if I'd made the right choice. I was twenty-four when I started working at the FSS. But perhaps any age feels too young to learn about what it's possible for one human being to do to another using only their bare hands. The question I asked myself during the evening after my experience with the vinyl handbag was whether I had done the wrong thing. Did I really want to abandon the fascinating study of harmless, clever little sea slugs in order to spend hours in a stuffy, oppressive laboratory examining the blood-spattered personal belongings of victims of brutal murder? It was a question that was made even more difficult to answer by the fact that I didn't feel able to air my concerns with my work colleagues, who were clearly all coping splendidly – or so it seemed. So I had no one immediately available to help me put things into perspective.

I was wrong about my colleagues though. It turned out that I wasn't the only one trying to decide whether they were cut out for a life in forensic science. I don't know whether Ron Outteridge's disparaging behaviour was deliberately intended to be part of a process of natural selection, so that only those who were tough enough to deal with everything the job entailed stayed on. It certainly had that effect though, and several people who had been taken on as assistants – both male and female – left after just a few weeks. In the end, I was one of those who stuck it out, and suddenly, after I'd been at the FSS for six months, Ron's attitude towards me changed. From that point on, he seemed to accept me completely and was very supportive, although he did tell me when I challenged him about it several years later that he considered me to be 'an honorary bloke'. Which I realised was meant as a compliment!

Most of the work I was doing as a forensic biologist during my early days at the FSS involved relatively 'simple' sex offences. What that usually entailed was looking at one or two swabs from intimate parts of a victim's or suspect's body and maybe a pair of knickers. I suppose I was given cases like that to work on because they were generally thought to be straightforward. Whereas, in fact, the interpretation of the results of the tests involved was often quite complicated.

Incidentally, it was the chemical we used to test for semen that was responsible for the blood-coloured stains I'd noticed on the lab benches on my first morning. It was a chemical we all sprayed in the open laboratory, until it was discovered to be highly carcinogenic and banished to a fume cupboard, where it could only be used while wearing a mask, gloves and other protective clothing. We eventually stopped hanging out clothes to dry in the open laboratory too – blood stained or other-wise – as soon as we began to understand the potential health hazards rather better. As with almost every other aspect of forensic science, our knowledge of health-and-safety issues has advanced considerably during the last forty-five years.

2

The Yorkshire Ripper

After the merger of the laboratories in Harrogate and Newcastle in 1977, I moved to the new FSS laboratory that was created in Wetherby, where we worked with police forces in Northumbria, Durham, Cleveland, Humberside, West Yorkshire, North Yorkshire and South Yorkshire. A few months later, I was promoted to Senior Scientific Officer and started going out to crime scenes.

There was no DNA profiling in the 1970s, and blood grouping was far less discriminating, often providing only very limited evidence of specific links. So forensic investigations relied heavily on fingerprinting – which, for historical reasons, was usually done by the police – and various other types of evidence that constituted some of the primary tools in the forensic scientist's armoury. Included among them were hair and textile fibres, paint and glass fragments, shoe and tool marks, firearms and ballistic materials, handwriting comparisons, illicit drugs and poisons, and traces of them in body fluids and tissues.

What I was looking for at my first crime scene in the wood yard in Huddersfield that cold February night in 1978 was anything that might give some clue as to what had happened there, or to the identity of the killer. Car-tyre, footwear or drag marks, for example; or any fragments of clothing, hairs, traces of semen, a used condom or discarded cigarette butt.

The police had already been in the wood yard for some time when my boss and I arrived. And after we'd orientated ourselves and helped them to search it for evidence, we went to the mortuary to see the body of the victim, who had already been identified as eighteen-year-old Helen Rytka. I hadn't seen a dead body before, and I was nervous about what my instinctive reaction might be. What struck me as I walked into the brightly lit room with its scrubbed stainless-steel tables and angular surfaces was the distinctive smell of disinfectant and other chemicals. It wasn't just when visiting crime scenes that we wore our own clothes in those days, before it was common practice, in some laboratories at least, for everyone to be issued with hospital-type scrubs. And that was the first of many evenings when I'd get home after visiting a mortuary, strip off whatever I'd been wearing and put it straight in the washing machine, to get rid of that smell.

After death, gravity causes fluid to accumulate in the lower parts of a body, leaving the upper surfaces drained of blood. So I wasn't surprised by the fact that Helen Rytka's skin had a waxy paleness that gave her an unreal appearance. What I hadn't expected was that someone who had been so brutally killed would look so peaceful. Maybe it was because I'd read too many Agatha Christie novels in my youth that I imagined all victims would look tortured or surprised, which, for medico-scientific reasons, they actually never do.

Helen had clearly been an attractive girl, and it was the thought that she was *real*, that she had been someone's daughter, sister, friend, that enabled me to focus on the job I was there to do. After discussing with the pathologist conducting the post mortem what had happened to her, I watched as he examined her wounds in detail for any indications of the type and size of weapon that had caused them. Then I helped collect debris from the surfaces of her body that could have been transferred from her attacker, and looked for any other evidence that might conceivably assist the police in their investigation.

By the time Helen Rytka's body was found, police suspected that the Yorkshire Ripper had killed other women, mostly in and around Leeds, Bradford and Halifax, and had probably brutally attacked several more, leaving some of them with life-altering injuries. And Helen's injuries certainly fitted his *modus operandi*, which was to strike his victims on the head, sometimes multiple times and usually with a hammer, then stab them repeatedly with a knife or a screwdriver-type implement.

Shortly after Helen's death, the Assistant Chief Constable of West Yorkshire Police received a number of letters and an audiotape from someone purporting to be the Yorkshire Ripper. The police were under constantly mounting pressure to find the serial killer who now appeared to be taunting them. And with no other obvious leads to follow, the investigation ended up getting stuck down a blind alley for almost three years, by which time the Yorkshire Ripper had claimed more victims. In fact, the police interviewed the real killer on several occasions during those three years. But because he didn't match the profile of the man they were looking for – someone with a Sunderland accent like the man on the tapes, who turned out to be a hoaxer – he was discounted as a suspect.

Fourteen months after Helen Rytka's murder, I attended my second Yorkshire Ripper crime scene when the body of another young woman was found in a park in Halifax. Nineteen-year-old Josephine Whitaker had been attacked as she was walking home at night. But it was light by the time her body was discovered the following morning. And one of the first thoughts that struck me was that an area of open grassland in full view of anyone who happened to look across the park seemed an odd place to assault and kill someone, even when it was dark.

One of the many things I was to learn over the next few years was how critical it is to examine the scene of a crime very thoroughly. Getting as clear a picture as possible of the likely sequence of events tells you what the forensic opportunities might be and enables you to plan the most effective strategy for testing. So, on that particular occasion, we returned at night and stood on the edge of the park, looking in towards the crime scene. And what we realised as we did so was that when the lights encircling the grassland were on, the central area was plunged into almost total darkness, creating a visual barrier to anyone outside it. Even so, whoever had killed Josephine had still taken a huge risk by attacking her in the open. Perhaps it had been a spur-of-the-moment decision. Or, if her killer *was* the Yorkshire Ripper, as police suspected, maybe he was beginning to believe he was invincible.

There were no computers or computerised databases in the 1970s to help West Yorkshire Police in their search for suspects. All they could do was follow every lead, create some new ones – by correlating 'cross-area sightings' for example (i.e. sightings of vehicles in more than one of the areas where the murders had taken place) – and log all the information on a cross-reference card-index system. It was a process that generated a massive, almost overwhelming, amount of paperwork. But it was because the police were determined to pursue every potentially useful avenue of inquiry that we were asked to examine a house in a small mill village near York.

Suspicions had been raised when a man wearing a bra over his shirt and 'behaving very oddly' had answered the door to an 'Avon lady'. And although the narrow-terraced house that I visited with a colleague seemed unremarkable from the outside, there was evidence inside it of some very bizarre activities.

The police reported that the man had a peculiar pattern of burn marks on either side of his face and between his legs. And, in one way or another, fire was absolutely a theme in the house. As well as an unusually large number of matchboxes and cigarette lighters, there were scorch marks on an archway in the cellar, a vat of solvent containing some large wooden stakes with tights wrapped round one end of them, and several paintings of people burning or gathered around funeral pyres, some of them clutching similar flaming stakes. In a locked room, there were also some semen-stained women's nighties and Indian-style pantaloons. Clearly, something very peculiar had been going on. Which was an impression that was reinforced by the discovery in various places around the house of bowls containing blood-soaked tissues.

I had been working at the FSS for almost five years by that time, gaining invaluable experience and learning something new almost every day. And I knew that one of the most important principles underlying any forensic investigation is 'never make any assumptions', because truth often really is stranger than fiction. It was a principle that was well illustrated in that particular case when we realised that, however potentially incriminating some of our observations in the house might appear to be, the man was not the suspect police were looking for. He was just someone with a fetish that involved dressing up in a wig and pantaloons and setting fire to himself. And the blood-soaked tissues had been used to staunch his bleeding gums after he'd had all his teeth removed the previous day.

It was the first of many madhouses I was to see during the next forty years. What was almost more incongruous than all the fire-related materials, however, was a note that had been left by the man's wife, which said, simply, 'I've had enough. I'm leaving you. You owe me three shillings and fourpence.' It was a debt I think *I* might have forgiven, in the circumstances!

I don't think any of us really expected to find anything in that house that could be linked to the Yorkshire Ripper or one of his victims – a weapon, for example, or some blood-stained clothing. There was certainly nothing there to suggest that the man with the peculiar fetish was a serial killer. In fact, there was no evidence to indicate that he had committed any crime, apart, perhaps, from putting his neighbours' lives and property at risk every time he held a match to one of his homemade wooden stakes.

Back in the laboratory, we started going to extraordinary scientific lengths to see if we could link the Ripper crimes with each other. What we were looking for particularly were any traces in common that could conceivably have come from the killer. From our tapings of the victims' bodies and clothing, we recovered what must have been hundreds of thousands of individual microscopic textile fibres, which we systematically compared by various means, focusing on any from different victims that looked similar. One of the methods we used was a relatively new technique at that time called microspectrophotometry (MSP), which provides an objective assessment of colour in the form of a graph by shining light of different wavelengths at small things – in this case individual textile fibres – and recording how they react.

The work was well underway by the end of the following year when, after the deaths of three more women, Ron Outteridge was brought in to help find the Yorkshire Ripper. Ron was the Director of the FSS laboratory at Nottingham by then, and the man he chose to assist him was a forensic scientist called Russell Stockdale, who was later to play a very significant role in my life.

Installed in police HQ at Bradford, Ron and Russell systematically reviewed each of the Ripper crime scenes and all the work that had been done in relation to them. They collated critical information about basic things like the possible nature of the weapons used, surviving victims' descriptions of their attacker, and any forensic evidence in each case, for example semen, and footwear and tyre marks. Then they drew up two lists, one summarising 'things we know about the Ripper', and the other, 'things we think we know about the Ripper'. As well as being an effective means of helping to bring some sense of order to the 'paperwork' that was swamping the investigation and making it difficult to 'see the wood for the trees', the process also helped identify some new avenues to explore.

In a separate exercise, Stuart Kind – who, at that time, was the Director of the FSS Central Research Establishment (CRE) – started to think about some techniques he had become familiar with as an RAF navigator during the war. First, he plotted the locations and times

– insofar as they were known or had been estimated – of all the murders and assaults for which the persistently evasive serial killer was thought to have been responsible. Then he looked at factors such as the killer's need to be able to get home as quickly as possible after each attack – any that had taken place earlier rather than later in the evening were likely to be further away from where he lived.

The conclusion Stuart came to using the technique that subsequently became known as geographical profiling was that the man they were looking for lived somewhere between the towns of Manningham and Bingley, in the borough of the City of Bradford. It was a conclusion that was at least a contributing factor in the police's decision to shift their focus from the area they had been led to by the hoaxer. Not long afterwards, and as a result of some good, observant police work, a thirty-four-year-old lorry driver called Peter Sutcliffe was arrested in Bradford.

After spending so long desperately trying to find any evidence that might identify the Yorkshire Ripper, my colleagues and I couldn't help wondering what Sutcliffe was like. So some of us took the unusual step of travelling down to London to watch part of the trial proceedings. I think we were all a bit surprised by how insignificant he seemed to be for someone who had inspired such terror over a large part of the north of England for so long. But I expect we would have felt differently if we'd encountered him somewhere late at night, rather than in the dock at the Old Bailey. In fact, whenever I had to drive through Leeds alone at night after I'd been out to a crime scene or at a police event before he was apprehended, I was always relieved to get out into the open countryside and be on my way home.

In May 1981, after being found guilty of murdering thirteen women and attempting to kill seven more, Peter Sutcliffe was sentenced to a recommended minimum term of thirty years in prison.

Coincidentally, I went into business some thirty years later with a very talented police officer called Chris Gregg, who had joined West Yorkshire Police in 1974, the same year I started working at the FSS, and whose first Ripper crime scene was also that of Helen Rytka. In fact, it was Chris – who was by that time Head of West Yorkshire CID – who eventually uncovered the true identity of the hoaxer, John Humble, aka 'Wearside Jack'. And in 2006, having been traced through his DNA, Humble was sentenced to eight years in prison for perverting the course of justice.

3

Some peculiar behaviour

As well as learning about forensic science itself, I was discovering a lot about people too, and about how peculiar some people's behaviour can be. Emotion of one sort or another is probably always involved in crime. Some of the most horrific cases I've worked on over the years have been prompted by anger, jealousy or greed, often heightened by alcohol and the presence or absence of money. But it was difficult to relate to the motivation for what was possibly the most chilling case of all.

One Saturday evening in February 1980, the body of a man in his thirties was found by a passer-by on a footpath in a town in Humberside. After being examined at the scene by Professor Alan Usher, who was one of the leading Home Office pathologists of the day, the body was taken to the mortuary for a full autopsy.

What the post-mortem examination revealed was that the man had been stabbed at least thirteen times, from in front and behind, during what appeared to have been a sustained attack. Some of the stab wounds were relatively superficial. Some had occurred as he tried to ward off the blows. At least four were more serious, causing damage to his neck, spine and soft abdominal tissues. And one, beside the scrotum, had probably been inflicted while he was lying on the ground, possibly when he was already dead. What the post-mortem report also stated was that the weapon used could have been the large clasp knife police had recovered from one of the two suspects they had already arrested.

A watch, some blood-stained clothing and various other items were removed from the man's body and passed on by the police to the FSS laboratory at Wetherby, where I was working at the time. But what was particularly interesting were the statements of the two suspects, who I'll call Daniel and Davey.*

According to Daniel, while the two young men were in a pub earlier in the evening, they had been discussing ways of getting hold of some money when Davey started talking about 'bumping off and robbing a taxi driver'. Then they left the pub, and while they were walking to another one, Davey attacked a total stranger in the street, at which point Daniel ran away. Catching up with Daniel a few minutes later, Davey told him he'd killed the man, then handed Daniel a knife, which he put inside one of his gloves.

In a discussion that followed while they were in the second pub, Davey said that it was now Daniel's turn to do something similar, so that he wouldn't 'have something' on his friend.

'I can't recall exactly what was going through my mind at that moment,' Daniel said in his statement to the police in reference to the attack he subsequently launched on an elderly man they came across when they left the second pub. 'It was like a bad dream. Instinctively, with the knife in my right hand I threw a blow towards his throat . . . it

* The names have been changed.

had only broken the skin and didn't do any damage . . . I looked at his face and he acted as if I'd never touched him . . . Then I heard him tell me he was only an old-age pensioner. That only made me feel worse. I think the next blow I threw him was more in disgust at myself . . . I couldn't get quick enough away from the guy . . .'

Whatever the truth of it was, the attack was curtailed and, unlike the first victim, the elderly man survived. And after burying the knife – which Davey later retrieved and threw into a pond – the two young men returned to their respective homes.

Davey's account was similar in some respects, except he claimed that during their original conversation they had asked each other if they thought they *could* kill someone. Then they *both* decided to kill a randomly selected man that night, just to see if they were capable of doing it. He said also that *he* was the one who got scared and talked Daniel out of killing a taxi driver. And although he admitted to stabbing the first man, who died in the street, he said Daniel kicked the stranger in the head when he tried to get to his feet.

The incident occurred almost forty years ago, and I don't have access to any lab notes related to the case. But part of our job as forensic scientists was to try to find anything that might prove the validity of one version of events rather than the other. So we looked at the first victim's clothing and at the knife the police had found, which I think provided some evidence of a connection between the suspects and the dead man. Although I don't know what the outcome was for Daniel, Davey was sentenced to life in prison for the entirely random murder – just to see what it felt like – of a man who happened to be in the wrong place at the wrong time.

It was a different type of emotional detachment that I witnessed during an investigation into the suspicious death of a young child in a mill town in West Yorkshire. Police suspected that the child's head had been struck numerous times on a bed post. So I expected the mother to be inconsolable when my colleague and I arrived at the house to carry out our investigation. In fact, she seemed quite cheerful, and sat watching *Dynasty* on television the entire time we were there. She did turn away from the TV screen briefly at one point, to offer us a cup of tea, which we declined, for professional reasons, and because the walls of the house were smeared with dog excrement. I suppose *Dynasty* was as good a form of escapism as any. It just seemed strange that she clearly wasn't making any comparisons with her own immediate situation and surroundings.

It isn't only human beings who are the victims of people's odd behaviour, as was illustrated by a case that was investigated by one of my colleagues, Alf Faragher, in the lab at Wetherby. A man had been admitted to hospital in a very serious condition, with a punctured colon and peritonitis, the cause of which left medical staff absolutely baffled. What particularly perplexed the doctors was the presence in the patient's abdomen of a jelly-like substance, the origins of which were mystifying to them and, apparently, to the man himself. Eventually, someone explained to him that unless the substance could be identified so that he could be treated appropriately, there was nothing more that could be done for him and he would probably die. Which is when he finally admitted to having had sex with a boar.

Apparently, boars have sharp, corkscrew-shaped penises that match the similarly shaped cervical canal of a sow (a left-hand thread, for anyone who likes to know all the facts) – which explained the damage to the man's colon. The fact that they also produce relatively large quantities of semen, which requires a plug to keep it in the sow for the required length of time, accounted for the jelly-like substance in his abdomen.

The man was lucky to survive. But as bestiality is a crime in the UK, Alf was asked to test a sample of the 'jelly', as evidence if the case went to court. There was a strong sense of camaraderie among everyone who worked in the large FSS laboratory at Wetherby. And although we obviously all took our work very seriously, it was perhaps inevitable that when Alf asked if anyone had any ideas about what he should look for, the answers would include suggestions such as, 'Trotter marks up the back of his jumper'! What he ended up with was a positive reaction to anti-pig serum and some rather odd-looking sperm that were subsequently confirmed to be boar sperm.

It was goat hairs and witness statements that formed the basis of the evidence in another case involving an act of bestiality that we worked on some years later. There was no mystery on that occasion, however, as the act in question took place on an allotment next to a railway line, in full view of the passengers on a slowly passing train, one of whom pulled the emergency cord.

By the time I left Wetherby in 1981 and went to work at the FSS laboratory in Aldermaston in Berkshire, I thought there was nothing more anyone could do that would surprise me. I was wrong, of course, although I don't think anything ever surprised me quite as much as some of those early cases, when I was still learning about what some human beings are capable of doing.

*　　　*　　　*

Towards the end of my time at Wetherby, my husband Peter and I split up. We had been together since I was fourteen, and had probably simply married too young. It was all very sad. But I had already met the man who would eventually become my second husband – the forensic scientist Russell Stockdale, who had assisted Ron Outteridge in the search for the Yorkshire Ripper. And it was largely because Russell got a job as Head of Biology at CRE in Aldermaston that I moved too, to work at the FSS operational laboratory next door.

The lab at Aldermaston did all the forensics for the police forces in Hampshire, Surrey, Sussex, Kent and the Thames Valley (which covers Oxfordshire, Buckinghamshire and Berkshire). As soon as I started work there in 1981, I realised that some things were very different from the way they were in the north. What was particularly noticeable was the different relationship that existed between the police and forensic scientists, who were only ever called out to assist at crimes scenes when the police were desperate. I think that was at least partly due to the fact that the scenes-of-crime officers employed by the police in the south had a much higher profile than they did in the north. In some ways, their greater involvement was a good thing, because it meant they did more than just show up, take photographs, test for fingerprints and collect some items on which they thought there might be evidence. The problem was that, because they didn't always know what we were capable of doing in the laboratory, they didn't always ask for the most appropriate tests or provide us with all the necessary background information.

It was because of that gap in understanding that I started producing a magazine called *Lab Link* a couple of times a year. The aim of the magazine was to make the police more aware of what we were actually doing in the laboratory, and what we needed them to do to enable us to be as effective as possible. And as well as commissioning articles from some of my own colleagues, I encouraged the police to raise issues too, which they seemed to respond to quite well.

Another of the obstacles I had to overcome at Aldermaston was the misogynistic attitude of some police officers, which although not all that 'odd' in the early 1980s, was very frustrating. Ron Outteridge's comment about women and the kitchen sink notwithstanding, I was accustomed to being treated with respect by the officers I worked with in Harrogate and Wetherby. So I was deeply disappointed on attending my first crime scene in Sussex to be met by the senior investigating officer's obvious scepticism and disappointment, which he made no attempt to hide. It wasn't long, however, before he started actively asking for me for his particular crime scenes, and would express almost grudging approval if I said I was going to attend. That was really the turning point for me, when the police we were working with started to think a bit more broadly about both forensic science and the role of women in forensic investigations.

4
Specialisms

Forensic science can involve absolutely anything and everything you'd find in everyday life. The trick is to work out what's most relevant, then where and how it might be best to look for it. The main types of forensic evidence used routinely today are body fluids and tissues and the DNA associated with them, fingerprints, and, increasingly, mobile phones, laptops and other digital devices. But other types of traces and marks can be critical too, such as textile fibres from clothing and furnishings, hairs, glass and paint, and footwear and tool marks. Theoretically, we can analyse and compare any kind of trace to try to work out what it means in the context of a case.

It's actually very difficult to do anything in life without leaving traces, even if they're only indirect such as – at the simplest level – via gloves. One of the most interesting principles underlying any forensic investigation is Locard's Exchange Principle, which can be summarised as 'every contact leaves a trace'. Coined in 1910 by the French criminologist Dr Edmond Locard, I've learned from experience over the years that it's completely right. Always. In every case. The only variable is whether or not you find the trace that has been left, because sometimes it may not be at all obvious. So forensic scientists need to be imaginative – as well as meticulous and tenacious – when conducting their investigations.

Also crucial to any forensic investigation is teamwork between specialists in each of the evidence types that may be involved. Take the case of someone who has been hit over the head with a hammer. If they die, which is likely in that scenario but not always the case – some of the Yorkshire Ripper's victims survived just such an attack – a pathologist will examine the body. During the post-mortem examination, the pathologist will take the dimensions of any hole(s) in the skull that might correspond to the dimensions of a particular hammer that has been recovered. The police will look at any fingerprints. A forensic biologist will examine the blood patterns on the hammer, any skin and hairs that might have been transferred to it, and any textile fibres or glove marks that might be present in the blood on its shaft. A forensic chemist might get involved too, to look at the mark(s) the hammer made in the victim's skull, and at any other marks on the body where it impacted but didn't break the skin. Then, of course, there are various types of examinations that may be relevant in relation to the victim's and suspect's clothes and to the crime scene.

There's crossover, of course, between the different specialisms. Basically though, as well as looking at marks and traces on bodies and elsewhere, forensic chemists specialise in what used to be called 'crimes against property', i.e. crimes that involve breaking and entering, damage to or use of vehicles, arson and explosions etc. Forensic biologists, on the other hand, are mainly concerned with 'offences against the person' (and animals), which includes the full range of sexual and violent assaults – so anything from pushings and shovings to stabbings, shootings, bludgeonings with heavy instruments, and kidnappings.

Forensic chemists will examine things like glass, paint and other building materials, footwear marks, tyre and tool marks, as well as fire damage and any accelerants that may have caused it, which can provide incredibly powerful evidence. For example, if someone breaks into a house through a door using a jemmy, there will be tool marks on the door, and flakes of paint will transfer from the door on to the jemmy. If they effect entry by breaking a window and climbing in, tiny fragments of glass will stick to their sleeve, some fibres from their clothing may get caught on the sharp edges of the glass, and they may leave a footwear mark on the windowsill or in a flower bed outside. Chemists understand the chemical constituents of all those things. They can tell from just a tiny fragment of glass whether it's from something that has been broken recently, and whether it's container glass, from a drinking glass or bottle, or from a flat pane of what's called float glass, which is used to make windows. They can match fragments of glass by looking at their refractive index and chemical composition; they can tell whether they are fragments of toughened glass; and, by looking at stress marks and cracks, they can ascertain from which side a pane of glass was broken. They can also identify a flake of paint from a house or car by looking at the composition and sequence of layers, and compare things like paper and polythene by examining the marks made during the manufacturing process.

Drug chemists specialise in identifying drugs of abuse and clandestine drugs factories, determining the amount and working out the quality (purity) of any drugs found.

With cannabis plants, yield is important – i.e. how much of the active constituent tetrahydrocannabinol the plants are going to produce – in order to distinguish between possession (for personal use) and intent to supply. Drug chemists also compare drug seizures to see if they came from the same source. And they profile the chemical constituents by looking at the cutting agents and any adulterants there might be from the manufacturing process. Sometimes, the packaging provides more powerful evidence than the drug itself in terms of linking seizures and establishing supply chains, and chemists can learn a lot from folded-up bits of paper from magazines, cling-film wraps, and fingers of disposable gloves. They are also able to compare the stress marks on plastic bags, and superficial score marks from beads of polythene, that build up at the edges of the 'dye' through which the bags are extruded during the manufacturing process, thereby identifying bags produced in the same sequence.

The job of a toxicologist, who is another type of forensic chemist, is to examine body samples and body fluids for different kinds of drug substances and metabolites, which are the compounds the drugs turn into once they're inside the body. The fact that some metabolites are short lived, while others take longer to be eliminated from the body or change into other compounds, can help a toxicologist to work out when a drug was taken. By knowing how to interpret the toxicology results in the context of the specific circumstances of a particular case, they can then assess whether the drug substance was affected by anything else that might have been going on at the time and the extent to which those involved might have been 'impaired'.

Then there are the forensic biologists, like me, who

identify blood and other body fluids, and the patterns they produce, which can be very useful when trying to work out the sequence of events during an assault. Biologists were also responsible for blood grouping, and now do the DNA profiling that has superseded it, as well as examining biological traces such as skin, nails, teeth and hairs, and textile fibres, although some, particularly synthetic, textile fibres are often dealt with by chemists or, latterly, by specific textile-fibre experts. Biologists look at damage too – to clothing and weapons, for example – and play a central role in interpreting the more complex crime scenes, which is why they are often responsible for pulling all the scientific evidence in a case together.

There are other types of scientists who get involved with forensic investigations these days. For example, there's a whole new area of digital forensics, which reflects the way people live today and includes all the information that's stored on mobile phones and personal computers. With phones, digital forensic scientists can tell who was talking to whom – based on their mobile numbers – and when, and even roughly where they were at the time. They can also identify what Internet sites someone has looked at and can pull up information about all the items they've ordered online and a whole history of what they've been doing. And they look at CCTV footage too, which now gives such broad coverage they can usually find something, somewhere that's relevant to a specific crime.

There are also some specialisms within forensic science that you only need to bring into play occasionally. Forensic entomology, for example, which involves the study of insects and which, although complicated, can be extremely useful. Flies are attracted to the smell of a decomposing body for quite a while after death. And if the body is outside and easily accessible, they arrive in a sequence that reflects the state of decomposition. So it's possible to gauge the time since death by looking at the stage of development of specific types of insects, maggots or eggs found on the corpse. A forensic entomologist can also sometimes determine from the species of insects present whether a body has been moved after death.

Other examples of less common forensic specialisms are described later in the book in relation to specific cases.

5
Blood: grouping, identification and patterns

It was the chemistry departments that were huge in forensic laboratories when I started working at the FSS. Today, biology is the primary focus, all because of the impact of DNA profiling, which was first used in a case in the mid-1980s. In those days though, when we relied on blood grouping, the power to discriminate between different people as potential sources of some body fluid found on a critical item was of a whole different order of magnitude from that provided by DNA profiling. So we were always very careful to err on the side of caution in interpreting and reporting our results.

A forensic scientist might say in court that the blood in a blood stain on a suspect's clothing, for example, occurred in one in twenty-five (or 4 per cent) of the UK population and matched that of the victim but was different from the suspect's own blood. The problem was that the jury might focus more on the word 'match' and less on the statistic. So, unless the 'one in twenty-five' was clearly explained, I'm sure it sometimes carried more weight with at least some jurors than it should have done. Because what it actually means is that in a town with a population of 200,000, there would be approximately 8,000 people with a matching combination of blood groups from whom the blood could *technically* have come. Therefore, there obviously had to be other evidence, either forensic or something else that helped to locate the defendant at a particular place at the relevant time.

Blood grouping relies on the presence in blood of various chemical substances that exist in a number of different forms. The blood is classified according to which particular form(s) of each substance – referred to as the blood-grouping system – it contains. The oldest blood-grouping system is ABO, in which all human beings belong to one of four blood groups – A, B, AB or O – based on genetically determined antigens. Of the raft of other blood-group systems available to forensic science, the most commonly used in the 1970s and 1980s were PGM (phosphoglucomutase), EAP (erythrocyte acid phosphatase) and Hp (haptoglobin).

The PGM system has ten different groups – plus some rare variants that we can ignore for the present purpose – each of which is determined by the presence of one or two of four different factors known as 1+, 1–, 2+ and 2–. The groups are therefore designated as 1+, 1–, 1+1–, 2+, 2–, 2+2–, 2+1+, 2+1–, 2–1+, 2–1–. The enzyme EAP includes just three factors, A, B and C, which give rise to six different blood groups, A, B, C, BA, CA, CB. And the protein Hp exists in two different forms, 1 and 2, giving rise to three different groups, 1, 2 and 2–1.

It was possible to establish which form(s) of each of the substances was contained in the blood of a particular individual. Then you could say that a sample of blood at a crime scene, for example, *could* or *could not* have come from that person. What you couldn't say with the same certainty was that it *had* come from someone in particular. In other words, you could exclude but not uniquely identify a specific person as the source. But knowing how commonly blood with that combination of blood groups occurs in the general population would give an idea of how strong the link provided by blood grouping might be.

Blood-pattern analysis, or BPA as it's known, is the other side of the coin. Looking at the size, shape and density of a blood stain, together with its location, can provide valuable information about how it might have arisen. So BPA is one of the most powerful forms of evidence for understanding what happened at the scene of a violent crime and the sequence of events that occurred.

There are three basic elements of blood-stain patterns, which can tell you a great deal when you know how to interpret them. (1) Blood that has dripped passively from a wound, been flicked off finger ends or a weapon, or spurted rhythmically from a breached artery gives rise to distinctive spots and splashes that tend to be relatively large. (2) Forces such as gunshot, punching, kicking or the use of a blunt instrument split up the blood into smaller droplets. The pattern of blood spatter that is produced is of spots and splashes of characteristic shape and size, which can indicate the approximate position of the victim at the time, how many blows were struck, and sometimes even the shape of the weapon. (3) Blood stains arising through direct contact with something with wet blood on it will be in the form of smears, swipes and wipes, or patterns such as fingerprint, footwear or fabric marks.

Normally, the patterns you find at crime scenes tend to be combinations of these three basic elements. Sometimes, they are augmented by additional elements such as clotted blood, indicating that an attack has occurred over a period of time, or the air bubbles that are characteristic of blood emanating from coughing and sneezing.

Unless it's extremely severe – someone's head being crushed by a lump of concrete, for example – the first blow in an assault may just break the skin and start the blood flow. It will only be with the second and any subsequent blows that blood will start to be transferred on to surrounding surfaces – which can include any surface, not just floors, walls or clothing – in a characteristic pattern of blood spatter.

Despite what detective novels may suggest, it's actually very difficult to erase all traces of blood following an attack. Sometimes though, a vital clue becomes immediately apparent, as occurred in one case that was worked on in the lab, which, admittedly, is a rather extreme example. Presumably, the suspect thought he'd covered his tracks pretty comprehensively. But when the police went to his house, he answered the door wearing spectacles that were covered with tiny specks of blood. Although he obviously couldn't see the blood himself, when looking out through the lenses, it was clearly visible to the officers who arrested him.

One fascinating case I worked on while I was at Wetherby illustrated very clearly both the significance of blood patterns and the importance of actually visiting the crime scene. When the body of a woman with a wound on the side of her head was found in a lay-by a few miles from where she lived, the police thought at first that she might have been struck by the wing mirror of a lorry as she was walking along the road in the dark. Their suspicions were raised, however, when they went to the house to break the news to her husband.

Although I'd been reporting cases in court for a while by that time, I was still learning how to do crime scenes – what to look for, how to select items for closer examination, and how best to take samples from surfaces that couldn't be transported to the laboratory, such as walls and floors. So I went to the house as an assistant to a more senior forensic scientist called Peter Gregory. The woman's husband was still there when we arrived, and while he sat talking to police officers in the living room, we started our investigation in the hall.

The reason the floor in the hall was bare, the man explained to the police officers, was that he and his wife had taken up the carpet with the intention of replacing it, but hadn't yet got round to doing so. It was a reasonable explanation, and it was quite possible that the absence of any floor covering might prove to have no bearing at all on our investigation.

The walls in the hall were papered with a type of wood-chip wallpaper we used to call 'donkey's breakfast', which had an uneven surface that made any stains or discolouring quite difficult to see. But when I looked at it carefully, I noticed a couple of very small splashes of something that could have been blood. And when I examined the paper more closely using one of our very powerful scene lamps (which were actually glorified torches), I could see some more.

One of the two presumptive chemical tests commonly used for blood is the leucomalachite green (LMG) test. When the LMG reagent followed by hydrogen peroxide is added to a suspect mark or stain, the LMG turns from colourless to a bright blue-green colour in the presence of peroxidase activity, which exists at quite a high level in haemoglobin. However, because peroxidase activity is also present in substances such as raw horseradish root, additional tests also need to be performed to confirm a positive result for blood. An alternative presumptive test, the Kastle-Meyer (KM) test, involves a similar process using the chemical phenolphthalein instead of LMG, which reacts to the haemoglobin in blood by turning a strong magenta colour.

At Wetherby, we tended to favour the LMG test, which was the one I used that day. After gently rubbing part of one of the stains on the wall with the tip of a folded disc of filter paper, I unfolded it and added a drop of LMG to its centre. If it changed colour at that point, I'd know that the stain wasn't blood but something like paint or rust that was reacting directly with the reagent. So I waited a few seconds, and when nothing happened, added a drop of hydrogen peroxide, then watched as the damp patch on the filter paper turned from colourless to a distinct blue-green.

Further tests would need to be run back at the laboratory to confirm the positive reaction before we could say categorically that the marks on the wall were human blood. In the meantime, we took samples of the wallpaper with splashes on it, completed our examination of the hall, then went into the garage, which was where the police told us the carpet had been found.

A quick inspection *in situ* showed that part of the carpet was damp and there was a faint smell of disinfectant associated with it. What we also noticed were a few hairs in the same area that might prove to be of interest. Later, when we examined the carpet in more detail back in the laboratory, we were able to confirm the presence of blood on it, and that the hairs matched the head hair of the woman whose body had been discovered in the lay-by. When questioned by police, the man said that, some time earlier, his wife had had 'an accident while menstruating'. It was another potentially plausible explanation. Or, at least, it might have been if it hadn't been for what we discovered when we put all our findings together.

In the orientation in which the carpet would have been fitted in the hall, the damp stain on it was adjacent to the area on the wall where we'd found the small splashes that had now been confirmed to be blood. What was even more significant was that the nature and pattern of the splashes suggested that the blood had been split up – from a blow, for example – rather than being passive bleeding from menstruation. There was blood on a pair of the man's shoes too. And when the police questioned him again, he suddenly remembered that he and his wife had been messing around in the hall one day when she'd fallen and banged her head on the radiator.

Being able to visit a crime scene and see blood patterns *in situ* is an important aspect of any forensic investigation and can often provide quite a clear picture of what might have happened, as it did in that case.

Another case I worked on, for which being able to piece together the course of events proved useful, involved a brutal attack on the wife of a restaurant proprietor. Fortunately, despite some very severe injuries, the woman survived the assault. But she was left with no memory of what had happened to her.

I was working at Aldermaston at the time, and the restaurant where the attack took place was in a small town in the Thames Valley. L-shaped, quaint and cottagey, the restaurant might have been a bit less popular than it apparently was if any of its customers had ever looked inside the dustbins at the back of the building and seen the maggots that were crawling all over their contents. But it appeared to be clean enough inside the restaurant itself. Or it probably had been before its surfaces were spattered with a substantial amount of blood.

At first glance, the interior of the restaurant looked like a scene of random carnage. Then, on closer examination, quite a clear picture began to emerge of what had taken place the previous evening, after the last customers had eaten their meals and gone home.

Splashes of blood on some of the tables and heavy pooled staining on the carpet nearby indicated where the woman had been attacked and subsequently lain. A trail down the narrow corridor that ran alongside the dining area showed her route to the toilet, where she had obviously gripped the edges of the basin with blood-stained hands and coughed, spattering blood on to the mirror. Then, still leaving a trail of dripped blood, she appeared to have made her way along another part of the corridor to the door that opened out on to the street. She obviously hadn't gone through the door though, and the last part of the trail led back to the restaurant, where she had finally collapsed.

The investigating officer looked sceptical as I explained what I thought the sequence of events had been. And he was clearly completely nonplussed when I added, 'Oh, and the victim is 5 foot 3.'

'She *is* 5 foot 3,' he told me. 'How could you know that?' It was a reasonable question. But because I was rather enjoying his astonishment, I didn't answer it.

Sometime later, I had a phone call from the same police officer, who told me that the woman had undergone hypnosis. 'And do you know?' he said, in an almost reverent tone. 'The sequence of events she recalled exactly matches what you said had happened.' I think that was when I finally relented and explained how I'd known how tall the woman was. In fact, 5 foot 3 inches was the distance from the floor to the underside of a leaf on a large plant in the restaurant corridor where I'd seen a special sort of mark made through contact with wet, blood-stained hair. Knowing that the victim had sustained severe head wounds and that her hair would have been dripping with blood, I'd realised that the mark must have been left on the plant when she walked or ran underneath it.

I think the police suspected that the woman's husband had paid someone to carry out the assault on his wife. What was also interesting about the case was that it was an example of how important it is to have the knowledge and experience to interpret what you're seeing at a crime scene. As well as being able to fill in the gaps for the investigators, it also gives you the best chance of collecting for closer inspection the items that are most likely to have evidence on them. In fact, lack of appropriate knowledge and experience in relation to crime scenes has contributed to various shortcomings in forensic investigations in the past, including some that have been brought to light in recent times.

Another fascinating, and in some respects unusual, blood-related case I worked on when I was at Aldermaston involved the murder of a retired bank manager. The victim had clearly been bludgeoned to death in the sitting room of his house in Sussex. But examination of the crime scene yielded little useful information, other than how the assailant had gained access to and left the premises. What *was* interesting was a blood-stained outline on the bed that appeared to be of some sort of pole-shaped implement. Most of the drawers and cupboards in the house had obviously been opened and roughly searched, presumably for money and other valuables. And it looked as though, having attacked and killed the householder, the assailant might have placed whatever weapon he had used on the bed while he was searching the chest of drawers in the bedroom.

As with any murder by a stranger, it was going to be difficult for the police to identify a possible suspect. But I can't remember what it was specifically that made them decide to bring in, or accept support from, a medium. It was a decision that, for any scientist, would probably fit unambiguously into the 'interesting but unlikely to help' file. Even so, I did try to keep an open mind when I was told, after the event, about what had happened.

Apparently, an arrangement had been made for the medium to meet two police officers outside the deceased man's house. When only one of the officers had arrived by the specified time, she told him, 'I need to start walking *now*.' Then she turned abruptly and set off down the road, with the officer following a few steps behind her.

They had walked about half a mile when the medium stopped in a small close that was lined on all sides by the back gardens of several properties. After hesitating briefly, she pointed towards some fencing and told the officer, 'I think there's something deeply significant to the murder very close to here.' And when the police searched the gardens, they found a blood-stained section of scaffolding pole.

A lucky coincidence, perhaps? The thought might even cross the mind of a sceptical person that the medium knew more about the murder than she admitted to, although there was never any suggestion that that was the case. It was certainly absolutely extraordinary, and provided a critical lead that enabled the investigation to move forward – because the section of scaffolding pole matched exactly the dimensions of the blood stain that had been found on the victim's bed.

It wasn't all plain sailing, however, and when we examined the pole in the laboratory at Aldermaston, we found that the blood on it belonged to the same combination of blood groups as the dead man, except for one – the EAP group. For a while, the discrepancy was baffling and frustrating, because even if there was just one group that didn't match, it wasn't possible to say that the blood on the scaffolding pole could have come from the victim. Clearly, logic seemed to indicate that it was too much of a coincidence for it *not* to be the weapon that had been used to kill him. As well as having been found so close to the scene of the crime and being precisely the same size and shape as the blood-stained outline on the bedding, the pole had blood on it that matched all of the victim's blood groups, with that single exception. So surely there had to be *some* explanation for the mismatched blood group.

I knew it was technically possible for an EAP group to change as blood ages. But that couldn't be the cause of the discrepancy in this case, because if the blood on the pole *had* come from the victim, it had only been there for a matter of days. So maybe it was something to do with the galvanised nature of the pole itself. To test that hypothesis, we did some experiments. After putting blood of different known groups on another, similar scaffolding pole and then on to an unstained section of the pole discovered near the crime scene, we watched to see what happened. What we found was that we effectively got accelerated ageing of the blood. And when we used blood of the same EAP group as the victim's, we were able specifically to demonstrate that it could have changed in the time available to the mismatched group we had found in the original blood sample from the pole.

Zinc is a strong reducing agent, and our chemist colleagues were able to explain why the zinc coating on the galvanised scaffolding pole might have been responsible for the blood-group change that had occurred. So it was the breakthrough everyone had been hoping for. Because now we could say that the blood on the scaffolding pole could have come from the victim, backing up that claim with the evidence from our experiments.

When the assailant was subsequently identified, he was convicted of murder and sentenced to life in prison – thanks, in part, to a combination of science and (don't quote me on this) psychic detective work.

6

DNA profiling

In 1984, Dr Alec Jeffreys (later Professor and now Sir), a geneticist at the University of Leicester who was studying hereditary diseases in families, realised that people could be identified on the basis of variations in their genetic code. Four years later, after he went on to develop the technique of DNA fingerprinting – which is now more commonly referred to as DNA profiling – a man called Colin Pitchfork became the first person in the world to be convicted of murder based on DNA evidence, and the first person to be identified as the result of mass DNA screening.

There is absolutely no doubt that DNA profiling has been the single most significant development in forensic science during my career. It has transformed the strength of the link between individual people and traces of saliva, semen, blood and even skin flakes left on clothing, for example. Also, since the early days of its use in the mid-1980s, the technology has advanced and the techniques have been refined to such an extent that results can be obtained from amounts of material that are so small they aren't visible to the naked eye, that have been degraded by the environment they've been in, or that are mixed with DNA from one or more other people – or from a combination of all those scenarios.

DNA – or deoxyribonucleic acid – is the main component of the chromosomes that are present in the cells of almost all living organisms, both animals and plants. It can replicate itself to create copies as the cells divide. And it carries the genetic information that is inherited from one generation to the next.

DNA can be collected from an item by a range of techniques, including swabbing, scraping, cutting out bits of fabric, and removing surface debris using sticky tape. The sample is then placed directly into a small test tube, together with chemicals into which the DNA is to be extracted. As far as analysis is concerned, the first step is to multiply up (or 'amplify') the amount of DNA in the extract so that there is enough to analyse. This is achieved using a complex mixture of chemicals and exposing the whole thing to a series of heating and cooling cycles – the amount of DNA doubling with each cycle. A sample of the amplified extract is transferred to a reaction plate, together with a series of known samples – some of which contain no DNA, while others contain DNA of known types, as a check that the system is working properly. The reaction plate is then inserted into a big grey box with flashing lights that is known, imaginatively, as an analyser. The analyser separates out and identifies the specific component (of several possible types) at each of a number of particular sites. And it's the combination of these specific components that provides the profile of the DNA.

The fact that it's possible to obtain a result from tiny amounts of DNA means that you have to be particularly careful to rule out any alternative explanation for it. Could there have been some sort of contamination, for example, either before or after the relevant item reached the lab? Or could the DNA be related to an entirely innocent event before the incident occurred? It's therefore very important to understand as much as possible about the context of cases and the items and samples that have been collected and tested in connection with them. For instance, has the suspect been at the crime scene before? Has he or she been in contact with key items from the crime scene? Or together with the victim? Or at the same venue as the victim before the crime was committed? Any one of those eventualities, or variations of them, could conceivably result in the innocent transfer of DNA, which could later be mistaken for evidence in connection with the incident.

By the same token, you have to ensure that systems and processes within laboratories are sufficiently robust to be confident that nothing in the lab itself could have compromised the results. So laboratories have to be much cleaner than they were before the advent of DNA, and scientists have to wear much more protective clothing than they used to. When I started work at the FSS, a lab coat was all that was required, plus a pair of disposable gloves if something was particularly nasty. We didn't always wear the gloves though, as it was sometimes easier to 'feel' stains with ungloved hands than it was to see them. Since the advent of DNA, however, protection is just as much for the exhibits being looked at as it is for the scientists themselves.

The standard technique currently in use in England and Wales is called DNA17, because it analyses components at seventeen different sites on the DNA, including the site that tells you about gender. A full DNA profile will typically occur in fewer than one in a billion people. And as there are only about 7.5 billion people in the world, you can see how powerful DNA profiling is. By comparison, from traditional forensic blood grouping, you'd be lucky to get a frequency of occurrence of the combined blood groups of one in a few thousand.

Despite the impressive statistics, it's still possible to make mistakes. In the early 1990s, for example, a man who was suspected of having committed a burglary was convicted on the basis of a DNA-profiling result with a frequency of occurrence of what I think was 1 in 37 million. The suspect always denied very vociferously that he had been involved in the burglary, and when his case later went to appeal, further work was done. By that time, additional areas of DNA had been added to the test that made it even more discriminating. And while the new results confirmed that there was nothing wrong with the original test result, the man's DNA didn't match in the new areas. So the crime couldn't have been committed by him after all. The finding came as a bit of a shock to the forensic community, which was still getting used to the vastly improved statistics DNA could provide, only to discover that, even at that level, they still weren't good enough.

DNA profiling has proved to be a critical factor in helping to solve many of the cases I've worked on since the late 1980s – in the cold-case investigations into the murders of Stephen Lawrence and of Gwenda and Peter Dixon on the Pembrokeshire Coastal Path, for example. But as well as helping to prove the guilt – or innocence – of countless numbers of people, it has also been used to test historic convictions, such as that of the 'A6 murderer' James Hanratty.

Michael Gregsten and his mistress, Valerie Storie, worked at the Road Research Laboratory near Slough.

On 23 August 1961, they were in Michael's car in a field near Maidenhead when they were accosted by a stranger. Having forced them at gunpoint to drive to a lay-by on the A6 between Luton and Bedford, the man shot and killed Michael. Then he raped Valerie, before shooting her too, leaving her alive but paralysed from the waist down.

The following day, a .38 revolver was found, wrapped in a handkerchief, under a seat in a bus. A few days later, two cartridge cases from the same gun were discovered in the room in a guesthouse in Maida Vale where James Hanratty had stayed on the night of the attack. After he had been identified by Valerie Storie, twenty-five-year-old Hanratty was tried and convicted of the crimes, then hanged in Bedford Prison in April 1962.

Hanratty had protested his innocence to the end, and in 1991, I was approached by Bob Woffinden, an investigative journalist working for Yorkshire Television, supported by a solicitor called Geoffrey Bindman, who thought there might have been a miscarriage of justice.

During the original investigation, some mixed seminal and vaginal staining had been found on Valerie's knickers and half-slip. But after blood-grouping work had been done on it by scientists at the Metropolitan Police Forensic Science Laboratory (MPFSL), it was generally agreed that the test was 'an exclusion test and not an inclusion test'. In other words, the blood-grouping evidence should not be used as a positive link between Hanratty and Valerie Storie, although it could be the basis for excluding someone as the source of the semen.

Various evidence items had been destroyed in a fire. But when I visited Bedfordshire Police HQ in July 1991, I looked at a number of exhibits relating to the case that were still being held there. A couple of months later, I went to the MPFSL in Lambeth to examine the original forensic case file. The file was thin and rather battered. But among its few sparse pages I found two small snippets of fabric that proved to be just the sort of critical samples we were looking for, and hadn't really believed we'd be fortunate enough to find.

The snippets, which had been stored in separate, sealed and labelled plastic bags, were what remained of the samples of some of the semen staining that had been discovered on Valerie Storie's underwear during the original investigation. But although several attempts were made over the next few years to get a DNA-profiling result out of extracts of the snippets of fabric, the tests all failed to produce any results. And after leaving the precious samples I'd unearthed in what I knew were very good hands at the MPFSL, my direct association with the case came to an end.

Consequently, I was no longer involved in 1999, when the handkerchief that had been wrapped around the murder weapon apparently turned up, and DNA tests were carried out on some mucus staining on it. Samples of DNA from members of Hanratty's family were used for comparison. And what the tests showed was that the 'evidential DNA' was 'two and a half million times more likely' to have come from James Hanratty than from anyone else unrelated to him and selected at random.

In view of all the controversy surrounding the case, Lord Chief Justice Woolf then decided that Hanratty's body should be exhumed so that comparisons could be made with DNA directly from him. When that was done, the results confirmed that he was very likely to have been the source of the DNA on the handkerchief and of the semen staining on Valerie's underwear, which had eventually yielded results to more modern forms of DNA profiling. (Other male DNA identified on the underwear was thought to have come from Michael Gregsten.)

At the appeal court in 2002, the possibility was raised by Michael Mansfield QC, acting for the Hanratty family, that the DNA results could have arisen as the result of contamination. It was a suggestion that was dismissed by the judges as 'fanciful', and as there was also other evidence to implicate Hanratty, including identification by eyewitnesses, the appeal court judges decided that there was overwhelming proof of the safety of the original conviction.

The general point about contamination was well made though. And it's particularly relevant in cases that stretch back over many years, to a time before the advent of DNA profiling, when exhibits were handled and tested in conditions that wouldn't be acceptable with today's technology. Having said that, it's not enough merely to suggest that contamination could be a factor. Specific routes need to be explored, and the likelihood of transfer and persistence of any traces that could conceivably be mistaken for evidence needs to be evaluated. What the case also highlighted was that, sometimes, a sample kept in an old file, that might easily have been overlooked, can prove to be the key to confirming – or otherwise – a verdict in a historic case.

Since they were introduced into the forensic-science armoury more than thirty years ago, DNA-profiling techniques have evolved and developed hugely, and will no doubt continue to do so for many years to come.

7

A new type of forensic service

One of the things I learned quite quickly after I started going out to crime scenes for the FSS was that although they may not be visible to the naked eye, many – or all – of the pieces of the puzzle are there somewhere. You just need to understand what happened in order to know where to look for them so that you can start to fit them together to create a coherent picture. Context is vitally important in almost every case. And one of the things that can be very useful in helping you to understand the context is reading the statements of surviving victims, witnesses and any suspects. So there was considerable consternation – expressed by many of my colleagues and by me – when a notice was issued by the Director of Public Prosecutions towards the end of 1981 saying that forensic scientists would no longer be routinely supplied with statements before they examined evidential items.

Apparently, it had been decided that, 'The danger of supplying statements in advance is that the scientist, under cross-examination, is liable to be accused of having "tailored" his findings to fit in with his knowledge of the alleged circumstances of the offence.' While that may have sounded sensible in theory, the new regulation was a nightmare in practice. Because what it meant was that we were denied a proper framework for choosing the most useful items to examine and test within the context of the specific circumstances of each case and to understand the potential significance of the results. Fortunately, the police officers who submitted work to us understood that, and often bent the rules, until eventually everyone just seemed to forget about them.

Meanwhile, scientists at the six FSS laboratories – at Wetherby, Chorley, Birmingham, Chepstow, Huntingdon and Aldermaston – were becoming overwhelmed by cases. Service levels dropped, and morale dropped with them. The Home Office, which had invested heavily in new laboratories, obviously wanted to find a solution to the problem that would enable the scientists to get through more work more quickly. So they decided to send inspectors to one of the FSS laboratories to do a sort of time-and-motion study.

We all understood why the Home Office was keen to work out how many forensic scientists were actually needed and how big the labs ought to be to enable the work to be done as efficiently as possible. What was so exasperating was the fact that the people employed to do the assessment and write a report clearly had no understanding of what was involved in forensic investigations. Nor, apparently, did the people whose job it was to read and interpret that report. The laboratory they chose to inspect was the one at Chepstow. And as everything that was said about it was also true of all the other FSS laboratories, including my own at Wetherby and then Aldermaston, there can't have been many forensic scientists who weren't absolutely incensed by some of the comments that were made.

One infuriating 'observation' concerned some scientists who had gone out to a crime scene and then 'just stood around' for the first half an hour, instead of immediately getting down to testing things. Apparently, no one thought to ask the scientists what they were actually doing. If they had, they would have discovered that they were trying to work out what might have happened before deciding what tests they needed to do and which items to take back to the laboratory for further examination. It was a misunderstanding that I addressed in a subsequent letter of protest I wrote, which was just one of many irate and indignant letters that were written in response to the Chepstow report.

One of the things I said in the letter was that, 'Scene examinations have been glossed over in the report, yet this is one of the most testing areas of the forensic scientist's work ... The scientist needs an inquiring, alert and scientifically trained mind to interpret signs correctly, to distinguish between the significant and insignificant in an overwhelming mass of clues, to know which items need to be examined in depth and which may safely be ignored – an increasingly difficult task in the face of mounting selectivity.' The word 'selectivity' was a reference to attempts to improve efficiency by cutting down on the number of items we examined, focusing on those that were of most apparent relevance. Obviously, if you weren't going to look at everything, you had to be particularly careful not to exclude anything important.

The points I was making are still relevant today, to a greater or lesser degree. As my director at Aldermaston used to say, going to a crime scene can save two weeks in the laboratory. To which, in view of some relatively recent changes in the commissioning and delivery of forensic services, one might now add the addendum, 'but only if you know what you're doing'.

Reaction to the Chepstow report notwithstanding, what was becoming obvious was that change to the FSS was badly needed, and that it *was* coming.

Since the early 1980s, I'd been thinking about the effect the changes that were already taking place within the service were going to have on my own future as a forensic scientist. After becoming responsible for managing a small team of assistants and junior reporters, the next step would have been for me to manage a larger unit, or perhaps a whole department. Although I thought at the time that was something I wanted to do, I'm not so sure in retrospect, particularly because it would have meant doing much less of the science I enjoyed so much. As things turned out, however, it wasn't a decision I had to make, because by the time the opportunity might have arisen, the FSS had put a freeze on promotions. The organisation had expanded massively around the time I started work at Harrogate, and there was now a glut of experienced scientists with nowhere to go, career-wise.

The Controller of the FSS from 1982 to 1988 was a forensic scientist called Margaret Pereira, who had begun her career at the MPFSL. Known as 'Miss Murder', Margaret was something of a novelty. On the scientific side, she was probably best known for her work on minia-turising ABO blood grouping, and for investigating the murder of Lord and Lady Lucan's nanny, Sandra Rivett. But she'd done some other interesting things too, includ-ing, in one case, discovering a physical fit between differ-ent parts of a fresh chrysanthemum flower. Having been the only female candidate for the Controller's job, there had been the inevitable complaints from some of her

male colleagues about positive discrimination in favour
of women. But despite what were becoming increasingly
difficult circumstances, she seemed to be doing a good
job. So before I decided what my next move should be, I
went to see her.

Basically, as there didn't seem to be any real prospect
of being able to advance my career within the FSS, I
thought I was going to have to leave. And when I explained
that to Margaret, her response was pretty much what I
thought it would be: she completely understood my situation, and although she didn't want to lose experienced
people, she simply didn't have anything suitable to offer
me. It was an amicable discussion and we parted on good
terms, as I like to do with everyone. In fact, Margaret
Pereira was later to provide tremendous support when I
was involved in setting up a laboratory in competition
with the FSS, even though doing so made her a bit
unpopular at the Home Office.

I'd been very happy during the last twelve years and
had learned a great deal. But having reached the end of
the road as far as the FSS was concerned, and with some
ideas of my own that I wanted to pursue, I left Aldermaston
in 1986 and started my own company.

During the years I had been working at the FSS, I'd
become increasingly aware of the fact that defendants
didn't have any proper access to the qualified, experienced forensic experts that were readily available to the
police and prosecution. So my main purpose in setting
up Forensic Access was to try to redress what I saw as a
fundamental imbalance in our adversarial justice system
in the UK by providing forensic services for the defence.
It was fairly rare for defendants to have the scientific
evidence against them checked independently, and even

rarer for it to be done by properly trained forensic scientists, and the need for it appeared to be great.

What I'd also realised was that when scientists were working almost exclusively for the police – which was the case at all the FSS laboratories – they tended, especially in those days, not to think very much about alternative explanations for their evidence. Scientists in that position – working at the 'front end' of an investigation, often before all the necessary information has been gathered from house-to-house inquiries, witness interviews and so on – are at a disadvantage anyway. So it's doubly important that when forensic-science evidence is critical to a case, you have two scientists. While one of them discovers what the prosecution proposes is evidence, the other makes sure that that evidence has been interpreted appropriately in the light of all the circumstances, including what the defendant has to say on the subject.

The situation is rather healthier today, with more companies now doing what Forensic Access did in the 1980s, including some that work predominantly for the police. What also helps is the fact that judges today sometimes insist that prosecution and defence experts get together in advance of trial to discuss and decide which bits of the evidence they can and can't agree on. Then jurors can focus particularly on the issues that are in dispute. At that time, however, there must inevitably have been some miscarriages of justice as a direct result of the courts' reliance on the evidence of just one – unchallenged and not always entirely understood – expert forensic witness.

Another reason why things tended to be biased in favour of the prosecution at that time was that defence lawyers often didn't have the knowledge to look at the evidence that had been presented from a different perspective. As a result, they frequently didn't have the confidence to ask the right sort of questions that would enable them to find out if there might be an alternative explanation to the one being proposed by the prosecution.

Take, for example, a situation in which textile fibres have been found on a suspect that could have been transferred from something the victim was wearing. The suspect is insisting that that isn't possible, because he didn't do it and he wasn't there. It's a claim that could be tested if the suspect is able to point to an item of his own clothing that might contain the same sorts of fibres. But, because of the amount of work involved, the police and prosecutors are unlikely to offer to go through his entire wardrobe on the off-chance of finding an alternative match. So the possibility that the fibres came from an item of the suspect's own clothing rather than something the victim was wearing is never investigated.

To make matters worse, if the defence asked for the work to be done, they had to send their request – and receive the results – via the police. And if the results of the tests weren't what they expected or hoped they would be, and weren't helpful to their case, the police and prosecution lawyers would know about them before the defence did. Which meant that a lawyer acting for a defendant might end up bringing to light some evidence that would help to convict his or her own client.

Firms like Forensic Access changed all that by providing defence lawyers with an authoritative source of expertise of their own, through which they could understand the strengths and weaknesses of the scientific evidence their client was facing. What it also meant was that they could test out any alternative theories about why that evidence might be present in the same privacy as that afforded to the prosecution.

The fact is that forensic scientists are witnesses for the court and can, theoretically, be called to give evidence by either side. But as lawyers always like to know in advance the answers to the questions they are asking, it's a risky business calling witnesses that have been instructed by the opposing legal team. So, in practice, if a forensic scientist is called at all, it's usually by the side that instructed them.

I didn't know when I set up Forensic Access whether I would be successful in what I wanted to do. Obviously, I was concerned about whether I'd be able to attract enough clients to make it a viable business. And there was also the risk that I'd become disillusioned if they consistently wanted me to say something I couldn't say – I was never going to be an 'expert for hire'. But I was, as ever, optimistic and determined to give it a try.

Russell Stockdale and I were married by that time and had a young son, who had become – and remains – the main driving force in my life. So we had Russell's income to fall back on. But it still felt like a huge risk when I borrowed the equivalent of my final year's salary at the FSS from the bank.

Our house in Newbury, in Berkshire, was a typical 1960s' suburban bungalow, to which we had added a porch and pitched roofs that made it look a bit like a single-storey Swiss chalet. Now, we converted a six-by-eight-foot room into an office by installing a white kitchen worktop along one wall that served as a desk, as well as another, slightly higher, one along an adjacent wall on which to examine things and keep a recon-ditioned comparison microscope and some electrophoresis equipment. There was enough space underneath the worktop to house a small fridge, which held all the chemicals I needed to enable me to do blood grouping and textile-fibre analysis. By the time I'd added two bright-red filing cabinets to the room, plus a trolley to hold the state-of-the-art BBC Master home computer I bought, it was pretty much full.

Once the office was set up, I got some leaflets printed and sent them to every address on a long list of solicitors specialising in criminal law. Then I put an advertisement in the *Yellow Pages*, and did everything else I could think of to make people aware that I was open for business as a well-qualified, independent forensic biologist.

For some reason, I've always been very keen on stationery, so I was very pleased with the logo my brother Adam designed for my new company. Depicting the labyrinth created by Daedalus, in which King Minos of Crete kept the Minotaur, it had a direct route from its centre to the periphery, which represented the direct path through the maze I would create for my clients. It's an image that absolutely sums up what I was hoping to be able to do: after looking at the scientific evidence, some of which can be quite maze-like in its complexity, I would interpret and explain it to my clients in a way that could be easily understood by someone without a scientific background. In fact, the logo worked so well that we still use it on all our stationery today.

So I had the stationery, a small but functional office, and all the equipment I was going to need for the sort of cases I'd be taking on to begin with. Now all I needed were some clients.

My first case came from the advert I'd placed in *Yellow Pages*. I was an experienced forensic scientist by that time. So looking at a pair of knickers for a man who suspected his wife of infidelity wasn't the sort of case I particularly wanted to work on. But you do what needs to be done when you're starting up a company.

You have to be very careful when testing for semen, because the colour change you are looking for in the presumptive test can, to the untrained eye, look rather like the colour change you can get from vaginal secretions. In fact, I'd come across a number of scientists who took on forensic work who didn't know the difference. And what concerned me was that, by reporting false-positive reactions in their tests, they might have been responsible for wrecking some perfectly good marriages. So at least I would get a chance to address an issue related to semen tests that I'd been concerned about for quite a while.

My second case was quite different, however, and involved a murder that a pathologist friend of mine called Stephen Cordner was working on for the defence. The forensic evidence for the prosecution, which was being presented by scientists at the MPFSL, focused mostly on blood patterns, particularly a limited amount of impact spatter that had been identified at the crime scene.

As well as visiting the laboratory in London, talking to some of the scientists there and examining key items for myself, I had read all the relevant reports and statements. The conclusions I came to were that the prosecution's interpretation of the evidence wasn't the only possible explanation for it, and that some of it might actually exonerate the suspect. I don't remember the details of the case now, but I do recall feeling that the report I wrote should at least make people think about the fact that just because something *could* have happened in a particular way didn't mean that it *did* happen that way. It was an important distinction, and one that lawyers for the defence often didn't emphasise enough. Of course, their expertise was in law, so it wasn't surprising they didn't understand all the scientific detail I'd spent the last twelve years learning about. But maybe that was about to change.

8

'This is my life'

As more work began to come in, I would sometimes look at the critical witness statements in a case that was being prosecuted, examine the most important exhibits on behalf of the defence, and end up wondering how it had ever got to court in the first place. One such case involved a doctor who had been accused of sexually assaulting one of his patients. After reading all the statements and other relevant papers, I examined various evidential items, including two pairs of trousers, a disposable examination glove and other debris that had been collected from the waste bin at the doctor's surgery.

The upper part of the thumb of the glove had been removed for testing by the forensic scientist employed by the prosecution, who had apparently found traces of semen on it. The thumb section was no longer available, so I wasn't able to check it myself. But the lab records supported what had been reported. And I *could* corroborate the other findings, including the presence of traces of semen around the fly area of the doctor's trousers.

When considering these findings in the context of the rest of the case, there were three main reasons why I thought they lost any impact they might otherwise have had. (1) No semen had been found on any of the swabs taken from the alleged victim or from the couch and blanket she said she was lying on when the alleged assault occurred. (2) There was no seminal staining on the doctor's underpants. (3) The semen on the doctor's trousers only represented a very small part of a normal ejaculate – so where was the rest of it?

Also missing from the equation was any evidence on the glove of the 'profuse white (vaginal) discharge', which was apparently the woman's reason for visiting the doctor in the first place. One of the fundamental principles of forensic investigation is that absence of evidence can't be assumed to be evidence of absence. In this instance, however, it was starting to look as though the woman's version of events was unlikely to be true. In my opinion, I wrote in my report for the defence, there was actually no scientific evidence to indicate that the complainant had had sexual intercourse on the night in question. In fact, taken together with all the other evidence, or lack of it, it seemed more likely that there was some alternative explanation for the original forensic scientist's findings.

By presenting evidence based on sound scientific tests but without putting it into context or talking about other possible explanations for it, there is a very real and ever-present danger of blinding people with science – including lawyers, judges and jurors. That was something I'd wanted to try to combat when I set up Forensic Access. And the fact that it was absolutely highlighted by that case is one of the reasons I still remember it after all this time.

As a forensic biologist, most of the work I was doing involved blood and other body fluids such as semen and saliva, textile fibres from clothing, furnishings etc., and a wide variety of weapons and the damage caused by them. Some of the cases were fairly straightforward. Like the case of the cheese-and-tomato sandwich, for example, when I was able to confirm the suspicion of an officer from the Department of Health that the reddish-brown smear on one of the pieces of bread was human blood. Or the case of the six foil-wrapped chocolates that had obviously been unwrapped and then clumsily wrapped up again. In that instance, the fears of the well-known chocolate manufacturer proved unfounded and there was no evidence that anything had been injected into the chocolates or smeared on their surface, or that they had been tampered with in any other sinister way. Then I started getting requests from other barristers, solicitors, pathologists, various police forces and investigation bureaux. And, before long, I was very busy.

A few months after I'd left the FSS, I was alone in the house one early-winter's evening, sitting in my little office, when I became aware that it had gone dark outside. The rest of the house was dark too, and completely silent. All I could see was the pool of brilliant white light that was being cast by the Anglepoise lamp on my desk. The sense that I was surrounded by absolute nothingness was clearly an optical effect. But it was a surreal experience, and I can remember looking at the circle of light and thinking, 'That's all there is. This is reality now. This is my life. I won't ever forget this moment.' And I haven't.

Perhaps the reason it felt so strange was because I wasn't used to being alone. My brothers Jonathan and David were always around somewhere in the house when I was a child. And I saw my other brothers Adam and Jeremy, and then, later on, Sam, and my stepsister Kate, fairly often. Then, for the last twelve years, after being at school. and university, I'd worked with friends and colleagues in busy laboratories at the FSS. So I suppose I was still in the process of adjusting to the sense of isolation that came with working alone in a silent house, while wondering if it was all going to work out. It wasn't a thought that depressed me in the slightest though; I was just interested, even excited, to find out what the future might hold.

Mainly because of the confidential papers we now held in the house, we'd had an alarm fitted when I started working from home. But I never felt nervous or threatened, until the day a man came to hear the results of some tests I'd done for him in yet another case of suspected infidelity.

The man had been perfectly pleasant, almost cheerful, when he brought me his wife's stained skirt. I'd explained the limitations of the tests I could do, and that even if the stain did test positive for semen, it wasn't possible to say how old it was, so it could have been there for some time. He seemed to accept and understand everything I told him. And he was pleasant when he came back for the results too, until I said that the stain on his wife's skirt *had* tested positive for semen.

Even though I reminded him about the caveats we'd discussed on his earlier visit, I expected him to be upset by the news. But I was caught off guard by the speed with which his demeanour changed from politely attentive to incredibly tense. For most of the time I'd been talking, his arms had been hanging loosely by his sides. Now though, they stiffened as he clenched his hands into tight, white-knuckled fists. Fortunately, I managed to manoeuvre him out of the room to the front door, which I locked swiftly behind him. A few days later, we had a panic button fitted, which rang at the local police station and made me – and Russell – feel a lot better.

At the other end of the spectrum of suspected infidelity cases was one I did for a woman who sent me numerous hairs she had recovered from her husband's underpants. Clearly very meticulous by nature, the woman had stuck the hairs to Sellotape strips, to which she had also added reference samples of her own and her husband's head and pubic hair. The test results required no qualifications or explanations and prompted no extreme emotions on that occasion, however. In fact, I was able to reassure the woman that the 'suspicious black hairs' she had noticed in her husband's underpants were actually very fine grey-blue textile fibres – probably transferred from an item of his own clothing.

By the autumn of 1987, when Forensic Access had been in existence for about eighteen months and I was struggling to cope with all the work that was coming in, it had become clear that I needed some help. Russell had been transferred to work in London some time previously and was fed up with all the travelling involved. So, rather than me finding someone else, he decided to give up his job and join me. Then, having rebuilt the garage at our house in Newbury to create an L-shaped laboratory and a couple of offices, we took on a secretary, and subsequently a chemist as well.

My income during the first year at Forensic Access was about the same as I'd been earning when I left the FSS – and just a few hundred pounds less than the overdraft I'd obtained to set up the company. So taking out a mortgage on our house after our chemist joined us felt like another risk when we were only just getting over the first one. But it wasn't long before the company had outgrown the converted garage and we moved it to a small office in Newbury, where we employed a practice manager to take over some of the management tasks Russell and I had previously shared between us. Then, when the time came for the company to expand again, we moved into larger premises in Thatcham. The new premises, which had previously been used by the charity Guide Dogs for the Blind, had a training kitchen that made an excellent laboratory, and we were able to take on another chemist and a DNA expert, as well as some more office staff.

Because we were usually employed by the defence, I often had to drive to FSS laboratories around the country, where I'd spend the day checking and discussing what had been done by the scientists there, before driving all the way home again. What was even more tiring than the physical effort, however, was the vast amount of nervous energy involved.

My role was to check the results of examinations and tests on critical items, and to highlight any alternative explanations that might be suggested by specific case contexts, of which the FSS scientists might be unaware. To be able to do that, I needed to have useful conversations with them about the work they'd done. So, in order to ensure that they saw me as a sort of safety net rather than as an enemy, I had to reassure them that I wasn't there to pick holes gratuitously in their work. What helped was the fact that, having worked at the FSS for so many years, I knew every minute detail of what was involved in the job they were doing. And I understood the pressures they were constantly under to deal with more cases in less time. Sometimes, I would crack jokes to try to keep the atmosphere light. But striking the right balance could still be very tricky, and it certainly wasn't a job for anyone who didn't like people.

By that time, we were working on a wide range of investigations. As well as murders, sexual and violent assaults, thefts, armed robberies, suspected arson, drugs of abuse and toxicology, we did various one-of-a-kind, sometimes quite odd, cases, both in the UK and abroad. One rather unusual case we were asked to look at involved a blackmail demand that had been sent to the President of Cyprus in 1987.

The letter, which was signed 'Commander Nemo', was from someone who said he represented an organisation called Force Majeure and claimed that chemical weapons had been positioned around the island of Cyprus in 'poison injection generators'. Unless the Cyprus government paid a ransom of US$15 million, the letter said, the chemical weapons would be activated to release the toxic gas dioxin, which would contaminate the country for centuries to come.

A few days after the letter had been received, someone calling himself Colonel Digsby phoned the presidential palace in Nicosia. Claiming to work for British Military Intelligence in London, the man said that Force Majeure was a known and serious threat, and that the government of Cyprus would be well advised to hand over the money that had been demanded. A little while later, when the money still hadn't been paid, a man visited the Cyprus High Commission in London and offered, for a fee of £25,000, to help detect the hidden generators by flying over the country in a helicopter fitted with a magnetometer. This time, an agreement *was* reached. But when the man returned to collect the money, he was arrested by detectives from the UK's anti-terrorist squad.

We became involved two years later, when the case against British-born Greek Cypriot Panos Koupparis went to court. It was a representative of the government of Cyprus who asked us to assess the possible threat that had been posed by Commander Nemo and the various members of his family who constituted the 'terrorist group' Force Majeure. Having accepted the case, we then had to work out how we were going to deal with it, which was when I had the bright idea of asking my brother Jeremy for advice.

The second oldest of my five brothers, Jeremy was at that time a distinguished Professor of Chemistry at Harvard University. (He went on to become Dean of the Faculty of Arts and Sciences from 1991 to 2002, then again from 2006 until his death in 2008.) After consulting an eminent professor who was a colleague of his, Jeremy gave us some very funny advice, in a letter that included the following observations.

This is hilarious, and 'Digsby' is inspired. The defendant should be recruited for TV script writing instantly . . . A proton magnetometer can, with good sensitivity, detect metal (actually iron-like metals), but it is extremely unlikely that it could be used from a massive moving lump of metal like a helicopter, and even if it could (some such devices are used on long ropes in submarine detection), it would detect every old car, new car, dumped fridge, etc. (i.e. this, too, is nonsense).

In summary, this letter (exhibit 20) would only confirm for me the hilarity of the whole exercise! I await exhibit 21 with hungry anticipation . . .

In other words, the whole scheme really was as crazy as it sounded. There were no poison injection generators, no Colonel Digsby working for British Military Intelligence, no Commander Nemo, and no terrorist group called Force Majeure. The attempt to extort money from the government of Cyprus had been real enough though. And following a trial at the Old Bailey in London in July 1989, Koupparis was found guilty of blackmail and sentenced to five years in prison.

Not long after the Koupparis case, we became involved in another 'imaginative' case when we were asked to examine some boots belonging to a former police officer. The work was done by Dr Clive Candy, who had been a Principal Scientist at the MPFSL before coming to work with us at Forensic Access. And his report made interesting reading.

The details we were given about what had happened were fairly brief. Apparently, the police officer had been driving his own car in the early hours of a dark winter's morning in 1980 when he was involved in an incident that rendered him temporarily unconscious. Before he regained consciousness, the officer believed he was removed from his car by aliens, who exposed his feet to some sort of bright light resembling a laser beam, then returned him to his vehicle.

According to the information we were given, the boots the man was wearing at the time were fairly new and in good condition. But when he looked at the sole of his left boot the next morning, he found a split across it that corresponded to an itchy burn mark on the bottom of his foot. What he now wanted to know, his solicitor told us, was whether there were any marks or debris on the boots that might shed some light on where the aliens had taken him.

The alleged incident had occurred some ten years before we became involved in the case, during which time, the police officer said, he had only worn the boots indoors. So, with the open mind that's required of any good forensic scientist, Clive examined the boots very carefully. What he found was extensive cracking and creasing to the uppers, discoloration and compression of the insoles and heel linings, and signs of wear on the existing soles and heels. Both boots had also been re-soled and re-heeled at least once. Therefore, based on the evidence, Clive wrote in his report, it was his opinion that the boots had been worn extensively.

What was perhaps most informative of all was Clive's finding that the original sole of the left boot had been completely worn away or had cracked across the ball of the foot – as had the replacement sole – creating a jagged edge. There was also a nail in the sole of the left boot that had penetrated through the insole in the region of the ball of the big toe. So perhaps that was what had caused the 'itchy burn mark' the officer had described on his foot. It was certainly a more probable explanation than that the sole of his foot had been burned by a laser. The very diffuse type of laser light used for entertainment purposes etc. wouldn't be powerful enough to inflict an injury. And there were no signs of burns on the boots of the type that would have been caused by an industrial laser beam.

There was also nothing among the traces of mineral grit, vegetable matter and bitumen that you wouldn't expect to find on almost any pair of boots. And although there *was* a small amount of loose debris, mainly between the tongue and the underside of the lace eyelets, when examined under a microscope, it proved to have been derived primarily from polish and the leather itself.

Again, Clive expressed his opinion with polite restraint when he said there was nothing that warranted further investigation. So, unfortunately, we weren't able to unravel the mystery of the aliens and the police officer's boots – which, I suspect, may remain unsolved to this day.

9
The case against
Massimo Carlotto

In 1989, I became involved with a case in Italy when I was asked to provide a critical appraisal of the forensic evidence on behalf of the International Federation for Human Rights. Once again, it was interpretation of the evidence that played a critical role.

On the evening of 20 January 1976, a nineteen-year-old student called Massimo Carlotto went to a police station in Padua in northern Italy and told the following story.

As he was passing the building where his sister lived, he said, he heard someone crying out for help. His sister's flat was on the ground floor, and she was away at the time. But realising that the voice had come from the flat upstairs, and finding the door to the street unlocked, he entered the building. Inside, he found a young woman he knew slightly, lying naked and covered in blood on the floor of a built-in wardrobe in a dressing room off an upstairs bedroom.

Frightened and in a state of shock, Carlotto bent down with his right side next to the woman's left side. Then, just as he was reaching across her chest towards her face, she lifted her right arm in an arc-like motion before letting it fall to the floor on her right side. When the woman's eyes closed, Carlotto thought she was dead. So he ran out of the flat and went to the house of some friends, who advised him to tell his story to the police, as he was now doing.

When he finished explaining to the police what had happened, Carlotto was arrested and charged with the murder of twenty-five-year-old student Margherita Magello. By the time his case was heard in the court in Padua in March 1978, and he was acquitted for lack of evidence, he had spent two years in detention.

In England at that time, only the defence could appeal against a conviction or sentence. But the legal system in Italy was different, and in 1979 the Italian Ministry of Justice began appeal proceedings to try to get the original verdict overturned. This time, the case was dealt with by the Appeal Court in Venice, and Carlotto was convicted of murder and sentenced to eighteen years in prison.

For some reason I've never been clear about, Carlotto was allowed to leave the courtroom following the hearing and ended up living at home for a while before going to Mexico. Then, in 1985, he was expelled from Mexico, and was arrested and imprisoned on his return to Italy.

Having always categorically denied any involvement in Margherita Magello's murder, Carlotto began to gain support after his imprisonment, both within Italy and elsewhere, particularly in France. As a result, the Italian Supreme Court ordered a retrial in 1989, which was the point at which I became involved in the case.

The undisputed facts, as far as I understood them, were that Margherita Magello had been stabbed approximately sixty times, in what appeared to have been a frenzied attack. When her mother returned home from work that evening to the flat they shared, she found her daughter's naked body in the built-in wardrobe. Other than that, the details were less clear cut. And while some of the very substantial amount of medical and scientific evidence that had already been presented by various experts seemed to incriminate Carlotto, other aspects tended to exonerate him.

Included among the various documents, which I read in translation from the Italian, were a post-mortem examination report and reports by the police and various experts about the murder scene. There were also details of the laboratory examinations of Carlotto's clothing and of items removed from the scene itself, as well as Carlotto's own account of events, and the statement from the victim's mother.

According to the post-mortem report, there was no semen on Margherita Magello's body to indicate a specifically sexual motive for the assault. The numerous defence wounds on her arms indicated that she had defended herself vigorously against the knife attack, but she had died as a result of cuts involving her vital organs. A hair was caught between two fingers of one of her hands. And there were some patterned marks in the blood on the inner aspect of her right foot that were thought to have come from the sole of a shoe – although not from the shoes Carlotto was wearing when he was arrested that night.

By the time I became involved in the case, the patholo-gist had already re-examined some of the evidence for the prosecution. The clothes Carlotto had been wearing had been taken in and out of bags and had been looked at by various people on countless occasions. But I wasn't allowed to examine any of the clothing or other items myself, or visit the crime scene, or check any of the original records relating to the scientific analysis. And as the various photographs lacked linear scales and were all technically poor – even allowing for the fact that they had been taken some fourteen years earlier – it was often difficult to understand exactly what I was looking at. There were also problems with regard to some of the medico-scientific documents, which had apparently been translated by someone who wasn't a specialist in the relevant fields, so didn't always manage to convey the real meaning of what had originally been written.

One thing I quickly realised was that there were also problems with the blood-stain identification and analysis that had been done at an early stage of the investigation. The forensic tests that had been performed for the appeal hearing in 1979 were reasonably thorough, and in keeping with good scientific practice. But even by the standards in existence in 1976, the techniques that had been used during the original investigation fell far short of those that were in use in the FSS laboratories at that time. Also, the fact that the blood grouping had been restricted to the relatively undiscriminating ABO system meant that any link with the victim's blood was more circumstantial than the result of objective analysis. For example, after the victim's blood group had been identified as O, there had been a tendency to assume that all group O blood found at the scene was hers. Which was a conclusion that completely overlooked the fact that, as O is a very common blood group, occurring in something like 39 per cent of the Italian population (and about 45 per cent of the population of the UK), some of it might have come from her attacker.

It's not uncommon in frenzied knife attacks for offenders to cut themselves as their hand slips in wet blood down the knife from handle to blade. Just that unconsidered possibility alone would have cast doubt on some of the inferences drawn about the potential significance of some blood stains found at a distance from the body. The assumptions were further exacerbated by the fact that no extensive blood-grouping tests had been applied to blood stains in the bedroom and bathroom and on the banisters. In fact, when some blood found in the laundry room downstairs was tested, the results showed that it could not have been either Margherita's or Carlotto's.

The prosecution's case insofar as blood staining was concerned was based on four propositions. (1) That some cuts in Carlotto's gloves were like those on Margherita Magello's body. (2) That Carlotto had washed his coat, and possibly his gloves. (3) That some visible stains on Carlotto's gloves were probably blood, even though they had not been analysed. (4) That the attacker need not necessarily have been heavily blood stained.

It was true that the blood stains on Carlotto's clothing *could* have come from Margherita. But there was nothing to suggest that he'd washed his coat. In fact, there had been no suggestion that blood on his coat had been diluted until the two scientific investigators were specifically asked to consider the possibility. They'd then conducted some experiments and concluded that some degree of dilution had, indeed, occurred after the blood had been deposited. Again, I wasn't able to examine the traces myself. So I looked at the original evidence, then drew on my own experience and knowledge of blood stains to come to a conclusion. And the conclusion I came to was that they could have been nothing more than light contact traces with one or two small splashes, as you'd expect to find if Carlotto had had the contact with the victim he described. There was no evidence to suggest that his gloves had been washed either, or, after exhaustive testing by the original scientists, that the stains found on the gloves were blood at all, despite what was claimed at Carlotto's trial.

Perhaps the most significant of all the prosecution's propositions concerned the blood found at the scene, most of which was on the floor of the wardrobe where the body was discovered. According to the two original scientists, Margherita would have been 'virtually supine' when the knife attack began, and because most of the wounds were on the front of her body, blood would not have drained out of them. The implication was that they would not have expected to find much blood on her assailant. And as there was only light blood staining on Carlotto's clothes – a few marks on the right sleeve of his jumper and on the lower left front of his coat, and a very small number of isolated marks on the crotch and lower legs of his jeans – they felt that he could not be precluded as her attacker. But it was a claim that ignored some very important facts.

For example, the fact that the main part of the attack had occurred in the confined space of the wardrobe made it difficult to see how victim and assailant could have avoided substantial contact. The large number of blows involved in the attack, some of which had been delivered with considerable force, would have resulted in a significant amount of blood staining on the assailant's clothing, as would Margherita's vigorous attempt to defend herself. Margherita had no clothes on, so there would have been nothing to absorb any blood emanating from her wounds. Her body – arguably the most heavily blood-stained item at the scene – had been removed by the time the Italian scientists got there, which might have affected their appreciation of the extent of blood staining. And if the blood in the adjoining bedroom had dripped from the assailant as he passed through it, as had been suggested, at least part of his clothing would have been heavily loaded with liquid blood. Consideration of all those factors led me to the conclusion that, on this occasion, one would have expected significant amounts of blood to have been transferred from the body of the victim to her assailant's clothing.

It was a completely different conclusion from the one the original scientists had come to. Fortunately, though, I had evidence from a past case to back it up. Forensic scientists don't tend to retain formal records of blood-stain distribution patterns, except on case files, obviously, and sometimes as reference for teaching or demonstration purposes. But I had a photograph of a man who had gone to the aid of a victim of violent assault in much the same way as Carlotto claimed to have done. The man wasn't ever suspected of having attacked the victim himself before the true culprit was identified by the police. Yet his upper clothing was spattered with many more spots and splashes of blood than Carlotto's.

It wasn't possible to establish a sequence of events from the information I'd been provided with. Ultimately though, I was confident that there was nothing in any of the documents or photographs I'd been allowed to see to suggest that the blood on Carlotto's clothing must have arisen in incriminating circumstances. Nor was there anything to indicate that it had not originated as the result of the sort of contact with the victim he'd described.

Carlotto claimed that it was hearing Margherita calling

out that had attracted his attention and led to him entering the flat, and that she had spoken a few words when he found her. According to the two Italian scientific experts, however, that could not have happened, because she would have died immediately from the injuries she'd received. It was an assertion that was subsequently refuted by another scientist, but it clearly went against Carlotto during his trial.

What should also have been taken into account was Carlotto's statement that when he found Margherita on the floor of the wardrobe, he thought she had just a few wounds on her body, and certainly not the sixty or more that were identified at autopsy. But that, too, was ignored by the prosecution. In fact, no one seemed even to have considered the possibility that when he rang the doorbell before entering the flat, Carlotto might have disturbed the real murderer. Perhaps Margherita's attacker had hidden in the bathroom, where some light blood staining was found. Then he could have returned to the wardrobe after Carlotto had fled, to finish what he'd started and make sure his victim didn't live to identify him.

It was certainly a hypothesis that seemed worthy of investigation. But it was discarded by the original scientists, who believed that all the wounds were inflicted within a short space of time, and that death had been almost instantaneous. However, it *was* upheld by the three scientists who subsequently became involved in the case, who maintained that the knife attack had occurred in two distinct phases, the first of which was not fatal.

What also seemed to lend support to the possibility that the murderer might have hidden in the flat while Carlotto was there were some apparent discrepancies between what he described at the scene and what was found there. For example, Carlotto mentioned in his statement that as he'd passed the doorway to the bathroom, he'd noticed some rags on the floor, but none had been discovered by the police. He'd described the bath as being half full of water, but he hadn't seen the tights and pants that were subsequently found floating at the end of the bath that was clearly visible from the doorway. He said that there were lights on in the bathroom and adjacent bedroom when he entered the house. But there was apparently no light on in that bedroom when Margherita's mother returned to the flat and found her daughter's body.

The fact that Carlotto had nothing to gain by lying about that sort of detail could suggest that he was actually telling the truth. And if he was, someone must have moved the rags and put the items in the bath after he left the flat. Perhaps the traces of blood found on the light switch in the second bedroom had been left there by someone with blood-stained fingers who had turned it off after Carlotto fled. Perhaps the traces of blood found on the door handle inside the bathroom and on a relatively inaccessible towel rail close to it had been deposited by someone with blood-stained hands. And perhaps that 'someone' had already begun to attack Margherita before hiding in the bathroom when Carlotto rang the doorbell.

What exacerbated some of the problems was the fact that the original scientists working for the prosecution might have been very experienced pathologists etc., but they didn't have forensic-science expertise. One very significant example of their lack of specific knowledge was the luminol test that had been used to detect blood.

The chemical luminol reacts with blood to produce a

chemi-luminescent reaction that glows in the dark. It's a test that had been in use in the UK long before I joined the FSS in 1974. In fact, it was so old-fashioned by that time that very few people still remembered or knew how to use it. It's actually a very sensitive test, in that it's able to detect blood at dilutions of up to one part in a million. So it's an extremely powerful tool for detecting blood traces and visualising blood patterns that you can't see with the naked eye. On difficult backgrounds such as dark, heavily patterned carpets, for example, or when attempts have been made to clean up blood staining, or to follow trails of blood-stained footwear marks long after they've ceased to be visible. But there are drawbacks associated with its use too, such as having to operate in the dark and record reactions that become progressively more diffuse while you're watching.

It was because of those negative aspects that luminol was dropped in the UK in favour of the more modern tests that are also extremely sensitive and can be used in broad daylight. But there *are* situations in which it can be useful, and I've used it often since then – although definitely not for the purpose for which it was employed during that investigation in Italy.

What compounded the problems in Carlotto's case was the assertion by the Italian pathologist that once blood has dried on a fabric, there's no way it can be transferred to anything else. But that isn't true. (Maybe the pathologist got confused with the fact that the older blood is, the more difficult it becomes to solubilise it, which is what you need to do for blood grouping.) When blood dries, it becomes susceptible to powdering if disturbed – if clothing fabric is flexed through being crumpled up while it's folded and unfolded, for example, or while being lifted in and out of evidence bags. Which means that even with a fairly modest stain on an item of clothing, dried blood powder can be spread to other parts of it. Then, when it's tested with the very sensitive luminol technique, the blood staining can appear to be much more extensive than it originally was.

To demonstrate that specific point, and to develop my own expertise with luminol, I carried out a large number of experiments at the time. What they proved was that, in certain circumstances, you can get a very misleading impression of the extent of blood staining on an item when using the technique. And I think that's what happened in Carlotto's case. Although the pathologist thought the test he'd done proved that Carlotto's clothing had been plastered with blood, there had only actually been very modest blood staining on it, which was absolutely consistent with Carlotto's description of what had happened.

The fact that the Italian legal system is inquisitorial – rather than adversarial, as it is in the UK – means that the courts have a slightly different function in that they investigate as well as adjudicate cases. As a result – certainly at that time – 'revered' experts can be given much more licence and be subjected to much less challenge than they should be. Having said that, it had happened in the UK, too, until perhaps seventy or eighty years ago, before it was discovered that people like the university academic and pathologist Bernard Spilsbury were fallible, and trust and confidence in them began to evaporate.

Certainly, the eminent pathologist who was giving much of the evidence when I attended the hearing at the court in Venice strayed well beyond his area of expertise, without anyone being prepared to question him. Like the police, the pathologist seemed to have made up his mind that Carlotto had killed Margherita Magello, and he was very confident when giving his evidence. Carlotto's family had been trying for years to get his conviction overturned. But although he had been released from prison because he was ill, he was still considered to be guilty. So I felt sorry for him and his family, having to sit there listening to all this deeply unscientific evidence and the outrageous conclusions on which his conviction had largely been based.

What was even more depressing than listening to the pathologist was something that occurred in a separate room behind the courtroom. The judges, barristers, members of the family and a few other people, including me and the director of a forensic laboratory in Paris, had adjourned to the room so that the pathologist could show us his slides of the blood on Carlotto's clothing. And he was just coming to the end of his presentation when we heard the sound of people chanting something over and over again. It seemed to be coming from the courtroom, and when I asked the interpreter what they were saying, she told me, '*Assassino.* It means murderer.' What seemed even more incredible than the fact that it was happening at all was that no one put a stop to it.

The director of the French laboratory had also been advising Carlotto's family, and her findings had pretty much agreed with mine. But, after much to-ing and fro-ing, it was decided that the defence wouldn't be allowed to put up their own experts. I couldn't have said categorically that Massimo Carlotto wasn't the murderer, but there simply wasn't any scientific evidence to show that he was. Yet these awful 'experts' had managed to convince everyone that such evidence did exist. It made me feel very impotent, knowing that I had evidence that cast very significant doubt on their assumptions, but that I wasn't going to be given the opportunity to explain it to the court.

In the end, Carlotto was again found guilty of murdering Margherita Magello and sentenced to sixteen years in prison. But his family remained determined to prove his innocence, and three years later, after an international campaign for justice, he was finally pardoned by the President of Italy. I understand that he went on to become a successful crime writer, helped, I imagine, by being able to base at least some of his plots on his own, very unfortunate, personal experiences.

10

Fibres and hairs

One evening in September 1990, the recently retired Governor of Gibraltar, Air Chief Marshal Sir Peter Terry, was sitting reading at his home in Staffordshire when several shots were fired through the window. Bullets from two of the shots lodged very close to his brain, while others shattered his face and also injured his wife, although less severely.

During his time in Gibraltar, Sir Peter had authorised a security operation based on British Intelligence reports of a planned attack on the island by the IRA. During the operation, three members of the Provisional IRA had been shot by the SAS. So it was assumed that the assault on his home had been an attempted revenge killing for their deaths. Two months later, three men were arrested and charged with the attack, which is when we were asked to have a look at the case by the solicitor acting for one of them.

After we became involved, Russell and Clive Candy visited the MPFSL laboratory in London, where scientists had already carried out tests on some of the many items that had been seized by police from several cars and addresses in London. Then I did some further fibre-analysis work, which included conducting detailed analysis of the fibres at the heart of the prosecution's case.

What we were particularly interested in were a few fibres that had been found in pockets of 'our' defendant's jacket and on his jumper and jeans when he was arrested. The fibres appeared to match the constituents of a black acrylic mask – which was actually a sleeve cut from a jumper – that had been found near the crime scene. According to the MPFSL report, the mask could also have been the source of a single textile fibre that had been collected from a window sill at Sir Peter Terry's house, and of two fibres found in combings from another defendant's hair.

The suitability of an article of clothing or any other textile as a potential source of transferred fibres depends on a number of factors. How deeply dyed the individual constituent fibres are, for example. How readily the item sheds its constituent fibres – a characteristic that forensic scientists have always called 'shedability'. And how commonly occurring the fibres are likely to be in the textile-fibre population as a whole. So it may not be worth spending what could be a considerable amount of time looking for fibres from blue jeans, for instance, because their presence would usually provide far too weak a link with any specific item.

The most common method of recovering fibres from the surface of an item involves systematically applying a series of strips of clear sticky-tape to the surface to pick up any superficial textile fibres and other loose debris. The strips – known as tapings, tape lifts or, simply, tapes – are stuck on to clear plastic sheets and their edges sealed with more tape before they are placed immediately and individually into protective envelopes or polythene bags. The envelopes and bags are then sealed and labelled to identify exactly whereabouts on the item the fibres on each strip were recovered.

When you re-investigate cold cases, you can be dealing with items that were first examined many years ago, when the protocols used by the police and in laboratories weren't as tight as they are today. So you have to be very careful to check that nothing that was done during the original investigation might be capable of undermining anything you wish to do now. Tapings are very useful in this respect because as well as always being the first samples to be taken from any item, before it has been handled to any great extent, they pick up a wide variety of traces. And they are then protected from contamination for however long a period of time passes before they are looked at again.

When forensic scientists talk about transferred fibres, they are not, as might be supposed, referring to strands of fibre, but to the individual components of such strands. Often no more than a millimetre or so in length, each fibre is so fine that it can be difficult to see with the naked eye. So comparison of recovered fibres with constituents of potential sources for them – so-called target or reference fibres – has to be done with the aid of microscopes. First, the fibres on a tape are compared under a low-power microscope with reference fibres of interest. Then any that look similar are removed, mounted individually on microscope slides, and compared in more detail in a process that involves a number of distinct phases.

In the first phase, the fibres are examined side by side under a high-power microscope to compare fibre type and perceived colour. Any that appear to be different from the fibres from the supposed source are then rejected. In the next phase, the perceived colour of the fibres is further analysed using microspectrophotometry, which gives a more detailed, objective assessment of colour. The chemical composition of synthetic fibres can also be determined using a technique called Fourier-transform infrared spectroscopy (FTIR), which enables acrylics, for example, to be distinguished from nylons, polyesters and a variety of other fibre types. The mixture of components of dyes in any particular fibre can be very complex. So, in the final phase, the dye stuffs in some of the remaining fibres may be extracted, analysed and compared using thin-layer chromatography (TLC), or instrumentally with high-pressure liquid chromatography (HPLC).

The problem with TLC is that some fibres are too pale or too short for it to be successful. However, during our investigation into the attack on Sir Peter Terry, it was the final phase that was potentially the most decisive. Because although one blue fibre might look very much like another, even under the microscope, the mixture of dyes used to create the colour in each of the two fibres might be different. Which would mean, for example, that two fibres that looked as though they could have come from the same item of clothing, carpet, towel etc. could prove to be distinctly dissimilar and have no connection with each other.

Although the fibres from the mask appeared black to the naked eye, when viewed under a microscope they were actually a mottled green-brown colour and of a type known as 'tiger tails'. There was a specific, primarily UK-based, textile manufacturer that produced most of the tiger-tail fibres at the time. And after they had confirmed that our fibres were, indeed, of a type sold by them, a forensic scientist at the MPFSL analysed the dye and identified it as being indistinguishable from a formulation from the same company.

A possible match between the mask retrieved from the crime scene and some fibres found in the pocket of a jacket belonging to one of the defendants might have proved to be useful evidence to the prosecution's case. What made it rather less incriminating, however, was the fact that the manufacturer had produced approximately 3,600 tonnes of similar yarn during a recent two-year period.

Further investigation failed to reveal information about any company that might have produced the specific item of clothing from which the sleeve-mask had been cut. But, ultimately, the source didn't matter. What *was* relevant to the defendant's case was that such a significant quantity of similar yarn had been produced. Because it meant that the fibres found in the defendant's jacket pocket could not be said with any confidence to have originated from the sleeve-mask rather than from any of the *millions* of other items that had been made from the same yarn. What was also interesting was that no saliva or head hairs had been found inside the mask, which you might expect there to be if it had been worn over someone's head for any length of time.

When Russell asked the defendant's solicitor to find out whether his client owned any other clothing containing black acrylic fibres that could conceivably represent an alternative, innocent source of the fibres, we were sent a number of fibre samples to look at. When two of these proved to be indistinguishable from the sleeve-mask fibres, Russell asked to see the actual items they had come from, which turned out to be two jumpers that were made of a mixture of fibres and were very different from each other in appearance. But when I carried out TLC and some other tests that were employed at the time, I confirmed that the two jumpers contained black acrylic fibres that were indistinguishable from the fibres that had been collected from 'our' defendant's clothing. And when scientists at the MPFSL subsequently conducted the same tests to check my findings, they agreed that the textile-fibre evidence wasn't as damning as it had originally been thought to be.

The reason I particularly remember the case is because it was a good illustration of the fact that you can't ever assume anything from evidence without having considered, and sometimes tested, other possible explanations. Even today, with all the advances there have been in DNA profiling, a DNA match isn't proof that someone has done something. All it establishes is that there's a link with that person, for which there might or might not be an alternative, innocent, explanation. What the case also highlighted is how important it is for all critical forensic evidence to be independently checked so that other possible interpretations of it can be taken into account.

About four years after that investigation, I worked on another case related to textile fibres and the Provisional IRA, following a bombing campaign in north London that took place between 2 and 8 October 1993. Three suspects were quickly arrested. But it was almost a year later when we were asked by a solicitor to look at some of the evidence relating to his client, who I'll call Suspect A.

The forensic investigation for the prosecution had been conducted by scientists at the MPFSL, who had done a lot of very good work on other IRA cases. Our job was to check the evidence and ensure that every possible explanation for it had been considered. Perhaps the most significant of the findings was what appeared to be two specific links. One of them was between some clothing and a bath mat in Suspect A's flat and some bomb-making equipment the police had discovered behind the bath panel there. The second was between the same items of clothing and bath mat and a device that had been planted in Highgate High Street but had failed to explode. Some fibres that seemed to match the bath mat were also discovered on clothing collected from the other two suspects, on a scarf Suspect A was thought to have left behind in a minicab, and on the driver's seat of a car he had formerly owned.

By the time I visited the MPFSL in early December 1994, most of the recovered fibres had been consumed in analysis. But after examining the few that remained, I was able to confirm that they were indeed indistinguishable from the sources proposed. What the significance of that might be, however, was another matter.

After checking the potential opportunities for cross-transfer, it seemed unlikely that the items had been accidentally contaminated before they were submitted to the MPFSL. Contamination wasn't the only alternative explanation for the textile-fibre evidence though. Apart from the explanations ascribed by the prosecution, it was also possible that the fibres found on the bomb-making equipment could simply have been picked up from the background fibre population in the flat itself. There was no dispute about the fact that Suspect A had lent his flat to the other two men; he just claimed not to know them and not to have been aware of any materials they may have concealed there. So it wouldn't have been surprising if there *were* fibres from the bath mat on their clothing.

When the case went to trial at the Old Bailey in 1994, the doubts our investigation had raised about the prosecution's evidence against Suspect A seemed to resonate with the jurors. And while the other two suspects were found guilty of conspiring to cause explosions and sentenced to twenty-five years in prison, the jury was unable to reach a decision about him.

On the other side of the coin are cases in which textile fibres provide quite compelling evidence of a link between a suspect and a victim or crime scene. But even in those cases, it's important to check for and rule out any possibility of cross-transfer or accidental contamination. Because, despite our current understanding of the risks, mistakes *are* still sometimes made. For example, the same police officer sometimes handles items from more than one location. Or fibres are transferred from a police officer's own clothes. Or items are packaged or repackaged in a room where they could pick up fibres from other items. Or even, as occurred when I was working at the FSS, bits of decaying binding can drop off a pathologist's notebook as he bends over the victim's body at the crime scene! We spent a significant amount of time trying to identify the strange blue fibres that were stuck together in an odd lattice pattern, before eventually realising what had happened.

One example of a situation in which there could have been cross-contamination occurred in another case I worked on for a defence solicitor. The defendant had been accused of attempting to rob the proprietor of a shop who was on his way to the bank with the day's takings. According to the forensic report, a couple of fibres that had been found on the anorak worn by the accused man could have come from the shop-owner's shirt. In the other direction, some fibres collected from the shop-owner's trousers and shirt and from the bag containing the takings could have come from the cardigan worn by the defendant at the time of the alleged attack. Therefore, it was concluded, the evidence was consistent with the two men having been in contact with each other.

After visiting the FSS lab at Wetherby, where I was shown the textile fibres by the scientist who had done the work, I conducted my own examination. At first, I thought some of the evidence might be even stronger than was being claimed by the prosecution. For example, four very distinct cotton fibres found on the bag were microscopically indistinguishable from some that had been collected from the lining of the defendant's anorak. However, the other fibre evidence was less compelling. And as I was reading all the reports and statements related to the case, something of potentially far more relevance almost leapt off the page at me.

Apparently, the police officer who had arrested the defendant had also come into contact with the proprietor of the shop *before* all the clothing and other items had been seized and bagged. There was doubtless a good operational reason why that had occurred. But the officer had still broken a cardinal rule by creating a situation in which he could, unwittingly, have transferred fibres from one of the men to the other. Despite the breach in protocol, the textile-fibre link between the bag and the anorak might still have carried some evidential weight if a substantial number of transferred fibres had been found. But the fact that there were just eleven microscopic fibres in total rendered it unsafe to rely on the findings of the original forensic investigation – and gave the defendant's solicitor something to work with.

As in many of the other cases we did for the defence, there wasn't anything wrong with the original forensic evidence; it was just that it might have had another interpretation. It was our job to try to put the evidence that had already been gathered into some sort of meaningful context. And while we might agree, on the basis of the available evidence, that a crime appeared to have been committed by someone with a 1+ PGM blood group, or while wearing a blue sweater, what couldn't be said was that that person was necessarily the defendant.

In more recent years, textile fibres have proved instrumental in helping to solve some high-profile murder cases. In the Pembrokeshire Coastal Path murders, for example, and in the murder of Stephen Lawrence, they not only provided excellent evidence in their own right, but also acted as a signpost to where to look for other types of evidence, including, critically, DNA.

As with textile fibres, I sometimes had reason to question hair-related conclusions that had been drawn by forensic scientists working for the prosecution. Before the advent of DNA profiling, the evidential value of human hairs was relatively limited. In fact, the only thing it was usually possible to state with any certainty was that a sample submitted as evidence was either human or from some other species of animal.

Reference samples from an individual can be compared with hairs recovered from evidence items with respect to their colour, length and microscopic appearance. If the recovered hairs are indistinguishable from the reference sample, or fall within the range of variation, you can say that they could have come from the same source. But there can be significant overlap between the features of the hairs from one person and those from another. Also, the hairs on one person's head can vary considerably in terms of colour and microscopic appearance. So the absence of a match could indicate either that they are not from the same source or that the reference sample provided is not representative of the complete range of hairs from that person.

If the hair has been bleached or dyed or is damaged or unusual for some other reason, such as being mixed with other hair in plaits, the link can sometimes be stronger. And if a hair has been pulled out by the root, there may be cellular material attached to it that can be analysed using DNA-profiling techniques. But without DNA confirmation, it isn't usually possible to say with any confidence that a hair sample of unknown origin is likely to have come from the same source as the reference sample – although the more hairs you have with similar characteristics, and the more unusual those characteristics are, the more likely that is to be the case.

The problem was, the prosecution often gave the impression that evidence that a particular hair sample *could* have come from the accused was tantamount to saying that it did. They might do it through some genuine misunderstanding, or to exploit uncertainties to bolster their case, even when it was very far from being what the scientific evidence had actually shown. Sometimes, it reflected what the forensic scientist had said. And sometimes it was due to the way the scientific evidence had been summarised in closing speeches by lawyers or judges in their summings-up – long after the scientist had left the court.

Because of all the difficulties inherent in hair evidence, there tended to be more emphasis in the UK on textile fibres. But the situation was reversed in the US, and we were always very uneasy about what appeared to be an inclination to overinflate the value of hair evidence there. It was a problem that came to a head in 2015, when the US Department of Justice, together with the FBI, identified 2,500 cases in the US that needed to be reviewed for that very reason. According to the report, 95 per cent of the examiners' testimonies in a review of 268 cases contained flawed evidence that 'favored prosecutors' and was based on a crude hair-analysis technique. The cases spanned two decades, and included thirty-two defendants who had been sentenced to death. And although some of the defendants might actually have been convicted on the basis of other, more compelling, evidence, the report provided a chilling reminder of how important it is to understand the limitations of hair evidence.

11

Roles and reconstructions

Everyone involved in the adversarial justice system that exists in the UK has a specific role to play. The role of the police is to investigate the circumstances of the crime. Drawing in various experts such as pathologists and forensic scientists as and when required, they attempt to work out what happened and to identify, investigate and then arrest the most likely suspect(s). If they amass what they consider to be sufficient evidence, they then present their case to the Crown Prosecution Service (CPS), which decides whether to prosecute and, if so, initiates proceedings. Lawyers for the defence are appointed, who take instructions from the defendant and make their own investigations, which sometimes includes employing their own experts. Advocates for each side – prosecution and defence – then present their respective cases to an impartial judge and jury. The judge instructs the jury in relevant aspects of law, makes sure all their questions are answered throughout the trial, asks any other questions they could have asked but didn't, and summarises the evidence they have heard at the end of it. Then the jury decides whether or not the defendant is guilty. Finally, if the defendant *is* found to be guilty, the judge passes sentence.

The requirement with regard to the police is that they are absolutely impartial. The prosecution's duty is to present the case in its entirety. Which means that as well as focusing on evidence that might suggest the guilt of the defendant, they also have to include any evidence that would tend to favour the defence. The role of the defence is to point out any weaknesses in the prosecution's case and to produce any other evidence that supports the case for the defendant.

I knew all this, of course. What I perhaps hadn't fully realised before I set up Forensic Access was quite how great the need was for a level playing field for defendants in the courtroom.

Forensic science represents an increasingly powerful form of evidence. As well as being objective – unlike eyewitness evidence, for example – it is capable of analysing and comparing tiny traces. Some of these aren't visible to the naked eye, and are therefore very difficult for an offender to appreciate and eradicate. So what is clearly also critical to the quality of justice is that forensic scientists are impartial too. Perhaps that's easier for them than it is for the police because, being one step removed from the heart of the police investigation, they don't usually have face-to-face contact with suspects. So they aren't exposed to the same level of risk of the cognitive bias that can lead to subjective judgements.

Take a hypothetical case in which a blameless old lady has been brutally murdered. The police strongly suspect her killer is an aggressive, thoroughly unpleasant man who has a known history of violence. Having witnessed the grief and distress of the old lady's relatives, some of the officers involved in the case are subjected to a barrage of foul-mouthed abuse by the suspect. But they must not allow their sympathy for the victim or their dislike of the man they think may have killed her to influence their investigation. The fact that it's possible to understand why that may sometimes prove difficult is one of several reasons why it's so important for both the defence and the prosecution to have access to the services of independent and *experienced* forensic scientists.

As Forensic Access became established, we were working for solicitors all over the country, which involved going to all the FSS laboratories to look at work that had been done on a wide range of cases. As well as discussing the forensic investigations with the scientists involved, we checked their results, examined key items ourselves, and did any further tests we thought might be necessary to get a more rounded picture of what might have happened. Sometimes, I found weaknesses in the forensic evidence that was being presented by the prosecution. And sometimes I agreed – even if only broadly – with the conclusions that had been drawn. On the occasions when the prosecution's evidence in a case was very strong, my job was to explain *why* it was to the defence lawyers. Because only by understanding the strengths and weaknesses would they be confident enough to know what parts of the evidence they could safely question and, conversely, what it wouldn't help their case to dwell on.

In a judicial system in which the accused is innocent until proven guilty, it's essential to have that sort of balance to prevent the defence being at a disadvantage. Because although prosecution lawyers have a duty to present the case in the round, they're inevitably going to focus on the aspects that support their side of it. That was certainly the way it was done in the 1980s and 1990s. Things are slightly different today though, since the

introduction of tight rules that require all relevant information to be disclosed, whether it's positive or negative
in terms of the prosecution's case.

Obviously, forensic scientists have to provide the results
of all the tests they've done, whether they've been employed
by the prosecution or the defence, and whatever potential
impact these might have on the case. Sometimes though,
if forensic scientists don't know the full context, they may
not realise the significance of the presence – or absence –
of something, so their interpretations may be flawed.

I had learned very quickly after starting to do defence
work how important it is to understand the circumstances
of every case and to look at each one as a whole. So my
reports always began with a note about what happened,
what the prosecution was alleging, and what the defendant said about it. Then I described the scientific evidence
the prosecution was bringing to bear, what I had looked
at, with a description of every item, what I'd found and
what I thought about it. Finally, at the end of my conclud-
ing summary, I'd give details of any extra work I thought
it might be useful to do, and why.

After having worked almost exclusively for the police
when I was at the FSS, I was slightly concerned when I
first set up Forensic Access that defence lawyers might try
to influence what I said, or the way I said it. It was something I wouldn't have allowed to happen – my clear duty
was always ultimately to the court. But refusing to do what
they wanted might have left me without much of a business. So it was a relief to discover that, in the vast majority
of cases, defence lawyers just wanted to know what the
evidence meant, and if there were any weaknesses in the
prosecution's case that they could talk about and exploit.

The work I did for defence lawyers was usually funded

by the Legal Aid Board. Occasionally, I would write my report and be told by the lawyer who'd employed me that there was something they didn't want me to say, and/or that they'd rewritten one of the paragraphs. I'm glad to say that it didn't happen very often. But whenever it did, I was always very firm and stuck to my guns. Unless, of course, the changes were purely cosmetic and made no difference to the opinion I was expressing.

As well as making sure that the lawyers understood the scientific evidence before the trial, there was the question of how to present oneself in court. All your evidence and answers to questions have to be addressed to the judge and jury rather than to the barrister who asked them. You also have to ensure that what you're saying is easily accessible to the judge (who may not have any specific scientific knowledge) and the jury (who almost certainly won't) while retaining its accuracy. (The 'teaspoons full' approach advocated by my first lab director, Ian Barclay, often proved useful in that respect.)

Forensic investigations can sometimes takes months to complete, and before you report a case, you have to be absolutely certain about every single part of it. Which means that as well as knowing exactly what everything looked like, you have to know what tests were done and in what order, and what the results of those tests are likely to mean in the context of the particular case. Also, while presenting your considered findings, you have to be prepared to revise them if new information comes to light while you're in the witness box. Giving evidence in court is a funny business, and while I can't say I ever actually enjoyed a court appearance, they were a very important driving force behind all the meticulous behaviours at the crime scene and in the laboratory.

The first case I ever reported, after I'd been at the FSS for a few months, was a suspected rape. Someone else would have checked and initialled all the different aspects of the forensic work that had been done, most of which centred on a set of intimate swabs. And before I left for court in the morning, I re-read all the records and notes. So I was confident that I could explain and substantiate everything I'd written, and that I would be able to comment on any alternative scenarios that might be suggested by the defendant's barrister. Even so, I was naturally nervous when I arrived at the old courthouse in York where the case was being heard.

What I wasn't prepared for was discovering that the door to the witness box wasn't, as I'd thought, a short walk along the corridor from the room where I was waiting to be called to give my evidence. It was actually immediately adjacent to it. Which meant that there was no time for me to take a deep breath and gather my thoughts before someone opened the door and pulled back a curtain, and I found myself facing a courtroom full of people.

There was a deep well in the courtroom that divided the witness box from the judge's bench and the jury. The decor was old-fashioned, with the walls painted cream, pastel-pink and green. And there was a lot of elaborately carved wood panelling. All of which contributed to my sense of having been thrust on to a stage in the middle of a Gilbert and Sullivan opera just as someone was about to burst into song. But I knew I couldn't allow myself to be unnerved. A lot of people had done a great deal of meticulous, complex work to bring the case to court. It was now up to me to present the forensic evidence and answer every question that was fired at me to the very best of my ability.

Some of the scientific evidence presented in any type of court case can be quite dry, and it's a horrible feeling to be answering a really important question and realise that the jurors' eyes have glazed over and you've lost them. So one of the many things you learn with experience as a forensic court reporting officer is to watch for any signs that their attention is wandering, and how to recapture it when it does. They seemed to be following everything I was saying on that occasion though, and I began to feel a bit more confident. Then, just as I was explaining about the evidence for cross-transfer of traces, with semen found on vaginal swabs and vaginal material found on penile swabs, the judge gave a slight chuckle and made a comment about it being like the cross-fertilisation of pollen by bees.

For a moment, I just stood there in silence, with what I hoped was a neutral expression on my face. In fact, though, my mind was whirring as I tried to decide whether he really *had* made a joke. Although that appeared to be the case, it seemed wildly inappropriate in the very serious circumstances. But would he be offended if I didn't smile? I knew my first experience of giving evidence in court was going to be daunting; I'd just expected it to be for rather different reasons.

Another aspect that can be a bit intimidating until you get used to it is the wide range of tricks employed by barristers to try to put witnesses for the other side off their stride. A common ploy is to flap the sleeves of their gown and turn their back on you. Another, which I quickly became familiar with, is cutting you off mid-sentence. Sometimes when that happened, the judge would interrupt the barrister and tell me to continue answering the question. But there were occasions when

I wasn't given the opportunity to qualify or explain something I'd said. And if I did try to do so, I might be told, very firmly, that it wasn't what I'd been asked. It all depended on the judge in those days. Things are a bit different now though, and expert witnesses do tend to get the chance to say if there's something they want to add or expand on at the end of their evidence. That's the way it should be, of course. There's nothing worse than leaving a courtroom feeling that you haven't achieved the necessary balance in your evidence because of the questions asked and the narrow latitude allowed for your replies. It's very important that if scientific evidence is to be relied upon, it really is the evidence, the whole of the evidence, and nothing but the evidence. Presenting just part of it and giving partial opinions can be misleading, and will inevitably risk miscarriages of justice.

Another strategy often employed by barristers when they don't like what's being said is to accuse the expert witness of incompetence or lying, either openly or by insinuation. Fortunately, I've only ever been accused of lying once – not in so many words, but certainly by very clear implication. The case I was reporting on when it happened involved a police officer who claimed to have been bitten in the stomach.

The man accused of biting the officer was adamant that he hadn't done so, and there was nothing in the report produced by the police to suggest that he had. We were employed by the defence lawyer to assess whether or not the claims against his client were even feasible. In fact, I think he just wanted someone to confirm the opinion of another forensic scientist, of rather dubious principles. Because by the time we became involved in the case, the other scientist had already pronounced that the damage to the officer's clothing could not have been caused by having been bitten in the way he described.

The pattern of tears in the police officer's clothing certainly looked odd. While there was little more than a thread broken in the jumper, there was a remarkably neat tear around three sides of a rectangle in the shirt, and a similar-sized rectangular piece of material in a corresponding position was missing altogether from the vest. What seemed particularly strange, however, was the fact that, despite the shirt and vest being made of very different fabrics, the tears along the weave lines in the two items were almost identical.

Forensic science involves a lot of testing and reconstruction. And having sourced a cotton-interlock, singlet-style vest, a cotton and polyester shirt, and a fairly chunky-knit jumper similar to those the officer had been wearing at the time of the alleged incident, I put them on. Then, without actually making contact with my body, one of my colleagues bit my clothing in as close an approximation as possible to what the police officer alleged had happened.

Having established that truth really is often stranger than fiction, you learn to keep an open mind when doing any kind of testing. But we were surprised to find that the fabrics tore in almost exactly the same way as the original clothes had done. Of course, damage caused to clothing in various types of attack isn't random. How something tears depends on many factors, such as what it's made of, its condition, whether there are any areas of weakness (lacy panels in knickers, for example), how strong the seams are, and the nature and strength of force applied. And although our test wasn't absolute proof that the police officer's allegation was true, it certainly confirmed it as a thoroughly viable possibility.

Obviously, that wasn't the answer the defence barrister had hoped for, and to say he was disappointed in me would be an understatement. But, somehow, the prosecution got wind of the fact that I had worked on the case, and they were the ones who called me to court. First though, they wanted to see what I'd written in my report so that they could feel confident about questioning me. So then there was a lot of wrangling about whether I should or should not disclose it. And, with the defence barrister resisting at every turn, I ended up going in and out of court while the two sides put their opposing positions to the judge.

In the end, it was agreed that I *should* release my report and then answer questions on it. What I hadn't bargained on was that, having lost the argument to exclude my evidence, the defence barrister decided that the best way to deal with the situation was to try to discredit me. He did it by suggesting that I was biased in favour of the police, and although he didn't actually use the word 'lying', it was clear to everyone that's what he meant.

Of course, any expert witness giving evidence in a courtroom should be required to explain precisely why they've reached their conclusions. But, in that particular case, I had to hide my feelings of outrage at the suggestion that I might have done anything improper and try to engage with the jury in a different way. Making, and maintaining, eye contact with the jurors, I attempted to convince them that I *had* done the tests properly and was simply stating the results. They were results that had surprised me, too, I told them. But they were supported by the photographs and other data I had in my case file. That's one of the things I like about science: even when you're dealing with circumstances that are full of emotion, your focus always has to be on the facts. After thinking about what tests you need to do, for example, you then do them as carefully as you possibly can, interpreting the results in the context of the case, and going over the background circumstances so that there can't be any misunderstanding about what information you've relied on.

Sometimes, people are wrongly convicted because the forensic evidence is misinterpreted or misunderstood. That certainly must have occurred in the days before forensic services became readily available to defence lawyers. Conversely, of course, there are occasions when the scientific evidence isn't strong enough to be able to help convict someone who *has* actually committed a crime. Whatever the circumstances, the suspect's guilt or innocence is not the forensic scientist's concern. That's the jury's job. What the scientist has to do is provide some of the evidence that may assist jurors in making their decision – evidence that is sometimes critical, of course.

A simple reconstruction in another case was instrumental in sorting out who was more likely to be telling the truth when a husband and wife were accused of murdering their boss and disposing of his body. The boss was the owner of the fast-food shop where the couple worked, and his death might never have come to light if the owner of the site on which the shop stood hadn't decided to redevelop it. While the area was being cleared and all the debris burned on site, the body was discovered, encased in concrete – which was degraded by the fire – and hidden inside a kitchen cupboard in an outhouse at the back of the premises.

The couple blamed each other for the man's death.

'My husband punched and kicked him,' the wife told the police. And when FSS forensic scientists examined the back of the restaurant where she claimed the attack had taken place, they found dilute blood under the floor covering and blood spatter low down on the adjacent wall, which was, on the face of it, consistent with her account.

'It was nothing to do with me,' the husband said. '*She* stabbed him, and there was blood everywhere. I just tried to help her out by cleaning it off the floor with a mop and bucket.'

I didn't go to the crime scene myself. I'm not even sure it still existed by the time I was instructed by the lawyer representing the husband. But I did see photographs and examined some of the critical items in the case. I also spoke to the FSS scientist who had carried out the original investigation, who confirmed the distribution of blood he'd found at the scene.

What struck me on closer inspection of the scene photographs, particularly those of the blood spatter low down on the wall, was that some of the blood spots were dilute and there were dilute streaks of blood in the same area. Mindful of what the husband had said about his involvement in the incident, I bought a string mop and bucket like the one I'd seen in the scene photographs.

Mopping a floor is something one normally does without thinking about it. But it can actually be broken down into several distinct phases. First, you wipe the head of the mop on the floor to soak up some of the liquid – some out-of-date transfusion blood in my reconstruction. Then you rinse it in the bucket of water. After lifting it out, you push and twist it down into the sieve-like basket on top of the bucket to squeeze out some of the water. And, finally, you lift it out of the basket and repeat the process.

After spreading the blood on a similar type of flooring adjacent to a wall, in the same position in which the blood was found at the scene, I set about mopping it up. What I found was that the action of pushing the strings of the mop head down into the basket sent out a spray of tiny spots of dilute blood. Also, it was very difficult to use the mop without at least some of the strings brushing against the wall in the same area. And the patterns produced, low down on the wall but above the skirting board – reflecting the height of the basket – were exactly like the patterns of dilute spots and streaks in the photographs.

It wasn't conclusive evidence, of course. But it did indicate that the husband's version of events provided a persuasive explanation of the blood pattern on the walls. It was certainly a more convincing explanation than the impact spatter that would have resulted from the punching and kicking described by his wife.

Over the years, my colleagues and I have designed, carried out and/or been involved in many reconstructions. Some of them have been simple, like those described above. Some have involved kicking and punching things with wet blood on their surfaces, tearing clothing, or stabbing through layers of clothing similar to that worn by a victim. And some have been more complex. Shooting a suspended pig carcass with a shotgun to ascertain where the shot went, for example. Or shooting into a blood-soaked sponge in the back of a model head to check on blood patterns on the adjacent wall. Or, variously, pulling clothing off colleagues or dragging them round the floor to look at drag marks or where best to sample for transferred DNA. The list is endless.

I didn't realise when I was doing the part of my university course that dealt with designing experiments how important it would turn out to be. But by recreating potential scenarios as closely as possible, it's amazing what you can discover, the surprises you get, and the insights you can then share with investigating officers, lawyers and the courts.

12

Murder or suicide?

What really opened my eyes to how powerful science can be in the forensic context was a case I worked on with my colleagues Clive Candy and Mike Isaacs at Forensic Access in 1992.

On the morning of 18 June 1982, sixty-two-year-old Italian banker Roberto Calvi was found hanging from scaffolding under Blackfriars Bridge in London. After untying the rope from around the dead man's neck, officers from Thames River Police transported his body by boat to Waterloo Police Pier. Photographs were taken, and bricks and lumps of concrete were recovered from the pockets and inside the crotch of Calvi's trousers and from the pockets of his jacket. Then his body was transferred to Guy's Hospital, where a post-mortem examination was carried out by the eminent forensic pathologist Professor Keith Simpson.

According to the autopsy report, Calvi's death was the result of asphyxia due to hanging and was estimated to have occurred between 2 a.m. and 6 a.m., on the morning on which his body was found. There were no injuries to suggest that he had been manhandled before his death, and no injection marks to indicate the possible administration of an incapacitating drug.

A month later, after various reports had been compiled by scientists from the MPFSL and elsewhere, an inquest was held in London, which returned a verdict of suicide. But Calvi was a devout Catholic, and his family were so convinced that he would not have committed the mortal sin of taking his own life, and therefore must have been murdered, they secured the services of the barrister George Carman to represent them. And when a second inquest was held a year later, it recorded an open verdict.

Roberto Calvi was the chairman of an Italian bank with close ties to the Vatican in Rome. Within days of his arrival in London, the bank had collapsed amid allegations of illegal transactions that had led the previous year to him being fined and given a suspended sentence. There were also suggestions of links to organised crime and membership of an illegal Masonic lodge known as Propaganda Due, or P2, which was sometimes referred to – coincidentally? – as *i frati neri* (the black friars).

Forensic Access became involved in the case in 1992, after Calvi's family hired the services of the New York-based investigation company Kroll Associates. Commissioned by Kroll's London investigator Jeff Katz, we were asked to carry out a forensic investigation to try to discover the true nature of Calvi's death.

All scientific investigations involve a series of exploratory steps, each of which is guided by the results of the one that preceded it. The first step in the Calvi case was to take a detailed look at the original investigation and the results of the various tests and examinations that had been carried out by the MPFSL ten years earlier.

The danger of making assumptions in any type of investigation is that you don't look for things that might actually be relevant. And, unfortunately, because the police assumed when Calvi's body was found that he had committed suicide, they had apparently untied rather than cut the rope by which he was suspended, thereby destroying potentially useful evidence, including any that might have been trapped inside the knot from whoever had tied it. In fact, because of that assumption, there had been a delay of several hours before a proper investigation was instigated. So the scene itself wasn't carefully examined in those first few critical hours that include what investigators call 'the golden hour'.

There were some discrepancies in the evidence too, although fortunately nothing particularly vital. For example, the man who discovered the body said that the buttons on Calvi's jacket were undone, whereas one of the police officers said they were fastened. What we did know for certain after reading the various reports, however, was that Roberto Calvi was 5 foot 9 inches (1.75 metres) tall and weighed approximately 13 stone 2 pounds (83.5 kilograms). Also, he had been carrying in his pockets and inside the crotch of his trousers three lumps of concrete and two part-bricks, all of which weighed an additional 11 pounds 11 ounces (4.3 kilograms).

Based on a comparison with similar bricks, stones and soil samples, it had been concluded that those on Calvi's body could have been taken from a nearby building site. It was a possibility that tied in with the report by another MPFSL scientist who had examined Calvi's shoes, in which it was stated that some minor damage on the insteps could have been caused by climbing or walking over rough, uneven ground. What the report also said was that Calvi could not have walked for a distance of more than about one kilometre (0.6 mile) after that, otherwise the damaged areas would have been worn smooth again.

Included among the original documents was a very interesting report by a senior hydrographic surveyor working for the Port of London Authority. By estimating the tides and water heights around the scaffolding from which Calvi's body had been suspended, the surveyor was able to establish limits for activity during the relevant time span according to the pathologist's estimated time of death. Also included in his report was information about when the eyelet in the scaffolding pole to which the rope had been attached would have been covered by water – until about 12.20 a.m. on the relevant night. And there was an estimate of the period of time during which Calvi's head, waist and feet would have been submerged. What was also stated was that in order to have reached the scaffolding via what could have been his 'suicide route' along the river bank between the relevant hours of midnight and 3 or 4 a.m. on that particular night, Calvi would have had to walk through water that was many feet deep for a distance of more than 25 feet (7.6 metres).

Another MPFSL scientist had examined the two Patek Philippe watches that had been found on the body. The watches were also examined by Mike Isaacs, who is, among other things, a clock and watch expert, to the extent that he makes his own clock parts from scratch. One of them, a wristwatch, had stopped at approximately 1.52 a.m. and had a very corroded movement that suggested substantial water penetration. So was Calvi already hanging from the scaffolding when the water rose and covered his watch, causing the movement to stop working? The second timepiece, a pocket watch on a chain, had less water damage and had stopped at 5.49 a.m. However, the fact that it started again when it was rewound indicated that it had not been similarly submerged. Unfortunately, no note had been made about when or where on Calvi's body the two watches and various other items had been found. So it wasn't possible to rely on that information together with information about the rising and falling of the tide to help refine the time period during which he might have been hanging there.

At the second inquest that was held in London, the foreman fitter who worked for the company that had erected the scaffolding some five and a half weeks prior to Calvi's death described how *he* would gain access to it. The route he outlined involved descending from the walkway on the bridge via a fixed metal ladder, then stepping across a gap of about 2 foot 8 inches (81 centimetres) on to two, apparently always slippery, wooden scaffolding boards. It was a route, the foreman agreed when questioned, that someone who wasn't used to clambering over scaffolding would find difficult to negotiate, particularly in the dark.

After reading all the original reports, we revisited the scene and examined all the other physical items that were still available at the MPFSL. Of particular interest were the stones and part-bricks that had been found in Calvi's pockets and inside the front of his trousers, the rope that had been tied around his neck, and the suit and shoes he had been wearing at the time. Calvi had apparently stayed in a flat in Chelsea Cloisters after arriving in England just a few days before his death, and the two suitcases that had been found there had been returned to Italy. So I also went to Milan to inspect some of the clothing and other items.

Unfortunately, as I was under strict instructions not to take any samples from the items I inspected in Milan, or carry out any tests, all I could do was look at things.

Which meant that I wasn't able to examine in any detail any of the stains on the other clothing it looked as though Calvi had been wearing at the relevant time. From the apparent tide marks and water damage on his clothes and the watches, however, and from knowing the ebb and flow of the tide that night, it was possible to say that he had probably been suspended from the scaffolding at some time between 1.50 and 2.45 a.m.

We then turned our attention to how he might have got there. Examining a situation from every angle and discussing all the different possibilities with colleagues are important aspects of any forensic investigation. What started to become apparent when we looked at and discussed the evidence in this case was that there were routes other than the 'suicide route' that was originally proposed via which Calvi could have ended up in the position in which he was found. In fact, there appeared to be two main routes he could have taken if he'd committed suicide, and two different routes by which his body could have been transported if he had been murdered.

Using a number of pairs of shoes and other items of clothing that had belonged to him but were unrelated to his death, we set about designing and then conducting a series of simple experiments and reconstructions. What we were looking for were the sorts of traces you could expect to find in the four different scenarios. Then we compared them with what had actually been found, or what we knew we could still look for on Calvi's clothes and shoes.

One of the two possible 'suicide routes' would have involved Calvi, with the stones already in place in his pockets and in the crotch of his trousers, climbing down the fixed metal ladder from the walkway on to the scaffolding, as described by the foreman fitter. He would then have had to walk across the slippery planks to the far side of the scaffolding, before suspending himself by the length of orange rope the police had retrieved with his body.

If he'd taken the other 'suicide route', he'd have walked along the embankment of the river and down a different ladder on to the foreshore, filling his pockets en route with the lumps of concrete and brick, which had probably been taken from the building site nearby. After walking for some distance along the foreshore – which would only have been possible at low water – he would have climbed on to the scaffolding and then a substantial way up it. To do so, he would have had to traverse the quite wide gaps – 3 foot 2 inches (97 centimetres) – between the horizontal poles, before suspending himself by the rope. What would have made that route even more complicated was the fact that the base of the scaffolding was always covered by water, even when the tide was at its lowest.

It turned out that the company that had erected the scaffolding under the bridge in 1982 had kept it. So after they'd erected part of it in the garden of our house, I managed to persuade Russell – who was roughly the same build as Calvi, although a little taller – to take part in some experiments. Wearing spare pairs of the dead man's shoes and trousers and one of his jackets, with stones of similar sizes and weights in the pockets and in the crotch of the trousers, he negotiated a ladder over roughly the same distance Calvi would have had to have done. Then he stepped across a 2 foot 8 inch (81 centimetre) gap on to a scaffolding pole. What we found was that the brick inside the trousers pivoted on the crotch

seam before eventually slipping off altogether and drop-
ping down inside one of the trouser legs, causing a series
of small abrasions on Russell's inner thigh. Of course, the
reconstruction wouldn't have been a precise reflection of
what had happened if and when Calvi had done it. But at
least it gave us an idea of what would have been involved.

In another experiment, Russell traversed the length of
two poles of the scaffolding, which was the minimum
distance Calvi would have had to walk on them to get to
where he was subsequently found. This time, what we
discovered was that the soles of the shoes became rough-
ened and picked up tiny fragments of rust and yellow
(and/or green) paint as they were first pressed on to the
bar with each step and then rotated over it. Some fragments of green paint had been recovered from the sole of
one of Calvi's shoes. But when Clive Candy examined a
sample of the fragments, he found that they were different from the paint on the scaffolding. So there was actually nothing to link them to the scaffolding poles at all.

We did other tests, too, in relation to the damage on
Calvi's shoes, which was originally ascribed to walking
over rough ground on the building site where he was
thought to have picked up the stones. What Clive discovered was that climbing down the ladder on to the foreshore near Blackfriars Bridge produced relatively little
damage to the soles of the shoes. Also, the damage that
would be expected to be caused by walking at low tide
along the foreshore, which was littered with large slippery
stones and angular lumps of concrete, was rather different
from the sort of damage that was actually observed.

When we immersed the leather soles of two other pairs
of Calvi's shoes in swirling water – to simulate the rise
and fall of river water – the incidental small, deep cuts

that were visible in them, and caused by normal wear and tear, became rather more obvious. Presumably, the water caused the leather fibres to swell, thereby emphasising any discontinuities, which didn't settle back down again properly on drying. So perhaps the damage observed in the similar shoes Calvi was wearing at the time of his death could simply have been an artefact resulting from their immersion in the river.

What was also interesting was that the rope from which Calvi was suspended was attached on the side opposite the ladder that was assumed to have been his means of gaining access to the scaffolding. So perhaps he had chosen that particular spot to hang himself because the rope was already attached there. But if that was the case, why had the rope been threaded through a small eyelet rather than simply tied around a horizontal scaffolding pole? And how had Calvi managed to climb down the near-vertical ladder and negotiate the gap in the scaffolding? Also, especially with stones in his clothing, why – and how – had a sixty-two-year-old man who apparently wasn't very fit made his way so far around the scaffolding? Why was no yellow and/or green paint or rust, like that on the scaffolding poles, found embedded in the soles of his shoes, as our experiments suggested it should have been? And, as he was apparently too short in stature to have noticed the scaffolding as he was making his way along the walkway above, how did he even know it was there?

In the end, we concluded that the scenario of the first suicide route was almost 'inconceivable', and that the second was completely 'untenable'.

So then we turned our attention to the two most likely 'murder routes'. One of them would probably have involved Calvi being either dead or drugged when his body was lowered over the parapet wall to whoever was waiting on the scaffolding under the bridge to tie the rope around his neck. In the other, he would have had to have been transported to the bridge in a boat. The second scenario seemed to be a more likely explanation for the presence of some dirty stains on the lower back of his shirt and trouser legs than that they had been deposited while he was being slid down something – the parapet wall, for example.

Blackfriars Bridge is the point at which the River Fleet joins the River Thames, and the level of swirling water rises and falls constantly. That fact, exacerbated by the wake of passing boats, made the circumstances of some of our investigations even more difficult than they might otherwise have been. But understanding the scene is always critical to being able to work out what might have happened. So when Jeff Katz decided to investigate the boat scenario, Clive and I went with him.

Following a route along the river at the same time of night, in the same tidal conditions, we were intrigued by the staggering level of noise made by what must have been many thousands of bats beneath some of the bridges we passed under. What we discovered was that, with the tide ebbing – as it was at the time when Calvi would have been transported along the same route – it was relatively straightforward to bring a boat in on the same side of the scaffolding as the body was found. And when we wedged the bow of the boat into the corner between the scaffolding and the river wall, the direction of the tide held it there, as it would have done while Calvi was being hauled up on to the scaffolding – stones *in situ* – and a rope was tied around his neck.

Visibility was reasonable too, thanks to the lights along the Embankment. But I don't think anyone looking *out* from the Embankment would have been able to see much of whatever was taking place on and around the scaffolding. Just as the lights in the park in Halifax concealed the actions of the Yorkshire Ripper when he attacked and killed Josephine Whitaker, the lights on the Embankment could have helped prevent Calvi and whoever might have been with him from being seen.

Another aspect of the case that I found intriguing was that Calvi had apparently always had a moustache, but was clean shaven when his body was found. Had he shaved it off himself before leaving the flat in Chelsea and going to the bridge to hang himself? The answer seemed to be no. Or, at least, he didn't seem to have done so with either of the two razors that were found in his suitcase at the flat, which had no obvious long hairs on them when I examined them, and didn't appear to have been cleaned. So maybe his moustache had been removed by someone else, perhaps because they thought it would take longer to identify him if he was clean shaven, or possibly for some symbolic reason. Like so many other aspects of the case, it seemed likely that, whatever the explanation might be, there *was* a reason for it.

Because of the delay in investigating the scene after Calvi's body was found, there were various potentially useful things we simply didn't know. Whether there might have been rope marks over the top of the river wall, for example. Or scrape marks on the face of the wall below to suggest lowering of the body. Or scrape marks on some of the scaffolding poles, possibly associated with minute fragments of paint, rubber, wood or plastic from a boat that might have drawn up briefly alongside it. Or any other scientific evidence to suggest that Calvi had been carried in one way or another to the spot where his body was found. It wasn't because there *was* no such evidence; it was just that no one had thought to look for it.

Ultimately, what our investigation seemed to prove was that Calvi had *not* walked along the foreshore to reach the scaffolding. Also, it was almost inconceivable for a man of his age and physical condition to have climbed down the access ladder and across, on to and along the scaffolding unaided, especially without there being any signs that he had done so. Which meant that the most likely scenario was that he had either been lowered or – the possibility that we thought to be more likely – transported by boat to the site under the bridge where he was found hanging. Therefore, we concluded, Roberto Calvi had *not* committed suicide, but had been murdered. It was a conclusion that brought some small comfort to his family, and was accepted both generally in the UK and, subsequently, by the Italian courts.

A few years later, after a suspect had finally been iden-tified and a prosecution was mounted in Italy, I was asked, via the City of London Police, to go to the terrorist court in Rome to give evidence at his trial.

The court was attached to a high-security jail and was very dark and forbidding. But I reminded myself that my evidence – which included all Clive's work too – was about my conclusion that Calvi had been murdered. It was for the Italian authorities to find out who might have been responsible. Even so, I couldn't help feeling a bit apprehensive during what turned out to be a very long, drawn-out process and when everything I said – and everything that was said to me – had to be translated. So I was grateful to the translator who sat next to me in the courtroom, who was a scientist himself and whose gentle light-heartedness helped to relieve some of the tension.

With the possible involvement of either the Mafia or the Vatican in Calvi's death, I was glad to be escorted to and from court. It was only after I'd given my evidence and was dropped off at the airport to catch my flight home that I began to feel a bit vulnerable. The high drama of the terrorist court had made anything seem possible, and I found myself breathing a sigh of relief when the plane eventually took off.

Despite everything though, being able to investigate that case provided me with a good opportunity and taught me a great deal. Perhaps the most important lesson I learned was that, however complex the circum-stances, a bit of imagination and a lot of tenacity will enable you to shed light on almost anything, even if you start with what you think is almost nothing. It was a lesson that stood me in very good stead some years later when I became involved in investigating cold cases in earnest.

13

Interpreting the evidence

It was the lack of any reliable scientific means of establishing the age of blood that was a factor in our examination of some of the prosecution's evidence following the murder of nineteen-year-old French student Céline Figard.

After working at a hotel in Hampshire during the summer of 1995, Céline had returned to England in December to spend Christmas with her cousin. She travelled for the first part of the journey – from her home in France to the coast – with a family friend who worked for a local haulage company, and crossed the Channel on the 19th. Then she was driven by another French lorry driver to Chieveley Service Station on the M4 in Berkshire, where she accepted a lift to Salisbury from a man driving a white Mercedes lorry. Ten days later, her body was found in a lay-by in Worcestershire.

A post-mortem examination established the cause of Céline's death as asphyxia due to strangulation and a fractured skull caused by at least four blows to the back of the head with a blunt instrument. A couple of months later, after police had released a Photofit image of the man who had given her a lift at Chieveley, a lorry driver called Stuart Morgan was identified by a colleague and arrested.

It was alleged by the prosecution that Céline had been sexually assaulted and fatally injured in the cab of Morgan's lorry. Her body had then remained there for several days, before it was abandoned near the A449. By the time a scientist from the FSS laboratory in Birmingham visited Morgan's home in Dorset a few days after he was arrested in February 1996, his lorry had already been examined by scenes-of-crime officers. The scientist found blood staining in several places in the cab, including on and just in front of the engine cover under the lower bunk. What she also found, in the garage at Morgan's house, was a slightly damp 'seat' that smelled strongly of decomposing blood and had a fabric covering very much like the upholstery in the cab of the lorry. In fact, the 'seat' was actually a bunk similar to the one that was still in the lorry. And when the scientist examined it in detail, she discovered that the internal part of it was extensively blood stained and there was pooled blood in the bottom and around the holes for the release knob.

Although DNA analysis of the blood in the cab indicated that it had come from Céline Figard, it hadn't been possible to establish the origin of the blood on the bunk. That was almost certainly because of decomposition of the DNA and blood-group substances in the blood during the two months that had elapsed since the body had been found. But assuming that it *was* Céline's blood, the scientist concluded that it had seeped through into the holes and on to the engine cover below during the period of time when her body had been left on the bunk.

Stuart Morgan had another explanation, however. According to him, some friends of his had borrowed the lorry in April or May 1994. And when one of them had suffered a serious accident, he had been driven from

Glasgow to Manchester, while bleeding heavily from a laceration on his leg that subsequently required approximately forty stitches. Following that incident, Morgan claimed, the mattress had remained in the cab of the lorry for more than eighteen months, until the contents of an overturned carton of battery acid had leaked on to it. He'd then removed it, placed it for an hour under a running tap, and left it in the garage, where it had been found by investigators a couple of months later.

Although the case was dealt with by Forensic Access, I wasn't directly involved in it at that stage. So it was my colleague Chris Handoll who visited the FSS laboratory in Birmingham after Morgan's trial had started. While he was there, he discussed the findings of one of the prosecution's forensic scientists and examined the blood-stained mattress from the bunk, which still smelled strongly of decomposition. Chris's brief was to establish, as far as possible, whether the blood might have been deposited in the manner and at the time described by Morgan, and whether there were any indications of acid spillage or of the mattress having been sluiced with water. What he found, after careful investigation, was that there were no obvious signs to indicate that the fabric had been rinsed. Also, although a faint white patch on the mattress cover could have been caused by fluid spilled after the blood was deposited, it could alternatively have been due to the blood itself reacting with some substance in the material.

Chris was unable to comment on the probable nature of the injury that would have elicited such severe blood loss. But as the blood on the surface of the mattress was confined to just one area, what he *was* able to say was that if Morgan's explanation was true, the injured man must have remained immobile throughout the journey from Glasgow to Manchester – a distance in excess of two hundred miles that would have taken at least three hours to complete.

As the age of blood can't be established by scientific means, it wasn't possible to say whether the blood had been deposited in December 1995, as alleged by the prosecution, or in April or May of the previous year, as claimed by the defendant. There are some other indicators that can be taken into account – for example, dried blood tends to become browner with age. But they didn't help in the specific circumstances of this case. Similarly, there was no scientific evidence to confirm that it had necessarily come from the same person as that found elsewhere in the cab of the lorry. Chemical components of blood, including blood-group substances and DNA, deteriorate and are progressively destroyed – some of them more rapidly than others – at a rate that's affected by factors such as temperature and moisture. In fact, it was bacterial decay – which was very active when the bunk was discovered in Morgan's garage – that was the most likely cause of the failure of the blood-grouping and DNA-profiling tests that had been attempted at the FSS laboratory.

So Chris contended that the scientific evidence wasn't much help in the case against Morgan. But there was apparently plenty of other incriminating evidence. And after a trial lasting fourteen days, Stuart Morgan was convicted of murdering Céline Figard and sentenced to a minimum term of twenty years in prison.

Although we assumed that was the end of the case, we became involved with it again a few years later, when Morgan lodged an appeal against his conviction and we were asked – by the prosecution this time – to look at some yellowish staining on the sides of Céline's hands.

I had set up a new company by that time, which involved forming an alliance with the technology offshoot of the UK Atomic Energy Authority (AEAT). The idea was to bring more powerful science and technology into forensic science in the most cost-effective way possible. And it was a brilliant scientist at the AEAT called Chris Pickford – who led our expanded technical capability working alongside our forensic scientists – who actually analysed the stain.

Standard forensic examination by the FSS at the time of Céline's murder had merely indicated that the yellow stain wasn't body fluid. But there was a wider range of powerful analytical techniques available in AEAT by 1998, when Chris looked at it. And what he discovered was that it had five components: nicotine; a metal alloy containing nickel, chromium and cobalt; diesel; cresol; and a substance that's used to kill mites and ticks in dogs' ears. The nicotine could be explained by the fact that Céline was a smoker. The nickel, chromium and cobalt were present in proportions that suggested they had come from high-grade stainless steel – possibly from the mortuary table on which her body had been examined at autopsy. Diesel is pretty ubiquitous, but could have come from a diesel lorry. The cresol – which is a chemical that's used in disinfectants – was in a very pure form and was identified as being of a type that was supplied to only seven organisations in the UK, including the mortuary where the autopsy had been carried out.

It was the veterinary substance that turned out to be both interesting and significant. After a bit of digging around, we identified the company that manufactured it

– and sold it in flat green cans of a specific size just like the one found in Morgan's garden shed. Maybe he'd had some on his hands after treating his dogs, and it had been transferred to Céline during the assault. Whatever the explanation for it was, it didn't matter in the end, because Morgan's application to appeal was rejected, so the evidence wasn't needed. But it was interesting in terms of the new dimension it added to the case, and because it showed just how powerful science really is – in the hands of the right kind of scientists.

The principle that 'absence of evidence isn't evidence of absence' is a very useful basis for any forensic investigation. Sometimes though, when you're trying to decide whether or not someone might be telling the truth, there's a point at which the absence of evidence is so overwhelming it seems capable of telling you something. That was the position I found myself in when I read the prosecution's scientific reports in what turned out to be one of the most interesting cases I've ever worked on.

It was alleged by the prosecution that in the early hours of a cold autumn morning in 1993, Yusuf Abdi had a fight outside his flat with a man called Frank Hobson.* After Hobson had been sick on the grass, it was claimed that he was taken upstairs to Abdi's flat and dumped outside on the floor of a small balcony that led off the kitchen, where he died from hypothermia. About twenty-four hours later, the prosecution believed, Abdi and a friend dragged or carried Hobson's body out of the flat and put it in the friend's car. They then drove to an area of tarmac in front of a pub, where they took the body out

* Both names have been changed.

of the car and hid it in a nearby culvert, which was where it was found the following day.

The forensic examination had certainly been thorough, with the prosecution presenting evidence from eight forensic scientists from various FSS laboratories. Each of the scientists had examined a particular aspect, such as the scene where the body was found, blood and textile fibres, Abdi's flat, fingerprints, vegetation, alcohol, cannabis etc. A biochemist at a London hospital had also analysed a sample of the vomit found outside the flat and compared it with some stains on Hobson's clothing.

About eight months after Hobson's death, I visited one of the forensic laboratories where part of the work had been carried out. While I was there, I examined some items myself, including Hobson's jacket, which had been found in the drainage channel about 100 yards (91 metres) away from his body. Then I looked at the car, which was housed in a police garage, and went to the culvert with my colleague Mike Jenkins, who was an experienced forensic chemist.

What was interesting was that most of the test results had been negative. For example, there was nothing to suggest that a piece of twig recovered from the car had come from the culvert or surrounding area. There was no evidence of a recent fight in the flat. No blood was found on any items collected from Abdi or his friend. There was no blood or textile fibres from Hobson's clothing in the car, or any other evidence to link him with either the car or the flat. Nor was there any evidence to support the theory that he had been left overnight on the flat's small, narrow balcony. In fact, some pieces of a broken, weathered mirror that were found on the floor of the balcony close to the door, and had obviously been there for some time, lay undisturbed. And there were no drag marks on his shoes or clothing to indicate that his body had been manhandled into the culvert.

What was also striking was that some of the evidence you'd expect to find if Abdi had been involved in disposing of Hobson's body was missing. For instance, there were no powdery deposits on Abdi's clothes like the sticky white deposits leached from the concrete ceiling of the culvert that clung to mine when I edged my way along it – and that proved surprisingly difficult to remove. Indeed, nothing was found on Abdi's clothes that linked him to the location where the body was discovered.

I think Abdi was known to be involved in illegal drug dealing and there was some suggestion that the alleged fight could have had something to do with money he was owed by Hobson. But some samples of cannabis resin taken from the flat and from Hobson's jacket did not appear to have originated from the same batch. And no fingerprints that might have helped in the investigation were found on the cling-film wrappings. When combined with some other 'absent evidence', the case against Abdi appeared virtually non-existent, and the whole scenario put forward by the prosecution seemed blindingly unlikely.

The conclusion I came to in the end was that several features of the scientific evidence seemed to suggest that Hobson had made his own way to the place where his body was discovered. What was interesting in that respect was that there was some bruising on his knees, and some areas of fading and abrasion on his otherwise unfaded and undamaged jeans, which indicated that he might have crawled. It was a possibility that was further supported by some injuries on his hands and forearms that had apparently occurred *after* his jacket had been removed. Described as being 'consistent with contact with a rough surface such as concrete', the post-mortem report also said that the injuries could have been caused 'by the young man raising his arms and hands to protect his head and face from a rough surface such as while struggling through the culvert'.

Another aspect that didn't seem to make sense was related to the fact that Hobson's jacket was found *upstream* from the body. It obviously hadn't been transported there by the flow of water. Which meant that it had either come off as his body was being dragged or carried along the drainage channel, or it had been left there. But if one of those scenarios was correct, why hadn't Abdi retrieved from the pocket of the jacket the cannabis the police believed he'd recently sold to Hobson? And why would anyone choose to dump a body in a culvert that could only be reached by carrying it along such an extensive, slippery route?

What was even more intriguing was the blood staining apparent in some photographs that had been taken by the police. At about 9 inches (23 centimetres) above the ground on the culvert wall, the blood was far more likely to have come from someone leaning against it or colliding with it while crawling, rather than while being carried or dragged.

All in all, the prosecution's evidence seemed to raise more questions than it answered. The only real support for their case was the biochemist's conclusion that the vomit found outside the flat and the stains on Hobson's jacket could have come from the same source. But when Mike checked it, it looked as though that might have been over-interpreted. What Mike did agree with, however, were the results of the original screening of the dead man's blood, which showed the presence of cannabinoids (the active constituents of cannabis) and a high level of alcohol.

Some men who had been working in the drainage channel two days before the body was found had confirmed that the culvert was clear when they left at 5 p.m. So that was the earliest Hobson could have got there, and about fifteen hours after he was last seen by an independent witness. He still had a fair amount of alcohol in his blood when his body was examined post mortem. Added to the amount he would have lost through metabolism before he died – equivalent to about half a pint of beer or a small glass of wine per hour – this suggested that, even if his last drink had been no later than the time at which he was last seen, he would have had a minimum amount that is sufficient to cause most moderate drinkers to pass out. And if he had arrived at the culvert and/or died much later than 5 p.m., his alcohol level when he was last seen would have been considerably more.

What I think happened after Hobson's body was found was that the police had looked at his associates to see if he'd recently fallen out with anyone, and had come up with Abdi. It was a reasonable suspicion, in view of the suggestion that Hobson might have owed Abdi money for drugs. But it was cold on the night he died, and he'd had a lot to drink, the effects of which would have been exacerbated by the cannabinoids detected in his blood. So the picture that began to develop as we examined the scientific evidence was more in keeping with him having crossed the field where he was last seen and stumbled into the drainage channel. Discarding his jacket because he felt hot – which is apparently a characteristic feature of hypothermia – he had then crawled along the channel to the culvert, where he banged his head against the wall, and died just a few yards further on.

Based on the prosecution's evidence – or, rather, the lack of it – the case should never have been brought to court. After they'd presented the little evidence they did have, the judge accepted a submission (at so-called 'half time') from Abdi's lawyer – including all our evidence – that there was 'no case to answer', and Yusuf Abdi was acquitted.

14

Who's telling the truth?

No justice system should ever rely on the police or anyone else 'knowing' that someone is guilty of a crime. And no one, whatever the circumstances, should ever be convicted on the basis of flawed scientific evidence. Even when someone has admitted to committing a dreadful crime, it's important that the true nature of that crime is understood and neither understated nor overstated. So when a defendant called Margaret Harrison* was accused of murdering her mother, one of the questions that needed to be answered was whether she was telling the truth about what had happened or whether, as the prosecution was suggesting, her attack on her mother had been far worse than she described.

Harrison had already moved out of the flat she used to share with her mother by the time cleaning contractors found a partially decomposed body under a mattress in the hall cupboard. Part of the focus of the prosecution's case was on some penetrating holes in the upper left back of the victim's cardigan. The forensic scientist at the FSS lab in Aldermaston thought the holes had been made by a sharp instrument such as a knife. But although Harrison

* The name has been changed.

admitted to having hit her mother on the head with a hammer, she denied having stabbed her.

According to Harrison's statement, the two women had been knocking a nail into the wall in the living room of the flat to hang up a clock when her mother attacked her with the hammer. In the struggle that ensued, Harrison grabbed the hammer from her mother's hand and, in the heat of the moment, struck her with it on the side of the head. Sandra Smith* then fell on the floor, bleeding profusely. And when Harrison realised that her mother was dead, she dragged her body into the hall cupboard, where it remained for nearly two years.

When the flat was examined, some blood staining was noted on the wallpaper and floorboards in the living room, and, in a much smaller amount, on a wall in the bedroom. What was also included in the original scientist's report was that the blood in the living room had the appearance of having been cast off a blood-stained surface, possibly of a weapon. Samples of blood from each of the different areas had been tested using what was then the current generation of short tandem repeat (STR) DNA analysis. But apart from a stain on the floorboards in the living room that matched the STR profile of the dead woman, attempts to identify the DNA were largely unsuccessful.

It was almost a year after the body had been discovered when I was asked to look into the case by the defendant's lawyer. And having visited the flat in Sussex, I went to the FSS lab at Aldermaston to discuss the forensic scientist's findings and examine some of the relevant items myself.

---

* The name has been changed.

Various assumptions that seemed to be indisputable were based on evidence related to blood stains and to some fatty deposits found on the floor in the cupboard that were presumably derived from the decomposing body. One of those assumptions was that Sandra Smith had died as a result of an incident that had occurred in the living room of the flat. Another was that her body had lain bleeding on the floor there for some time afterwards, before being transferred to the cupboard in the hall, where it had remained for some time. What was less certain was the manner in which the victim had met her death, and precisely where in the living room it had occurred.

During my examination of the scene, I noticed additional very small spots and splashes of blood on the living-room wall close to the hole for the nail on which the defendant said the clock was supposed to be hung. One of the first things we did was commission STR analysis on a sample I took of this blood staining, which, unfortunately, failed to yield any usable results. So we had no idea whose blood it was, or even if it was actually connected with the incident we were investigating.

The blood patterns themselves were more informative. For example, I agreed with the original scientist that the spots and splashes he'd found on the living-room wall could have been cast-off blood, as opposed to the cluster of mostly small spots near the nail hole that I'd found, which were more suggestive of blood that had been split up by a powerful force such as an impact. Also, the fact that these spots of blood had clearly originated from below suggested that they may have come from something, or someone, on or near the floor. And if the spots had been related to a blow, it would almost certainly have been delivered to a surface that was already wet with blood, although they were far too limited to suggest any kind of sustained attack.

Some spots and splashes of blood that appeared to have come from Sandra Smith were also found on a cardboard box in the cupboard. As what remained of her body was covered in at least two layers of clothing, they seemed more likely to have emanated from an exposed head wound – perhaps when the body was originally deposited on the floor of the cupboard – than from any injury to her back. So maybe the original forensic investigator's conclusion had been wrong, and the blood at the scene wasn't associated with the five holes in the back of her jumper that he thought were stab cuts.

When I examined the damage myself, I noticed that there were other holes in the jumper that had similarly sharp edges, some of which were inside the back of the collar. What became apparent on closer inspection was that the margins of the holes consisted of a series of loops, as if the section of yarn that had originally held them together in the knitted fabric was simply missing. It was certainly damage of a sort that was extremely unlikely to have been caused by stabbing with a knife. What was interesting was that no comparable damage had been observed in the coat Sandra Smith had been wearing over the jumper, or on the body itself. Also, there was other, rather similar damage in areas of the jumper where it couldn't readily be ascribed to stabbing. What was clear, however, was that the clothing and the body had been infested with insects. So what seemed to be a more plausible explanation than that Margaret Harrison had stabbed her mother was that all the damage to the jumper had been caused by insects randomly 'chewing through' short sections of yarn.

In the report I produced for the defence lawyer, I suggested some more tests and further investigations that could usefully be done. In conclusion, I noted that the scientific evidence seemed to sit more comfortably with the daughter's account of what had happened than with the prosecution's allegation. In other words, it was more likely that Harrison had 'simply' struck her mother on the head with the hammer than that she had also stabbed her.

It might seem like splitting hairs as far as the outcome for Sandra Smith was concerned. But it was a distinction that could prove to be important for her daughter. Because if, as Margaret Harrison claimed, she had killed her mother during an argument with a blow from a hammer, rather than as the result of a prolonged attack involving more than one weapon, she would quite probably receive a shorter sentence.

My job on that occasion was to check the scientific evidence and see if it contained anything that might suggest whether or not the defendant had been telling the truth. So, having shown that there was an alternative to at least part of the prosecution's interpretation of the evidence, my involvement was over.

It may sound odd not to be particularly interested, as a general rule, in the outcome of the cases we worked on. But what eventually happened was usually also dependent on a lot of other evidence that had nothing to do with us. Our satisfaction came from ensuring that the science was as good as we could make it, bearing in mind the various limitations we had to work with.

Forensic scientists are duty bound never to allow themselves to be swayed by the opinion of anyone else, and must check and examine any potential evidence for themselves before they suggest possible interpretations of it. Sometimes, that involves ignoring whatever you've read in the newspapers about a case, not least because there will almost always be something reported that isn't entirely accurate. But whatever else was said in the media about the murder of Jamie Bulger, it had clearly involved a very brutal attack. And it was largely because of that, and because of the young ages of Jamie himself and his attackers, that the case attracted an enormous amount of media attention.

Robert Thompson and his co-defendant, Jon Venables, were both just ten years old when they were accused of abducting and killing two-year-old Jamie Bulger. I was asked by lawyers representing Thompson to inspect the evidence against their client and advise on its strengths and weaknesses, so that they would be properly equipped to probe it in court.

What was known about Jamie's murder was that he was out shopping with his mother in the town of Bootle in Merseyside on 12 February 1993 when he was abducted and led away across the shopping centre, in a moment that was captured on CCTV. When his body was found two days later on a railway track serving Bootle docks, it was heavily stained with blue paint and had been severed in two by a passing train. Although Thompson and Venables admitted abducting the little boy, they blamed each other for part, if not all, of the assault, in what's called a 'cut-throat' defence.

The scientific evidence in the case was being presented by four different FSS scientists, each of whom was dealing with a specific aspect of it. One of the scientists had visited the crime scene and had examined a number of items back at the laboratory in Chorley, from the crime scene itself and from Jamie's body, as well as clothing and footwear from Thompson and Venables. Another was concerned with footwear marks, including some that had been found at the scene and on the body. A third dealt with the blue paint. While the fourth looked at oil stains on Jamie's clothing and compared them with samples taken from the undersides of a number of trains, in an attempt to identify which one had run over him.

The scenario that emerged from their collective efforts suggested that after blue paint had been spilt on Jamie, he had been injured beside the track, and again near the platform wall, in an assault that involved him being struck with at least one brick taken from trackside rubble. Then his body had been moved on to the track itself, where further bricks had been placed around him and where he was run over by a passing train.

Examination of some of the evidence had revealed various possibilities. Blood-grouping and/or DNA tests showed that blood staining found on both Thompson's and Venables' shoes could have come from Jamie. Some marks on the toddler's face could have been made by a blow from a shoe of the same general type as Thompson's. There were deposits of blue paint on the shoes of both older boys, as well as on other items of their clothing, including a mark on Venables' jacket that it was claimed could have been made by a small, blue-paint-stained hand. And a single hair like Jamie's was found on Thompson's right shoe, while another was stuck in some of the paint on a sleeve of Venables' jacket.

There was no evidence to suggest which train had run over the child's body. But as the testing had been fraught with complications, the scientist concerned hadn't attached much significance to this.

It was September 1993 when I visited the FSS laboratory at Chorley and talked to the main scientist involved about what he'd found. While I was there, he also showed me police photographs and a video of the scene, as well as the notes and sketch plans he'd made himself when he went there. Then I inspected many of the key items, briefly compared the hair found on Thompson's right shoe with reference samples from all three boys, and looked at the grouping results on blood from the same shoe. Meanwhile, my colleague Clive Candy dealt separately with the detail of the paint and footwear aspects.

You have to be stoical to be a forensic scientist. By the time you become involved in an investigation, there's nothing you can do to change what's already happened. But you *can* affect what happens next, in terms of helping to bring an offender to justice, and of giving some modicum of a sense of closure to the family and friends of someone who's been unlawfully killed. So you simply can't allow yourself to be thrown off course by your emotions. When a case involves a child, however, and you take a tiny item of clothing out of an evidence bag and lay it out on the bench in front of you, you can't help but be struck by the sadness of a little life cut short.

After my visit to Chorley, I was in a good position to describe more precisely what was likely to have occurred at the scene. I was also able to consider what the proposed blood, hair and paint links with Thompson could tell us about his involvement in the crime. And, as the two boys were blaming each other, I could assess, briefly, how those links compared with the evidence against Venables.

My report was, inevitably, a long one, as it picked its

way through all the fine detail. But, at the end of it, I gave a very comprehensive account of what I thought the sequence of events at the scene had been. Building essentially on what had been reported, I also highlighted some areas that needed careful consideration. One of those areas was whether and to what extent the forceful disturbance of the bricks surrounding Jamie's body by the passage of the train(s) over the top might have contributed to his injuries and exaggerated the nature of the attack.

Preparing simple visual aids was something I did quite frequently, as I found that they often conveyed information more quickly and accurately than written descriptions could do. So, after illustrating my analysis with a sketch plan, I added a transparent overlay on which I marked the locations of the main areas of blood staining and the key items and features. Then I addressed the links with Thompson.

The grouping of the blood on Thompson's shoe related to just one blood-grouping system: PGM. That particular system had been chosen by the FSS scientists because analysis of reference blood samples from the three boys showed that they each belonged to a different group within the system. Therefore their blood could be distinguished. But although I confirmed that the blood from the shoe matched Jamie Bulger's blood, I also pointed out that the same PGM blood group occurred in about 23 per cent (approximately one in four) of the UK population. So, on its own, the link it provided with Jamie in particular was very weak. Moreover, there was nothing to indicate that the blood must have been deposited on the day in question. But maybe none of that was going to be in dispute. In which case the only question that really needed to be answered was precisely how the blood had got on to the shoe. Which meant that what I needed to focus on was its nature and distribution.

Most of the blood on the shoe was in the form of fairly shapeless stains and smears, suggesting direct contact with something with wet blood on it. But a collection of tiny spots of blood on the front of the shoe was of potentially more significance. It was clear that the spots would have been formed from the tiny droplets that are created when blood is split up by some sort of force, and that are common on items in close proximity to sustained violent attacks. However, they weren't in a classic kicking pattern. In fact, they could conceivably have represented interception of blood spray produced during an assault by someone else. Which meant that Thompson could have been what is usually referred to as 'an innocent bystander'.

The other thing about the spots of blood was that they weren't part of the stain that was sampled for blood grouping. So it would be difficult to be entirely confident that they had necessarily come from the same source. The fact that there was also a small amount of what could have been Thompson's own blood on one of his shirts just goes to show how careful you have to be when drawing conclusions about the potential source(s) of a blood stain.

As far as the proposed hair link was concerned, I agreed that the hair could have come from Jamie, but not from either Thompson or Venables. What was also true, however, was that because there was nothing particularly unusual about it, it could alternatively have come from a fairly sizeable number of people selected at random. And the fact that it wasn't associated with any blood or blue paint and was reported to have been adhering only loosely to the shoelace meant that, all in all, it provided only the weakest of links with Jamie specifically.

Although Clive was dealing with the paint and foot-wear marks, I mentioned them briefly in my report so that all the evidence could be considered together. What Clive had found were some light smears and spots of paint on Thompson's blood-stained shoes – some of which were in the same area as the blood – and on his trousers and jacket. The paint smears indicated contact with something that had wet paint on it. And the spots of paint suggested that Thompson had been in the vicinity of the tin when the paint splashed out of it, although that didn't mean that he had necessarily been holding the tin at the time.

The marks on Jamie's face appeared to provide further evidence of contact with what could have been one of Thompson's shoes. But there was nothing to suggest that that contact had been related to the transfer of either the paint or the blood to the shoe.

There was blood staining on Venables' shoes too, which was also in the form of smears and small spots. In his case, however, DNA profiling had established with much greater certainty than blood grouping had done that the blood could have come from Jamie. In fact, DNA profiling indicated that the blood was likely to occur in only one in approximately three and a half billion of the population, including Jamie, compared to one in four of the population for blood grouping. What was also interesting was that the staining was rather more extensive than that on Thompson's shoes.

The fact that the hair similar to Jamie Bulger's that had been found on Venables' jacket had originally been described as 'loosely adhering to the paint stain' appeared to improve its likely association with the victim. But it was the paint itself that was most interesting, for three reasons. First, as Clive explained in some detail, it had been suggested that the paint staining on the left sleeve of Venables' jacket could represent the mark of a small (child's) hand. The second reason was that there was more extensive paint staining around the cuffs of Venables' jacket than there was on Thompson's, which suggested that Venables might have handled the wet paint and/or its container more than Thompson had done. And third, some of the paint staining on Venables' right shoe extended below the welt line at the front. Combined with light, streaky smears over the top of the toe, what that suggested was that the contact that gave rise to it could have been forceful.

Clive and I were sent the report that had been compiled by the forensic scientist appointed by Venables' lawyer and asked for our comments. (I expect he was sent copies of ours too.) What struck us when we read it was that he had linked the DNA results obtained from the blood on Venables' shoe with the evidentially much weaker blood on Thompson's. Also, in relation to Venables himself, the scientist had failed to point out the weaknesses in the suggestion that the mark on the jacket sleeve represented a small hand print in paint. Was it actually a hand print at all? In fact, though, that omission was made up for by the added strength that the paint smears over the toe of Venables' shoe gave to any suggestion of kicking.

It may all seem like a lot of nit-picking. But if you're going to rely on scientific evidence, it's critical that it's well understood and that the detail has been properly explored. For the criminal justice process to be carried out in the way it's intended to be, the jury must be able to consider and make judgements on both the strengths and the weaknesses of that evidence. The UK's adversarial system provides a good framework for doing that, as the Jamie Bulger case amply demonstrates. Being presented with all aspects of the scientific evidence may not change the anticipated outcome of a case – Thompson and Venables were both tried and convicted of what was a terrible crime. But at least when its weaknesses had been exposed, the court could be confident that they were outweighed by its strengths, and they were in a better position to judge the relative involvement of the two accused boys. Sometimes, of course, it works the other way round, as illustrated by various other cases mentioned in this book.

15
Great expectations

As Forensic Access expanded and we employed more scientists and consultants with more diverse expertise, we were able to take on a wider variety of cases. But even in the early days, we were involved in some extremely interesting investigations, as illustrated by the very different cases described in this chapter.

It wasn't long after Russell had come to join me that we were asked by a large scientific equipment supplier to go to Nigeria with them to advise on getting a new forensic laboratory up and running. It's relatively easy to build a laboratory, as they had done, but quite a different matter to get all the equipment functioning reliably. And my first impressions when we arrived at the lab in Lagos were how spacious, well equipped and eerily empty, dusty and humid it was.

Reminiscent of the room in Miss Havisham's mansion in Charles Dickens' novel, the laboratory represented the scientific equivalent of great expectations that had come to nothing. It turned out that a number of academically very well-qualified scientists had been recruited to work there. But none of them knew what to do with any of the high-quality, state-of-the-art equipment with which it had been kitted out, let alone how it might relate to police investigations. What they did know was that if they agreed that the laboratory had been finished, they would be expected to start doing casework, and would then be held personally accountable for any inevitable shortcomings – which, it was clear even to us, wouldn't be a good thing.

On paper, the job we had been employed to do had seemed fairly straightforward. In reality, however, it appeared to be impossible. Although we were able to show the scientists how to use some of their equipment, there wasn't anything we could do with the very expensive microscopes which had been damaged by the intense heat and humidity that built up after the air-conditioning was turned off in the empty lab quite some time earlier. Some of the larger pieces of kit also looked as though they needed some replacement parts. But even if they had been working properly, they were so specialised they required equally specialist scientists to run them.

The day after our initial visit to the laboratory, we wrote a preliminary report listing the steps we felt would have to be taken in order to achieve the main objective of creating a fully operational forensic facility. Basically, what we were suggesting was that the first task would be to establish the nature of policing and local crime priorities, and therefore the types of forensic science that would be most useful. Then they could do one of two things.

One option was to send the scientists to another country, where they could be attached to a busy police laboratory to gain experience of working on crime cases and using the type of sophisticated equipment they had in Lagos. The other option was to bring in experienced personnel from abroad for at least a couple of years to train a core group of scientists in the use of basic techniques and equipment. Better still, they could combine the two options to provide the Nigerian scientists who were being trained abroad with the assistance and guidance they were going to need when they returned to work in Lagos.

After some further discussions with those scientists who were bold enough to talk to us, and some more time spent poking around in the lab, we wrote a supplement to the preliminary report. Among the equipment that was gathering dust in various corners of the laboratory were a vastly expensive scanning electron microscope and an atomic absorption spectrophotometer. And what we noted in the supplementary report was that, even with the training we recommended, it was unlikely that the scientists would ever actually need, or be able to operate, equipment like that efficiently. Then we wrote about the health-and-safety issues related to biological hazards and the use of toxic chemicals, as well as the risks of electrocution, fire and explosion. No provision appeared to have been made to address any of the safety issues, in the form of fire extinguishers and emergency showers, for example. Nor was there any of the other essential paraphernalia and facilities that were commonplace in most forensic labs at that time – and that we'd had when I started work for the FSS in Harrogate more than fourteen years earlier, when we were still spraying dangerous chemicals in the open laboratory.

I don't know if any of the suggestions in our preliminary report were acted upon. Quite possibly not, as they would have had to scrap a lot of the equipment, and it would have been a huge job trying to get the rest of it working. But the trip to Lagos was an instructive experience for me, too, in various ways. I had never previously seen such strange-looking mosquitoes, for example, or been in any situation that warranted armed guards having to sleep on the porch of the house I was staying in. And I don't think I'd ever felt as vulnerable as I did when I realised the precariousness of our position after our host took our passports, for bureaucratic reasons, then refused to give them back to us! Most of all though, I was struck by the natural warmth and fantastic sense of humour of all the Nigerians we met. And by the clearly apparent desire of the scientists who had been employed to work at the laboratory to be able to do an efficient and effective job.

What had helped me to decide all those years ago whether I actually wanted to be a forensic scientist was the fact that the science I was doing was so immediately important to something as vital as criminal justice. With a few notable exceptions, I usually managed to disengage the emotional side of my mind and focus on whatever scientific puzzle I was trying to solve. Nevertheless, it was good sometimes to be able to work on something like the lab assessment in Lagos, or on a case with a different twist to it. So I was intrigued for various reasons when we were asked, in 1988, to examine a leather bag for a Swedish woman who wanted to know if the dying man from whom she had acquired the bag in 1947 had actually been, as she believed, the Swedish war hero Raoul Wallenberg.

Born in 1912, Wallenberg was an architect who served as a special envoy in Budapest during the Second World War. During the time he was in Nazi-occupied Hungary, he and his colleagues saved the lives of thousands of Jews by issuing them with passports and providing them with shelter in buildings that had been designated as Swedish territory.

Then, in 1945, when Soviet forces encircled the city during the Siege of Budapest, Wallenberg disappeared.

When I met the Swedish woman and her solicitor at our offices, she handed me the leather bag and explained how she had acquired it. Apparently, while working under cover for the Americans in 1947, she had gone to southern Poland, where she'd met a Swedish man who was dying from gunshot wounds and who told her that his name was Raoul Wallenberg.

'He certainly looked like Wallenberg,' the woman said. 'But in order to try to confirm his identity, I pressed the tips of his fingers on to the inner surface of his bag – to get his fingerprints. Then, before I left him, I swapped *his* bag for the one I was carrying.'

On her return to Warsaw, the woman gave the leather bag to her American associates for testing. But when it was given back to her a few days later, no one told her what had been found, if anything. So she took it with her when she left Poland and went home to Sweden, where she offered it to Wallenberg's family. When they declined to take it – on the grounds that they didn't believe it could have anything to do with him – she'd kept it in her house, apparently untouched, for the next forty years.

The woman had always believed that the dying man she encountered that day in Poland really was Raoul Wallenberg. Now, she had decided that the time had come to try to discover the truth. So she'd brought the leather bag to us in the hope that we would be able to find some scientific evidence to identify its origin. The burning question that was immediately obvious to me when the request was made was whether, if we did find anything on the bag, we would have access to any authentic reference samples with which to compare it – fingerprints or hair from Wallenberg, for example. Having agreed to cross that bridge if and when we came to it, we conducted a detailed examination of the bag.

The area to which we paid particular attention was the inside of the flap, on to which the fingertips of the dying man had apparently been pressed. Fingerprints are basically deposits of sweat. And because they're comprised – initially, at least – of approximately 99 per cent water plus some fats, amino acids and salt, which are also constituents of leather, they're difficult to identify on leather using chemical reactions. So we arranged for a specialist fingerprint expert to examine the bag using what was, at the time, a relatively new laser fluorescence technique that depended on the characteristic of some latent fingerprints to fluoresce when subjected to laser light. Unfortunately, no fingerprints were detected at all, either inside the flap of the bag or on its outer, polished leather surface, which had, of course, been handled very recently.

In addition to looking in vain for fingerprints, I applied strips of adhesive tape to the internal surfaces of the bag to remove any superficial debris. Then I brushed out the seams very carefully, and collected all the accumulated human hairs, textile fibres, grit and tiny splinters of wood etc. that had lodged in them. What was interesting about that part of the investigation was the absence of any traces of the charcoal, graphite, aluminium or talc used in the powder-based techniques for visualising fingerprints in 1947. The woman's claim that the bag had rarely been handled during the intervening years was borne out by its condition. So it seemed unlikely that *all* traces of those substances would have been lost if they had been used by the Americans in Warsaw to test the bag for fingerprints.

Which appeared to suggest that if they'd tested it at all, they'd done so using only conventional techniques involving illumination and photography, which are most unlikely to have been sufficiently effective.

By examining under a microscope the hairs that had adhered to the sticky tape, we were able to confirm that they were human, but not whether they had all come from the same person. None of the woman's hairs matched three pale hairs that had also been found in the bag, although it's possible that her hair had changed over the years. And while three darker brown hairs were indistinguishable in colour and microscopic appearance from some we'd collected from her for comparison, Raoul Wallenberg apparently had very dark hair too, to the point of it being a distinguishing feature. So, theoretically, they could have come from him. Unfortunately, however, we didn't have an authentic sample from him to compare them with.

In the absence also of any reference samples with which to compare the textile fibres, grit and splinters of wood collected from the seams of the bag, there was no point in us doing anything other than cataloguing them. We did get a strong reaction to a presumptive and then a confirmatory test for blood from part of a very small, dark-brown, crusty stain on the external surface of the bag. But there was no way of estimating how old it was. And there wasn't enough of it for us to do either a traditional blood-grouping test or to begin to think about DNA profiling, which was just starting to become available. These days, it would be an entirely different matter, and it's conceivable that DNA profiling might work. In order to make sense of any results, however, one would still need an authentic reference sample from Wallenberg

– or from some of his close relatives as a second-best option.

In the end, the results of all our investigations proved inconclusive. So we weren't able to confirm or deny the woman's belief that she had met the war hero Raoul Wallenberg in Poland shortly before he died. In fact, the mystery of his disappearance was never solved, and after a collaborative investigation by the Swedish Ministry for Foreign Affairs and Soviet authorities failed to provide any useful evidence, he was formally declared dead in 2016.

16

Errors of judgement

Unfortunately, no justice system is foolproof, and when it fails, there are two possible, potentially very serious, outcomes. Guilty people may be acquitted, and might go on to kill, rape, burgle or commit other crimes again. Or innocent people may be convicted and their lives might be irretrievably ruined by being sent to prison, or, in some of the countries I've worked in, they may be sentenced to death.

Having highlighted issues in other laboratories, I should add that labs in the UK aren't immune to problems either. For example, cost has become an increasingly important factor for the police since they started to pay for forensic services directly out of their own budgets, particularly now that those budgets are under such pressure in 'austerity Britain'. It isn't that forensic science is a large part of overall police expenditure. It's just that it's a large part of their external spend. So it's a cost that sticks out like a sore thumb when they're looking for areas in which economies might be made.

One of the things that became apparent during our visit to Nigeria was that however much expensive, high-tech equipment you buy and however many intelligent people you employ to use it, you won't get the results that are needed unless everyone knows what they're doing. I've never really understood why anyone would think that because they can do one type of forensic investigation, they can necessarily do another. Or because they can perform some simple forensic tests, they know how to identify and exclude any risk of contamination and how to interpret their results properly in the context of a specific case. Even though it isn't the whole answer, accreditation has helped enormously. But it isn't currently a uniform requirement, and unless and until it is – for both prosecution and defence experts – bad forensic science will continue to pose potential problems.

One early example of how bad things could get involved a forensic investigation that had been conducted in 1991 by the old British Rail laboratory on behalf of the British Transport Police (BTP).

The BTP are a very active police force, with responsibility for anything that happens in railway stations and on the rail network right across the country. We had done quite a few forensic investigations for them in the past in the FSS, although nothing drug related, as they did that aspect of the work themselves. But when their laboratory started branching out into other areas of forensic science that were well beyond the limits of their expertise, things began to go badly wrong.

The case we were brought in to look at by the defence involved two men who had been accused of attempted armed robbery of the booking office at a London underground station. One of the men was alleged to have threatened the booking clerk with a sawn-off shotgun, which he had apparently been carrying in a black holdall that was found under a van not far from where he and his accomplice were arrested.

Based on the transfer of textile fibres, two forensic scientists at the British Rail laboratory in Derby had found what they claimed to be very good evidence to link the men with the holdall and with a stolen car. So I visited their laboratory to check some of the evidence and discuss it with them, and was horrified by what I discovered. As well as examining various items, they had recovered superficial fibre debris from them, and compared fibres from one source with those from another. But the techniques and protocols that had been used fell far short of what would normally be required to suggest a link of the type they claimed to have established.

One of my concerns focused on the fact that they had taken just a single taping from each of the items of clothing (and two from each shoe) that had been collected from the suspects. However, a donkey jacket like that worn by one of the suspects during the alleged attempted robbery would have shed enough fibres to have filled up several tapes on its own. Which meant that the clothing tapes tended to be very heavily loaded with fibres and therefore difficult to search, and many fibres simply wouldn't have been picked up at all. Also, there was no indication as to whereabouts on the items any potentially relevant fibres had originally been located. And that's often very important when you're trying to work out what sort of contact someone might have had with someone else.

The fact that many of the fibres that are shed from textiles – sometimes in very large numbers – are microscopic in size makes them effectively invisible as they're transferred from one item to another through direct contact. Or when they're transferred by secondary contact via an intermediary item. Or when they're released from an item and drift in air currents to land on something else.

So one of the cardinal rules when investigating any kind of textile-fibre transfer is that different items must be examined in different rooms and at different times. Also, ideally, tapings should be taken by different scientists wearing standard laboratory coats and other protective clothing such as disposable cuffs and gloves. The search benches should be devoid of any nooks and crannies where fibres could become trapped and later dislodged. And every surface must be cleaned thoroughly after each item has been examined. It's all just standard forensic protocol – and basic common sense. But, amazingly, just one of the forensic scientists working at the British Rail laboratory had taken tapings from the holdall, the car seats and the footwells, and from every item of clothing that had been collected from both suspects. Then the same scientist had examined all the fibres from all the sources on the same narrow bench in the same room – making a mockery of his 'clarification' that he had 'placed each one of them on a clean sheet of paper'. This was the 1990s, and there was no excuse for any laboratory to be providing forensic services without ensuring that everyone they employed was properly trained and equipped.

There were also other aspects of the original forensic investigation in the BTP case that left much to be desired in terms of good practice. One of them, crucially, was the very crude way in which fibres from various sources had been examined and compared under the microscope. In particular, fibres had been left *in situ* on the tapings, which had then been flooded with chemicals to dissolve the adhesive and make the fibres easier to see. What had actually happened, however, was that they had created a sludge several millimetres thick and consisting of chemicals, dissolving glue and acetate from the tapings themselves. And there had been no attempt to identify precisely what sort of fibres they were, or to determine their detailed colour characteristics and dyestuff composition. The scientists hadn't even marked their positions on the tapings. So it wasn't possible to find half of them, or to be convinced that the others were the ones referred to in the witness statement. In short, the 'links' that had been proposed by the British Rail laboratory between the two defendants, the holdall containing the sawn-off shotgun and the stolen car were entirely unsafe. In fact, it was the worst scientific evidence presented by any police force in this country that I have ever seen – before or since.

In the report I wrote for the solicitor representing one of the suspects, I explained some very basic principles in an attempt to address the issues that had been raised. Then I ended with the words: 'Unless and until the British Rail laboratory ensures that its staff receive proper training in these sorts of examinations, and attain the necessary level of knowledge, experience and competence in them, it should neither permit nor require them to undertake any further work of this kind.'

I thought the prosecution would read the report I'd written, realise the fundamental errors that had been made, and drop at least that aspect of the case. Maybe the police did have the right suspect; but justice would not have been served if he had been tried and convicted on the basis of the extremely dodgy 'evidence' that was being presented. So I was very surprised when I was asked some time later if I would attend court while the prosecution's evidence was being heard.

By the time I arrived for the hearing at the Old Bailey, the scientific evidence had been withdrawn. And when the BTP officer involved was told the news, I heard him say, very irritably, to one of the British Rail forensic scientists, 'Next time, don't let her bully you.' Clearly, I was the 'bully' in question, and I was incensed by what was obviously a total lack of understanding of how appallingly bad their forensic investigation had been. What was even more infuriating was that they didn't seem to have any concept that forensic science is *not* a one-size-fits-all operation. Because although they had considerable experience of carrying out forensic investigations related to the seizure of drugs on trains etc., a completely different set of knowledge and skills is required to deal with the investigation of textile fibres. Unfortunately, that's a message I still sometimes find myself having to repeat today. Not in the context of British Rail, but because there are still some companies and individuals – in the UK and elsewhere – who are offering a range of forensic services that are way beyond their own experience and expertise.

What surprised me even more than being accused of bullying that day was being kissed on the cheek and thanked by the scientist whose work I had roundly trashed. 'It would have been the first time I'd given evidence at the Old Bailey,' he told me. 'And I think you might just have saved me from something!' So at least the experience seemed to have made him aware that there were limits to his forensic expertise. Or so I thought, until he rang me a few weeks later and said, 'You remember that fibres case, Angela? Well, I've got a hair case now, and I wanted to ask what you would do with—'

I don't know what his question would have been, because I interrupted to tell him, 'Don't even *think* about it. Hair is *much* more difficult than textile fibres. Just don't do it.' I can only hope that he took my advice.

Another possible miscarriage of justice that I still feel uneasy about today did actually result in a conviction, when Brian Parsons was sentenced to life in prison in 1988 for the murder of eighty-four-year-old Ivy Batten.

Ivy Batten died as the result of several hammer blows to the head, during what the police believed was a burglary that went wrong. When her body was discovered in her house in Devon, it looked as though her killer had gained access by breaking the glass in a window. Some textile fibres that were found on the broken edges of the glass matched the constituent fibres of a pair of hand-knitted woollen gloves that were recovered from a field near the house. And a hammer that was found with the gloves was stained with what appeared to be the victim's blood, with strands of her hair embedded in it.

I can see why the evidence against Parsons might have seemed to be quite compelling. Apparently, he'd had some contact with Ivy Batten before, and had been in her neighbourhood on the day she was killed, delivering invitations to his wedding. Of course, that in itself wasn't particularly incriminating. But there was also the fact that several different types of fibres matching those in the heather-coloured woollen gloves were discovered inside the glove compartment of his car. Added to which, there were similar fibres in the pocket of an old coat he kept at his workplace, which I think he'd borrowed some time previously from his father.

It wasn't until ten years later that Forensic Access became involved in the case, when Parsons appealed against his conviction and we were employed by the defence to look at the original scientific evidence.

Evidence is all about patterns. And something that struck me when I looked at the evidence against Parsons was that what there was appeared to be very strong, but that it just 'fitted where it touched'. In other words, it didn't form a convincing pattern. One aspect that seemed particularly odd was the fact that all the fibres on the coat were found in just one pocket. Unfortunately, not many areas of the coat had been sampled (taped) for transferred fibres, but none was discovered in the other pocket at all.

When you consider the sort of pattern involved in the normal handling and/or wearing of a pair of gloves, there are various things you'd expect to find. That the wearer would have fibres on both hands, for example. So if there were fibres in one pocket, there would almost certainly be some in the other, although not necessarily in the same numbers. It was the same in the car. The only place fibres matching the gloves had been found was inside the glove compartment, where, in my experience, most people keep a wide range of things, but rarely gloves themselves. What was also significant was that there were no fibres on the front passenger seat adjacent to the glove compartment.

The limited and highly specific distribution of glove-type fibres should at least have given the forensic scientist who originally worked on the case pause for thought. Because although there was no reason to think that anyone had planted the evidence, as was being claimed by Parsons' lawyer, it was absolutely what I would have expected to find if someone *had* done so.

There were other odd aspects too, such as a bit of yellow paper with the phone number of the murder incident room written on it. The paper wasn't listed as being in the pocket of the coat Parsons was wearing when he was arrested and the coat was first examined. But it was pulled out of it, like a rabbit out of a hat, when he was interviewed by police, after the coat had been returned to them from the forensic laboratory. Then, strangely, it was added to the list of contents found in the pocket as an undated afterthought in the lab case notes by the forensic scientist. Which was very odd, in view of the fact that the need for contemporaneous note making is drummed into us at an early stage.

Another odd aspect was the fact that the attack on the old lady had been particularly violent, which was apparently very much out of character for someone who was referred to by everyone who knew him as 'a gentle giant'. In fact, I think his nickname was 'Bunny'.

Although I did voice my concerns when I gave evidence at Parsons' appeal in 1999, I obviously didn't manage to convince the judges. And because Parsons refused to admit that he was guilty, he was turned down for early parole and ended up staying in prison until 2004.

DNA profiling wasn't generally available at the time of the original trial in 1988, but some DNA evidence was produced later that seemed to link Parsons with the gloves. What had become apparent, however, was that, prompted by the police during the initial investigation, the gloves had been tried on by various people. One of those people might have been Parsons himself, although he couldn't specifically remember whether or not he had actually put them on. It was bad practice even before the advent of DNA. And it was probably a fairly pointless exercise anyway, because the gloves were made of wool and would have stretched to fit a wide range of hand sizes. But when the Criminal Case Review Commission looked at the DNA evidence, they clearly decided it proved the case. Whereas, in my view, it raised as many questions as it answered within the specific context.

Maybe I'm wrong and there was nothing amiss with the scientific evidence. But I'd really like to get to the bottom of the case, perhaps by reviewing the DNA evidence and doing a bit more general investigation. Because, as it stands, it just doesn't feel right. It's a concern that I understand has been echoed by someone who was one of the prosecutors at the time, and by officers from Hampshire Police who reviewed the original investigation by Devon and Cornwall Police. And when police officers, lawyers and forensic scientists are all uneasy about the outcome of a case, it really does need to be looked at again, which is something the Cardiff University Innocence Project is still pushing for.

The investigation into the murder of Ivy Batten raised a common misconception that still exists today, which is that, being rooted in fact, forensic science provides an especially pure and objective form of evidence, and gives clear-cut answers that leave little scope for debate. It's probably largely our fault as scientists, because our reports have historically been long on jargon but short on explanations, with any room for doubt being hidden behind a façade of scientific precision and accuracy. What hasn't generally been recognised – and still often isn't – is the paramount importance of context in the interpretation of what we find. What also often isn't taken into account are the limitations that a paucity of background information can impose on the nature and extent of the work we think we ought to do, as well as on the conclusions we draw from what we *have* done.

Perhaps the best example of these dangers is DNA evidence. Frequencies of occurrence of individual DNA profiles are now reported as 'less than one in a billion'. But, right from the start, I think we have all been concerned that the sheer size of the statistics can effectively encourage leaps of logic. For example, the likelihood that DNA could have come from one person in particular can give rise to the conclusion that that person must have committed the crime – expressed simply, that DNA = impressive statistics = guilt. Like most things though, DNA is a double-edged sword. And while it's brilliant at indicating from whom a blood or other bodyfluid stain is very likely to have come, there's then a danger that not enough consideration is given to whether or not there's a contextually plausible alternative explanation of how it actually got there. What also doesn't help matters these days are the streamlined forensic reports (SFRs) that are favoured as one of the means of reducing the cost of forensic services and that report the facts about a profiling result but don't contain anything about context.

Another example of a case in which there seemed to have been too little attention paid to overall pattern – of the scientific evidence, at least – concerned a nineteen-year-old man called Raymond Gilmour.

Known to frequent the local woods, and with a previous conviction for indecent exposure, Gilmour was arrested within days of sixteen-year-old Pamela Hastie's body being found in woodland near her home in Scotland in November 1981. At first, Gilmour confessed to having attacked Pamela as she was walking home from school. Claiming to have knocked her to the ground and struck her on the head with a piece of wood, he said he had then dragged her into the bushes and tied a ligature around her neck before raping and strangling her. But he quickly withdrew his confession, which he said he had made under pressure from the police. And when it became clear that several aspects of his account were inaccurate in terms of the available evidence, he was released without charge.

Three months later, after a new detective superintendent had taken over the case, Gilmour was re-arrested, and subsequently convicted of rape and murder, for which he was sentenced to life in prison.

After withdrawing his original confession, Gilmour had always maintained his innocence. In fact, the solicitor who asked us to look into the case in 1994 had been working hard for some years to try to get it looked at again. By that time, it had already been the subject of a question raised in the House of Commons by Gilmour's MP, and of a television programme in the Channel 4 *Trial and Error* series. But appeals against the conviction were rejected by both the UK Court of Criminal Appeal and the European Court of Human Rights.

My involvement focused on assessing whether, and to what extent, the forensic findings in relation to Gilmour properly reflected what would have been expected if he had actually been the murderer. To do that, I read the various papers related to the original investigation, which included reports from forensic scientists, police officers, the pathologist who examined Pamela Hastie's body, and various civilian witnesses. Then I considered what further lines of inquiry might usefully have been pursued. What I found was that, despite a series of dogs failing to bark when they might have been expected to, almost no attempt had apparently been made to discover why.

The post-mortem report described bleeding from Pamela's vagina, but no blood had been found on a penile swab taken from Gilmour. That wasn't surprising in view of the period of time that had elapsed between the two events. But what *was* worthy of note was that although there was blood on Pamela's clothing, as well as cuts, scratches and abrasions on various parts of her body, no blood was found on any of Gilmour's clothes. Eye-witnesses had described what he was wearing around the time of the murder, and presumably those items were among the clothing that had been seized for examination from his home and car.

During the close contact that would have been involved in the assault prior to Pamela's death, textile fibres would inevitably have been transferred from her clothing to her assailant's, and vice versa. The absence of any evidence of transferred fibres on Gilmour's clothes might be explained by the delay before they were collected, during which time they could have fallen off and been lost. But there had been no such delay in examining the victim. So the absence of any transferred fibres on *her* clothes and body could be less easily explained, and should have raised a potential red flag during the original investigation.

What the forensic scientists did find was that the majority of Gilmour's clothing was contaminated with small fragments of blue, red and green paint. The source of the paint was apparently related to some work he'd been doing with a sander. But, again, nothing was found on Pamela's clothes or body. Which was odd, as you would absolutely expect some paint fragments to have been transferred during the sort of forceful and prolonged contact her assailant must have had with her during the attack.

Other 'missing evidence' included the absence of any traces of soil or vegetation on Gilmour's clothing like those that had been found on Pamela's. Nor were there any fibres from the sisal twine that had actually been used to strangle her – rather than the tie or strap from her bag that Gilmour 'confessed' to having used. There was no mention in the post-mortem report of any head wounds either. Which cast serious doubt on Gilmour's description in his original statement of how he'd struck her repeatedly on the head with a piece of wood. And there were no blood stains or, apparently, any hairs detected on the length of branch that was found near her body, which rather ruled it out as having been used as a weapon.

Something that *had* been noted by one of the police officers involved in the original investigation was a footwear mark on the ground near where Pamela's school books had been discovered. But although a photograph had been taken of what might have proved to be a vital piece of evidence, no attempt seemed to have been made to compare it with any of Gilmour's shoes.

Also mentioned in the forensic report were a purple nylon fibre and three hairs that were found on the branch of a tree at the scene. The fact that all three of the hairs were apparently like Pamela Hastie's suggested that she had come into contact with the branch at some point. So if the fibre was associated with the hairs, and assuming it hadn't come from Pamela herself, one obvious explanation would be that it had come from her attacker. But that was another loose end that appeared not to have been followed up.

As well as pointing out all the 'missing evidence' in the report I compiled, I also suggested looking at any superficial debris that might have been recovered from Hastie's body, especially the exposed parts. That was something else that could usefully have been done during the original investigation, because the debris could contain important transferred traces that might give the police some other avenues for investigation.

Perhaps even Locard himself didn't realise, when he formulated his principle more than a hundred years ago, how absolutely right he was when he said that every contact leaves a trace. Some people tend to believe it's only true to a certain extent and can always find reasons – as I used to – why in this or that particular case it's possible that no traces were transferred. Now though, I appreciate only too well that *every* contact really does leave a trace; it's just that sometimes no one finds it. What was clear in *this* case was that it wasn't possible that nothing – no textile fibres, blood, or paint fragments if Gilmour had been responsible – had been transferred between Pamela Hastie and her attacker. Apparently though, no one had been worried enough about it to wonder why.

The conclusion I came to after considering all the reports and other information from the original investigation was that there were holes in the scientific evidence sufficient to raise serious doubts about the safety of Raymond Gilmour's conviction. Unfortunately, it was to be another eight years before he was released from prison pending an appeal in 2002, and five more by the time his conviction was finally overturned.

I was already convinced of the need for defendants to have access to reliable forensic services. But if I hadn't been, cases like Gilmour's would have been all the proof I needed to persuade me that what we were doing was very worthwhile, even essential.

17

Stephen Lawrence

Stephen Lawrence was nineteen when he was attacked and killed while waiting for a bus on a street in south-east London on the evening of 22 April 1993. Although messages left on the windscreen of a police car identified the people suspected of stabbing and killing the teenager, it was two weeks before police made any arrests. And when the five white suspects – Gary Dobson, Luke Knight, David Norris and brothers Neil and Jamie Acourt – were subsequently released without being charged, it wasn't long before the Metropolitan Police were being accused of racism and of not trying hard enough to solve the murder because Stephen was black.

Two years later, I became involved in the case. Convinced that the original suspects were responsible for Stephen's murder, his family were planning to take out a private prosecution and I was asked by their solicitor to make sure that the scientists at the MPFSL had done everything they should have done. To that end, I spent a week at the lab in London, checking the work that had already been undertaken and helping the scientists to do a bit more in certain specific areas.

Stephen had been wearing several layers of clothing when he was killed, and these were likely to have helped clean the blade of the knife as it was withdrawn from the two stab cuts made in the upper part of his body. So I didn't disagree with the scientists' assumption that there would probably have been very little blood to be transferred to Stephen's attackers. And I wasn't particularly surprised that they hadn't found any blood on the suspects' clothing that could have come from Stephen.

What had also been assumed was that the suspects had probably worn their clothing during the two weeks before they were arrested, and therefore any textile fibres that might have been transferred to it from Stephen's clothing would probably have dropped off and been lost. It was an assumption that was made against a background of experiments which showed that around 80 per cent of transferred fibres will fall off in the first four hours or so if the person wearing the clothes is active. But Stephen had run just a few yards down the road before collapsing. So *he* hadn't been active before he was taken to hospital and the clothing was removed from his body. Which meant that looking for fibres from the suspects' clothing on what he had been wearing was the obvious next step in the forensic investigation. Although a few fibres had been found originally that could conceivably have come from two items of Dobson's upper clothing, they hadn't added up to anything sufficiently persuasive to put before a court.

After I'd acquainted myself with all the relevant items, I extended the search for blood on the suspects' clothes. I then checked Stephen's clothes for any more fibres that could have come from Dobson's upper clothing. And I instigated some searches for them on other items from Stephen – on his nail clippings, inside the plastic bags that had been placed over his hands to protect any evidence there might have been on them, and on the sheet of paper that had been put under his clothing while it was drying out before it was examined.

The trousers Stephen had been wearing at the time of the attack were made of a type of thick-stripe corduroy known as elephant cord, which shed its fibres very easily. Also, the fact that they were quite a strong green colour made them relatively easy to pick out from among a lot of others on tapings. So, despite concerns about whether or not they would have dropped off before items from the suspects were seized, I decided we should look for them on the suspects' lower clothing at least, and also on the two items of Dobson's upper clothing mentioned earlier.

In the report I wrote for the Lawrence family in 1995, I said that there was effectively no real scientific evidence (to date) to connect the defendants with the attack on Stephen Lawrence – only the weakest of links with Dobson. What I also said, however, was that this wasn't surprising, given the nature of the attack and the time interval that had elapsed before they were arrested. And I concluded that, in the circumstances, the absence of evidence need not be of concern to the prosecution.

I didn't actually give evidence at the private prosecution, which, unfortunately, collapsed when Duwayne Brooks – the young lad who was with Stephen at the time of the attack and had run off, expecting Stephen to follow him – was found to be an unreliable witness. I don't think Stephen's family ever really forgave Duwayne for that, which is sad, as he was clearly a victim too. And he *had* gone back to try to help his friend, in what must have been terrifying circumstances. So although I can understand why they thought he'd failed them, I can also understand that he must have been deeply traumatised himself by what had happened. Which wasn't helped by the fact that he had no proper support from the police; indeed, he has said that they were constantly 'on his case'.

I did give evidence to the inquiry that was commissioned in 1997 by the Home Secretary into what were referred to as 'the matters arising' from Stephen Lawrence's death. Basically, all I could do was confirm the FSS scientists' conclusions that there was only very weak evidence to link Stephen with any of the suspects' (Dobson's) clothing. Although, as I pointed out, that in itself was not a powerful argument for the defence.

When the Macpherson Report was published in 1999, it stated that 'There can be no criticism of the [original MPFSL] scientists' and said my evidence was 'noted for its clarity and fairness'. Which was nice, but didn't get us anywhere! More importantly, the inquiry found that the police investigation was 'marred by a combination of professional incompetence, institutional racism and a failure of leadership by senior officers', and that 'institutional racism affects the MPS [Metropolitan Police Service], and police services elsewhere'.

At the time of Stephen's murder, the UK had a law of double jeopardy, which prevented someone being tried again for a crime for which they had already been acquitted. And one very significant recommendation of the Macpherson Report was that the law should be repealed in cases of murder if new evidence comes to light. By the time it was changed in England and Wales in 2005, it had been extended to include other serious crimes carrying a life or very long sentence.

In 2006, William Dunlop became the first person to be tried for a second time under the new law. Having been cleared of the murder of Julie Hogg in 1989 when the jury failed to reach a verdict, Dunlop pleaded guilty at a second trial and was sentenced to life in prison. We worked on the second case. And following our discovery of some blood that had been missed on a pair of Mark Weston's boots when he was first investigated and acquitted of the murder of Vikki Thompson in 1995, he was found guilty and convicted in 2010.

It was also 2006 when I was approached again about the Stephen Lawrence case, ten years after I'd last been involved with it, by which time I was working with a company called LGC Forensics. As usual, and because it was such a high-profile case, which would bring pressures of its own, I selected a really strong team to investigate it.

As well as performing my usual role of leading and co-ordinating our effort, and managing the high-level liaison with the police, I also ensured that any new work was properly aligned with the old, so that nothing slipped between any gaps. I selected one of our most experienced forensic biologists to look after textile fibres and keep an overview of all the new work at operational level. Urbane, laid back by nature, Roy Green is a forensic scientist in the traditional mould, and very good with both textile fibres and DNA. In fact, it was thanks to him digging out an old FSS database that was in use at the time of Stephen's murder that it was possible to add some additional contemporaneous insights to the evidence. Deb Hopwood, who is another extremely experienced biologist of the old school, was responsible for work on the case involving hairs – animal and human – for which she had particular knowledge and aptitude. Ed Jarman, who was one of our talented, next-generation, home-grown scientists, looked after DNA – and found himself having to conduct a series of fairly complex experiments that he then had to explain to the satisfaction of judge and jury, which he did extremely well. And April Robson – who I mention elsewhere – was drafted in as chief forensic examiner, searching items and generally supporting the rest of the team.

One of the challenges with cold cases like Stephen's murder is that they inevitably have a complex history of investigation and re-investigation. And because that means that exhibits have been handled more extensively by a larger number of people than normal, there's more potential risk of contamination. So, in addition to the rest of the team, I took the unusual step of appointing someone to check the quality of everything the other scientists did. The person I chose for what was to be an entirely separate and independent role was Ros Hammond, who looked with a fresh pair of eyes at anything they found and were proposing as evidence, to decide whether or not any of it could alternatively be explained by some sort of contamination. As part of this, and before she gave evidence in court herself, Ros was able to sit in the courtroom listening to all the evidence from all the witnesses who'd had something to do with handling the key exhibits, in case anything was said that might change the conclusions she'd come to herself. It was a great piece of work from another very talented forensic scientist.

We had already helped to solve a large number of other high-profile cold cases by that time. And, with every success we had, the confidence people had in us and in our ability to help solve even the most complicated cases increased. We had learned from each case too, and the first thing we decided to do with the Stephen Lawrence investigation was to go back to the crime scene and try to understand precisely what had happened there.

There were various accounts of the attack on Stephen Lawrence. Among them was a statement by an eyewitness who mentioned seeing one of the attackers wielding a blunt instrument, which it was thought could have been a pole or bar of some sort. The only thing the police had come across that matched that general description was a short length of scaffolding pole, which had been found in a garden nearby. Scaffolders use paint to mark up poles so that they can fit them together more easily. So we started our laboratory investigation by examining the bit of scaffolding pole and noting the types of paint it had on it, then looking for paint on Stephen's upper clothing. And although we didn't find any paint on Stephen's clothes, we did notice a number of red fibres.

It was cold the night Stephen died and, as already mentioned, he had been wearing several layers of clothes, including a red polo shirt. So finding red fibres (that matched the polo shirt) on the other layers of clothing he'd been wearing wasn't significant, except that some of them were on the *outside* of his jacket. This meant that they would be available to be transferred on to the clothing worn by his attacker(s) – along with the constituent fibres of the jacket and his other outer clothing.

Then we looked at the tapings that had been taken of the suspects' clothes, and it wasn't long before we started finding red fibres of two different types. Some of them were made of the same twisty cotton and some were of the same polyester as the fibres from the polo shirt. We found them on the tapings from Dobson's clothes first, then on Norris's. And that was when we began to think we might be on to something.

We had already realised that the assumption made during the original investigation that most, if not all, transferred fibres would have been lost in the period between the assault and the suspects' clothing being collected, could be wrong. Which is why, after I became involved in 1995, we had started looking for fibres transferred the other way round – from Stephen to the suspects. Maybe 80 per cent *would* drop off in the first four hours, as was widely believed at the time, but only if the assailant continued to wear the clothes. If, on the other hand, he went straight home, took the clothes off and put them in a drawer, it was reasonable to expect some of the transferred fibres still to be there two weeks, two years, even two decades later. And that's exactly what he might well do, if he thought he could be identified by what he was wearing at the time of the attack.

The extent to which clothing fibres are transferred between people involved in a fight depends on what they're wearing, on the nature and extent of the contact between them, and on how long the contact lasts. It had always been assumed that the attack on Stephen had been very brief. But when we started considering in detail what would have been required to produce his stab wounds – aided by a study the police had commissioned into the medical dynamics of it all – we began to realise that a significant amount of contact would have been involved.

Encouraged by the red fibres we'd already found, we then started looking for the constituents of other items of Stephen's clothing, such as the knitted waistband and cuffs of his jacket and his green trousers. This time though, with our better understanding of the dynamics of the attack, we looked on the suspects' upper clothing as well as on their jeans and/or trousers.

The police had collected a number of items from each of the suspects. In relation to the Acourt brothers, they had apparently planned to seize clothing and other things from their house within two weeks of Stephen's murder. But, as we understood it, although the surveillance people got there at the appointed time, the police officers didn't. However, they did collect some jeans and several pairs of boots and shoes from the Acourt brothers later. There was also a green shirt that had some cuts in it on the lower right side that had clearly been made by a sharp instrument passing through folds of the fabric. But there was no blood associated with them. And although we did find a red fibre on it, there was nothing to indicate whether this had been transferred from its source directly, or indirectly via the other suspects' clothing, for example.

After discovering the red fibres on Dobson's and Norris's clothes, we found more evidence of transferred fibres. Some green cotton fibres on Norris's sweatshirt matched Stephen's trousers. And there were green/blue polyester fibres like those in the cuffs and waistband of Stephen's jacket on Dobson's jacket and cardigan.

During our detailed analysis of the colour of the red fibres using a microspectrophotometer, we noticed that the result from one of the red cottons from Dobson's jacket had an additional component that was reminiscent of what you get with blood. When we did a number of tests along the length of the fibre, we got this result from some parts of it and not others. Which raised the possibility that although the jacket had already been searched for blood a number of times without success, there might actually be some blood on it after all. Also, if there were fibres on the clothes themselves, might there be some more that had dropped off them into the seams of the paper bags in which they'd been stored?

Focusing our attention on Dobson's jacket and

cardigan and on a pair of jeans and a sweatshirt belonging to Norris – on which we'd found the other fibres – we brushed all the debris out of the seams of the paper bags, then looked at it under a microscope. What we found among the debris from the bag that had housed Dobson's jacket were numerous tiny fragments of blood, and then a larger flake of blood with two textile fibres running through it that matched the fibres from Stephen's cardigan. We then DNA profiled some of the blood in the flake, which showed that it matched Stephen's DNA.

If there was a flake of blood, we knew there probably should be a blood stain on the jacket from which it had come that must previously have been missed, by us and by the scientists at the FSS. But when we looked at the jacket again, we still couldn't find anything. So we decided to go over the whole thing again under a microscope that was capable of magnifying up to forty times normal size. Particularly on a grey jacket like Dobson's, that's a considerably more laborious, time-consuming exercise than it might sound, because that type of grey fabric is actually a mixture of black and white fibres. So your eyes are constantly having to adjust and compensate for dark versus light as you try to focus on each tiny area before moving on to the next one.

The first thing we found were some strange, very small, dark, blob-like specks of blood on the front of the jacket. At first, we couldn't work out what they were – or how we'd missed them! Eventually though, after Ed Jarman had conducted numerous experiments, we realised what must have happened.

There had apparently been lots of shouting during the attack, so we had looked for saliva on various items, particularly on upper clothing. The test we'd done involves putting damp blotting paper over the garment, then leaving it in contact for a while, before removing it and running water over it. The blotting paper is impregnated with glucose linked to a blue dye, and where there's saliva on the garment, the amylase it contains acts on the glucose, removing the link between the paper and the dye and leaving a white patch. What had also happened on this occasion, however, was that the damp blotting paper had partially wetted tiny particles of dry blood dust in the packaging – presumably from the flake – and stuck them to the jacket. So that was why the specks of blood looked so odd.

The experiments Ed conducted were meticulous and very time consuming. But it was because we were so careful and painstaking about everything we did that we eventually found something that proved critical to the case.

Inside the back of the neck of Dobson's jacket was a tiny blood stain measuring approximately 0.5 by 0.3 millimetres. It was quite different in appearance from the tiny blobs of blood, in that it seemed to have penetrated both within and between the fibres of the jacket and was much lighter in colour – just like a normal blood stain – and seemed likely to be the source of the blood fragment we'd found in the packaging. When DNA profiling showed that it matched Stephen's profile, our loose end had suddenly been tied up.

In fact, the position of the stain – inside the back of the neck of the jacket – wasn't unusual in the context of the kind of attack that had taken place. When an assailant uses a knife to stab someone, they often draw it back above their head. And as the direction of travel of the knife changes abruptly in that position, from backwards to forwards in preparation for the next blow to be struck, tiny amounts of any wet blood on the blade can be shaken off on to their clothing.

At a fairly early stage, we had noticed that there were a number of short lengths of cut hair on Stephen's, Dobson's and Norris's clothing, of the sort you get when you've just visited the hairdresser. While Roy was busy looking for fibres, and Ed was conducting his blood experiments, Deb was examining these hairs, as well as others that had been found through an extension of the microscopic searching we'd been doing for fibres. We were particularly interested in two very short lengths of 1 and 2 millimetres, the shorter of which had a reddish cast to it that looked like blood under the microscope. Although we weren't able to confirm this, and we knew it wouldn't be possible to get a DNA profile from it, we did manage to get a result from the longer (2-millimetre) hair. Or, at least, the laboratory in America we sent it to did. We couldn't test the hair for nuclear DNA, because you generally need a hair root for that, and neither of our hair fragments was rooted. So the test the US laboratory ran looked at mitochondrial DNA, which is different from the nuclear DNA we normally analyse and is only inherited maternally. Mitochondrial DNA isn't as discriminating as nuclear DNA, which means that we don't get the same powerful statistics from it. But what it showed was that the hair matched Stephen's hair.

The evidence we ended up with consisted of no fewer than five different sorts of textile fibre, some blood, and a hair. However, before we could make any claims about the value of that evidence, we had to make sure that none of it could have been due to some sort of accidental contamination.

During our investigation, we had drawn a diagram illustrating each of the links and their relationship to each other. Blood in the stain on the back of the neck of Dobson's jacket and in the packaging from the jacket linked Dobson with Stephen, for example. As did no fewer than four different kinds of textile fibres (from three different items) found on Dobson's jacket and some more on his cardigan. And fibres like those in Stephen's trousers and in his polo shirt found on the sweatshirt, and the hair like his on the jeans, linked him with Norris. What became clear as we mapped out the diagram was that there was actually a lot of evidence, in forensic-science terms, linking Norris and Dobson with Stephen.

The diagram provided a framework for Ros's work on where, when and how contamination might conceivably have occurred, and how likely it might have been. For instance, knowing that there were connections between Stephen's cardigan and Dobson's jacket, Ros checked who had seized every relevant item and bagged, sealed and labelled it; who else had subsequently handled the items; where that had happened; and what else might have been in the same place at the same time. Then she asked, and answered, the following questions. Were there any opportunities for evidence to be transferred, unwittingly, from the cardigan to the jacket, or vice versa? If so, how many transfer steps would that have involved? And what was the likelihood of each of those transfer steps occurring? It involved a massive amount of work, but we ended up with an overall understanding of whether or not contamination could provide a reasonable alternative explanation for any of the evidence.

Ros explained the principles in the very detailed statement she wrote at the end of it all, and said that, in her opinion, none of the possible mechanisms of transfer represented any realistic possibility of accounting for the significant pieces of evidence reported by her colleagues. She had also been asked to comment on the 'diligence and expedition' we had applied to the handling of the case. As well as a description of the detailed management of the scientific investigation, she wrote about the processing of the almost 500 tubes of DNA extracts, a vast number of tapings of clothing, the contents of 230 pots or bags of debris recovered by us and transferred on to an additional 700 tapings, 1,700 individual fibres recovered by the FSS and involving more than 2,500 specific comparisons, a further 4,500 fibres recovered by us and generating more comparisons, and hundreds of human and animal hairs examined and analysed. New experiments were also designed; new techniques, both photographic and related to microspectrophotometry, were developed and validated; and industrial inquiries were made into the production of several key items of clothing.

Part of the evidence I gave at court concerned whether or not what we'd found could have been uncovered during the original investigation. I said that, technically, the green cottons could have been found, because they'd been looked for by the FSS scientists, albeit not on the right item. What had changed in the intervening years, however, was our better understanding of crime scenes in general and greater appreciation that the attack on Stephen was likely to have involved significantly more contact with his assailants than previously thought. Aided by new imaging techniques to illustrate the medical dynamics of the attack, what this suggested was that a greater breadth of searching would be appropriate. Also, there was much greater knowledge and expertise in designing examination strategies and identifying and rigorously pursuing any potential leads. All of which meant that we were more likely to find tiny traces if they were there. Indeed, it was the combination of those two factors that led to the discovery of the red cotton and polyester fibres, then set the scene for finding the other fibres, the blood fragments (and further fibres), and the short, cut hair. So, all in all, it was most unlikely that the blood and hair evidence could have come to light in 1995. Even if it had, DNA analysis was almost certainly not sufficiently sensitive in the case of blood, or sufficiently advanced in the case of the hair, to have revealed the links they later provided with Stephen.

We had all the usual reasons for wanting to ensure that the scientific evidence and our interpretation of it was watertight. But, in this particular case, there was another reason too. We were acutely aware of the obstacles that had already hampered the Lawrence family's pursuit of justice for their son. So we knew that if we didn't have rock-solid support for every single bit of evidence that was capable effectively of ruling out the possibility of contamination, the evidence would fail and we would only be adding to their distress. That was the reason we all worked so hard and so determinedly on the investigation. And, clearly, the court was satisfied with what we found, because it was largely on the basis of that evidence that Dobson and Norris were arrested in 2010 and charged with the murder of Stephen Lawrence.

Before Dobson could be tried again for Stephen's murder under the new law that had done away with the double-jeopardy defence, his acquittal had to be quashed by the Court of Appeal. Then the CPS agreed to both men being retried in the light of what it deemed to be 'new and substantial evidence'.

When the trial began at the Old Bailey in November 2011, the forensic evidence was at the heart of it. And, this time, both Dobson and Norris were found guilty of the murder of Stephen Lawrence and sentenced to fifteen and fourteen years in prison, respectively.

18

Checking the prosecution's evidence

What a defence lawyer is hoping for when employing a forensic scientist to advise them is that he or she will be able to identify flaws in the prosecution's scientific evidence that will at least cast doubt on the defendant's culpability, if not undermine it completely. Whether or not there were any significant flaws to be found, we provided the equally important service of checking and verifying the original forensic evidence and its interpretation. In addition, we made sure that the lawyers understood the forensic evidence sufficiently to be able to question the prosecution's scientist effectively in court. The following are just two of many examples of cases in which those roles were put into practice.

On the night of 30 October 1991, twenty-four-year-old student nurse Julie Green worked the night shift at a local hospital in Greater Manchester. When her husband, twenty-seven-year-old CPS solicitor Warren Green, woke up at 10 o'clock the next morning, he was surprised not to find his wife asleep in the bed beside him. Although her coat and bag were downstairs, there was no sign of Julie herself. So Green began to search for her. He hadn't been looking for very long when he discovered that both the external garage door and the door that connected the garage to the kitchen were locked, and the keys were missing. Fortunately, a neighbour had a duplicate of the key to the external door. And when Green unlocked it and went into the garage, he found his wife lying dead in a pool of blood on the dusty floor.

At least, that was Warren Green's version of what had happened. What the prosecution claimed was that he had beaten Julie to death with the heavily blood-stained lump hammer that was found in the garage. Striking her sixteen times or more on the head, he had possibly also punched her in the face. Then he had tried to make it look as though she had been involved in drug dealing by planting an empty temazepam container and the corner of a £10 note beside her body.

By the time I was asked to look at the case for the defence, the prosecution had evidence from four scientists, one of whom I visited at the FSS laboratory in Chorley in August 1992. First though, I went to the Greens' house with Clive Candy, who would look after the chemistry aspects.

After an exhaustive search, the police had also found the missing keys behind a brick that had been wedged into the opening of a 4-inch-diameter (10 centimetre) pipe under the floor in the hall. So what we particularly wanted to do was look underneath the floor and get a better idea of the whole layout of the house and, especially, the garage.

Access to the under-floor void required the removal of six short lengths of floorboard, which had been cut for the purpose. And as the pipe wouldn't have been visible to anyone just looking down into the void from the hall above it, you'd have expected it to be a very good hiding place. But because the police clearly suspected Green, they had left absolutely no stone unturned in their search of the premises.

As well as visiting the crime scene and having discussions at Chorley, I read other prosecution reports and studied photographs that had been taken at the time. What I learned from it all was that Julie had obviously been attacked in the garage, where most of the blood had been found. But there were also some dilute blood stains in and around the basin in the bathroom, which suggested that an attempt had been made to wash blood off something there.

The forensic scientist who had done the bulk of the work had visited the crime scene on the day Julie's body was discovered and had taken samples of the blood staining in the garage and bathroom. Twelve days later, she'd returned to examine the site under the hall floor where the bunch of keys had just been found. Together with her colleagues at the Chorley laboratory, she had then conducted detailed examinations of the lump hammer, the pill container, the fragment of £10 note, the keys and key ring, the handle from inside the door leading from the garage to an alleyway that ran down the side of the house, and various items of clothing and footwear that had been retrieved from the house, including some from the washing machine that were still damp.

The lump hammer that had been found in the garage certainly appeared to have been the weapon used in the attack on Julie. Not only did the blood on it match hers, the twenty-seven hairs that had been recovered from it also looked as though they had come from her, and fourteen of the nineteen fibres appeared to have come from her cardigan. Also of particular note was some blood on the keys, key ring and leather fob – suggesting they'd been handled by someone with blood-stained hands – and on a pair of men's black shoes. What was especially interesting about the blood on the shoes was that it suggested they had been in very close proximity to the victim during what had been an extremely violent and sustained attack. In particular, the shape and position of some of the splashes indicated that they'd originated from a source very close to the ground. There were some elongated streaks on the sole of one of the shoes, for example, and some splashes on both of them that had travelled horizontally to land in the gap at the welt between the uppers and soles.

In addition, most of the blood staining was on the inner aspect of each shoe – consistent with the source of the blood having been somewhere between them. It was the sort of staining you'd expect to find if, for instance, the wearer had been standing with one foot on either side of a prostrate body. There were also areas on the uppers where the blood staining was confined to the pores in the leather, which could have resulted from an attempt to clean it off. If that *had* been the case, it might explain why the shoes were apparently damp when they were found by police in the airing cupboard at the house.

Photographs had been taken of a number of footwear marks that had been observed on the garage floor. Then the marks in the photographs had been compared with the sole patterns of numerous pairs of shoes belonging to Warren Green, his wife, and the police officers and ambulance staff who had attended the scene of the murder. But although some of the footwear marks could have been made by two other pairs of Warren Green's shoes, they hadn't been made by the blood-stained pair.

What *had* been established, by blood grouping backed up by early DNA tests, was that the blood on the shoes and key ring could have come from Julie but not from her husband. Renovation work was taking place at the couple's house at the time of the murder, and there were also some relatively small blood stains on various items of clothing that had apparently been worn as work clothes by Warren Green. But there was nothing to suggest that those stains or the stains on the washbasin in the bathroom had come from the victim.

Having examined the scene and checked as much of the evidence as possible, I wrote an extensive report on the case for the defence lawyer. A few of the points I made could conceivably be used in Warren Green's defence. For example, there was nothing about the blood on three items of his (work) clothes to suggest it was connected to the killing. Also, there was some evidence – in the form of possible fabric marks in blood on the rear door to the garage – that gloves might have been worn by Julie's killer. But although no fewer than fifteen gloves were collected from the house and submitted for examination, no blood was found on any of them. There was nothing to suggest that the blood on the basin had necessarily come from Julie, although it was likely to have been deposited when the basin was last used. And the rest of the £10 note left by her body was never found.

All those points paled into insignificance, however, in comparison to some very damaging evidence. For example, the missing keys had been found in a location that suggested they had been put there by someone with an intimate knowledge of the premises – stuffed down a pipe in an underground void beneath the hallway of the house. Even more significant was the evidence relating to the pair of Warren Green's damp, blood-stained shoes that had been found in the airing cupboard, which I thought was actually stronger than the prosecution scientist appeared to be suggesting.

The proposed motive for Julie Green's murder was money – her life was apparently insured for a fairly substantial sum. And in March 1993, based on the forensic and other evidence, Warren Green was found guilty of killing his wife and sentenced to life in prison.

A couple of years later, we were asked by a solicitor to look at another case involving a man who was suspected of having murdered his wife.

Carol Wardell's body was found in a lay-by a few miles from her home early on the morning of 12 September 1994. The post-mortem examination established that she had been asphyxiated, probably by a combination of pressure on her neck and smothering. The estimated time of death was during the afternoon or evening of the previous day, based largely on the examination of her stomach contents in the light of her husband's recollection of what she had eaten. Since the time of Carol's death was critical, her stomach contents became the focus of a long and painstaking investigation, during which they were examined by three different specialists: a forensic scientist at the FSS laboratory in Aldermaston, a consultant gastroenterologist at a hospital in Coventry, and a public analyst. (Public analysts are scientists who are responsible for testing and checking the safety of food and drinking water, and ensuring that they – and any labelling – comply with current legislation.)

The conclusion the scientists came to was that the

victim had last eaten between one and three hours before she died – certainly no more than eight – and that the meal in question had been the lunch and/or supper Gordon Wardell had described. That would mean Carol would not have been alive at 5.22 the next morning. The reason why that specific time was relevant was that Carol was the manageress of a local building society, which someone had entered at exactly 5.22 a.m. on the morning her body was found, using her code, before stealing a quantity of cash and other valuable items.

According to Carol's husband, he had last seen his wife alive when he returned from the pub at 10 p.m. on the night of 11 September and found her being held hostage at knifepoint by men wearing clown masks. After being attacked from behind, Gordon Wardell was apparently rendered unconscious by some sort of anaesthetic substance that was held to his nose. When he came round the next morning – some eight to ten hours later – he was bound, gagged and dressed only in his underpants. And Carol was gone.

A couple of days after his wife's body was found, Wardell appeared on television to appeal for anyone who knew anything about what had happened to Carol to get in touch with the police. Apparently too distressed to be able to walk, he sat in a wheelchair throughout his television appearance, with his expression masked by tinted glasses. The police officer who pushed the wheelchair into position in front of the microphones wasn't wearing glasses, however, and a perceptive observer might have ventured a guess as to what *he* was thinking. A year later, when Forensic Access became involved in the case, Wardell had been charged with murdering his wife.

Numerous scientists had already been involved in the investigation, and as well as the detailed analysis of Carol's stomach contents, the prosecution's evidence was largely based on textile fibres. A large number of apparently similar blue/black fibres had been found on her body and clothing, on her husband's jumper, on pillows from the matrimonial bed, on the strip of bed sheet with which Gordon Wardell had been gagged, on all the seats in his car and, to a much lesser extent, on the driver's seat of Carol's. Interestingly though, the fibres didn't match any of the many other items of Gordon's and Carol's clothing that had been examined. And, despite an exhaustive search, no potential source had been discovered.

What was even more intriguing was that the link between the fibres found on Carol's body and in her husband's car suggested that, whatever the source was, she had been in prolonged contact with it around the time of her death. It could have been something quite large, like a blanket, for example, which had been wrapped around her body. And it had been in Gordon's car as well as in contact with Gordon himself. What couldn't be concluded from that last bit of evidence was that Gordon Wardell had actually driven the car. What seemed to indicate that he might have done so, however, was the fact that his car keys had been found by police officers on a window sill in the house. Apparently, that was where Wardell said he'd left them when he got back from the pub and discovered his wife being held hostage by clown-masked men. So if he hadn't driven the car himself, someone else must have taken them from the window sill, driven Gordon's car to the lay-by to dispose of Carol's body, then gone back to the house and returned the keys to precisely the same place. Which seemed unlikely.

Some urine stains on Carol's trousers and underpants indicated that she had emptied her bladder while she was clothed, possibly at the point of death – which would explain why her bladder was found to be empty at post mortem. But there was no evidence of urine staining anywhere in the house or in her husband's car. So where was she when it happened?

Something else that seemed slightly odd was that although there was some disturbance to furniture and a rug in the lounge, and Carol's handbag and a briefcase had been emptied on the floor, all the ornaments and plants were still neatly arranged on shelves and around the fireplace. In fact, there was nothing to suggest that any significant struggle had taken place anywhere in the house. As far as Carol was concerned, that could have been related to the discovery of traces of chloroform in samples taken from her body. But her husband might be expected to have put up some resistance when he was bound and gagged, if not before that, when he came home and found his wife being held at knifepoint by masked intruders, unless he was too frightened to react, or had been struck on the head and anaesthetised before he had a chance to do so. Even so, it seemed strange that nothing was out of place after what had apparently happened in the house.

Some dirt staining around and between Carol's toes suggested that she might have walked barefoot, possibly on tiptoe, on dirt-covered ground. But there was no obvious dirt on the innersole of the sandal that was found next to her body in the lay-by – the companion to which was discovered in her office at the building society. The fact that there was no sign of a struggle in the lay-by, either, indicated that she was already dead when her body was dumped there. Indeed, the position of her clothing suggested that she had been pulled by the arms, or in bear-hug fashion from behind, before her head and the upper part of her body had been allowed to fall backwards on to the ground.

The robbery that had taken place at the building society was another intriguing aspect of the story. When the premises were entered at 5.22 a.m., the intruder alarm was disarmed by someone in possession of Carol Wardell's user code and keys. Silver paint had also been sprayed over two security cameras, which were transmitting to unmanned monitors at the time and weren't recording. Inside the offices, cash and valuables were taken from the safe, the chair and desk in Carol's office were moved, and, presumably, the sandal was left there.

According to my forensic chemist colleagues at Forensic Access, it looked as though the source of the silver paint had been held fairly close to the lens of the camera by the front door as it was being sprayed, perhaps by someone standing on a chair. So you'd expect some of it to have got on the person's hands, face and clothing, and possibly for footwear impressions to have been left on the chair itself. There was no silver paint on any of Wardell's clothing, shoes or spectacles. But there was actually nothing in the documents I read to indicate whether the police had looked for that type of evidence, which, I suggested in my report for the defence solicitor, was an avenue worth exploring.

Some plastic ties that investigators had found in the garage were the same type as, and with a serial number close to, the ties that had been used to bind Wardell's wrists. Even more interesting was the discovery in the garage of some sheeting that proved to be a physical fit with the piece of bed sheet that had been used as a gag.

The manner in which the gag had been tied – wrapped twice around Wardell's head, with the first wrapping incorporated into the knot – appeared to be unusual. And it was the opinion of one of the prosecution's forensic scientists that it was more likely to have been self-tied than tied by someone else. Indeed, when fourteen volunteers had been asked to tie a gag on someone else, none of them had apparently incorporated the first wrapping in the tying off. So the prosecution was claiming that Wardell had tied the gag himself. However, no similar experiment had been conducted in which volunteers had been asked to *self-tie* a gag. And when Russell did a separate piece of work involving some experiments with both options – which he later gave evidence on in court – he found that none of the volunteers incorporated the first wrapping when self-tying *or* when tying the gag on someone else.

I think Wardell had managed to attract the attention of a passer-by in the morning by shouting. When the police were alerted and arrived at the house, they found him lying on the floor in the lounge attached to a square-section metal bar that formed the backbone of a refuse sack holder. His knees were bent over the top of the bar, with his elbows underneath it, on either side of his legs, and his hands were bound together over the tops of his shins by two interlinked plastic ties like the ones found in the garage, one around each wrist.

A police officer of approximately the same height and build as Wardell subsequently demonstrated that it was possible for someone to gag and tie themselves up in the manner in which the defendant had been found. What he also showed was that, even when tied to the refuse sack, he could move around the floor using a rocking motion, open the lounge door with one of his feet, and call out quite loudly, albeit not very clearly. All of which raised questions about why it had taken Wardell so long to raise the alarm.

When I visited the FSS laboratory in Birmingham where the gag had been examined, I agreed with the findings of the forensic scientist about the garage being the likely origin of the strip of sheeting/gag and the plastic ties. I also agreed with his opinion that it was strange for an intruder not to have arrived at the house with whatever materials might be needed. Or not to have used the telephone or speaker cables that were close to hand in the lounge rather than searching the garage for something suitable. What I didn't agree with was the conclusion that Wardell must have tied the gag himself, or that none of the events could have occurred in the way he described, which is what the prosecution was claiming. They were conclusions that were based only on the evidence we were asked to look at. But balanced against that was other evidence, too, which seemed to indicate Wardell's involvement in his wife's death. For example, the police had taken statements from various neighbours who said they had seen lights going on and off in the house during the night. The fact that one of the rooms they mentioned was the bathroom might have explained why there was no urine on the floor in the area in which Wardell claimed to have been lying for several hours.

Perhaps the evidence that was most damaging to Wardell's case was some CCTV footage the police obtained after he finally abandoned the wheelchair for a walking stick. The recording began with Wardell hobbling into a shopping centre, barely able to walk. Then it showed him tucking the walking stick under his arm and strolling along quite happily, looking in all the shop windows. Finally, he can be seen emerging at the other end, using the walking stick again. Combined with the other evidence, I imagine it would have been difficult for the jury not to have been swayed by the CCTV footage. And in December 1995, following a trial at Oxford Crown Court, Gordon Wardell was found guilty of murdering his wife and sentenced to life in prison.

19

Redressing the balance

As well as providing a service for defence lawyers at Forensic Access, we worked for private individuals on a vast range of cases involving suspected infidelities, disputes between individuals and/or companies, and criminal cases for which defendants either couldn't get Legal Aid or wanted more help than it was able to offer them. People also sometimes came to us because they thought a case hadn't been dealt with sufficiently thoroughly by the police and they wanted to find out if there was anything further that could be done. That was how we later became involved in the Stephen Lawrence case, for example.

As I've already mentioned, a lot of the work involved going back into FSS laboratories where many of my erstwhile colleagues were still working – almost exclusively for the prosecution. Having looked at what they'd done, I would do any additional tests that seemed sensible, then write a report and, when necessary, give evidence in court for the defence. What I began to notice during the 1990s was that standards were starting to slip a bit, although not through any fault of the scientists themselves, some of whom were greatly concerned about it.

The year 1987 saw the publication of the Touche Ross Report, which had been commissioned by the Home

Office to review scientific support for the police. Among the report's recommendations were that the FSS should become an agency and that budgets for forensic services should be devolved to the police. The idea was that this might help to restrict the demand for forensic services, which had been spiralling out of control under the previous system that effectively allowed the police to commission as much work as they liked, because it was provided free of charge by the Home Office. Under the new system, forces would be encouraged to think more deeply about what they asked for, because they would be paying directly for it. What that also meant was that they would be free to use service providers other than the FSS, thereby opening up a market in forensic services, and introducing competition that would help to keep costs down.

What actually happened when the FSS became an executive agency of the Home Office in 1991 was that firms that were providing forensic-type services to other customers started to take on some of the routine testing the FSS had previously done. So competition did creep in at that end of the market, although not at the more complex, investigative end.

A good example was a company called LGC, which had been established (as the Laboratory of the Government Chemist) in 1842 to provide a very specifically forensic type of service related to the import and export of tobacco. What was happening at that time was that people were importing tobacco, mixing it with things like rhubarb and molasses, then exporting it again. Although they had to pay duty on it when they imported it, the customs charge was based on weight. Which meant they made a net gain when the duty was repaid on the bulked-up exports. It was a practice that the scientists at LGC were able to expose, thereby helping the government to curtail and ultimately put a stop to it.

Eventually, LGC's role expanded, and by the 1990s it was providing a whole range of forensic-type testing services, including questioned (suspicious) documents for the Department of Work and Pensions, drugs screening for the military, and drug-substances testing for Customs and Excise. So it was relatively easy for its scientists to switch over to police work and exert competitive pressure on the FSS. But what neither LGC nor any of the other analytical firms who entered the police market in a similar way could cope with at that time was the more complex investigative side of forensic work. There's a lot more involved than might be imagined in being able to use a range of different types of tests to find and make the most of any evidence there might be in a case while keeping costs at a reasonable level. As a result, there was a huge hole in the supply of forensic services as far as competition was concerned.

The Home Office's remit was to make the FSS more efficient, leaner and fitter so that it could compete well, and to halt the inexorable rise in the need for more labs, more scientists and more expenditure. With those aims in mind, a development plan was put in place, and overseen by the new Director General, Janet Thompson. This involved the closure of three of the FSS's seven laboratories – which, by 1996, also included the MPFSL. The first, and in the end the only one to go at that time was the lab at Aldermaston, where I used to work before setting up Forensic Access. The problem was that when Aldermaston closed its doors in 1996, all its work was transferred to other labs, thereby significantly increasing their already substantial workloads.

Meanwhile, the scientists were being encouraged to do less but more focused work on every case. And while that may have made sense from a financial point of view, the scientists themselves were starting to become nervous about the possibility of things being missed and mistakes being made, for which they knew they would get the blame. It was a concern that was well founded in the light of what had been happening following several high-profile miscarriages of justice that occurred in the 1970s and 1980s based on forensic evidence. The wrongful conviction for murder of the lorry driver John Preece in 1973, for example, and of the Birmingham Six in 1975, and of Stefan Kiszko in 1976.

I'd been working at the FSS lab in Harrogate for a year when Stefan Kiszko was arrested in October 1975 and charged with murder and sexual assault. The victim was an eleven-year-old girl called Lesley Molseed, whose body was found on moorland near Ripponden in West Yorkshire. My boss, Ron Outteridge, was the reporting officer responsible for directing and reporting the work on the case, which was conducted by various people in the laboratory. I worked on it too. But as I was still relatively new to the job, my contribution was limited to testing some samples of seminal fluid from Kiszko himself.

After his arrest, Kiszko made a confession to the police – albeit in the absence of his solicitor and subsequently retracted. He was also identified by three girls as the man who had indecently exposed himself to them just a few days before Lesley's body was discovered. So when he was found guilty of murder and sentenced to life in prison in 1976, I think everyone thought that was the end of what had been a very sad case. In fact, though, it was far from over.

Fifteen years later, following an appeal against Kiszko's

conviction, Ron Outteridge and two officers from West Yorkshire Police were arrested and charged with suppressing evidence that would have proved Kiszko's innocence. When the appeal was lodged in 1991, the three girls – who were adults by that time – admitted they had lied. Even more importantly, it was revealed that a potentially vital piece of evidence hadn't been presented at the original trial and that at least a few sperm heads had actually been found in some of the semen stains on Lesley's clothes. What might have made that particularly significant at the time was the fact that Stefan Kiszko had been having treatment for a hormonal problem, and there was a question mark over whether he could or could not produce any sperm in his semen.

After spending sixteen years in prison for a crime he didn't commit, Stefan Kiszko was released on appeal in 1992. A year later, he suffered a heart attack and died, just a few months before his mother – who had battled tirelessly to try to prove his innocence – also passed away.

As well as overseeing the scientific investigation, Ron had presented the evidence in court during the trial that led to Kiszko's conviction. He later explained that, at the time of his original investigation, he had requested a further seminal sample from Kiszko to check on the sperm question, but the police seemed reluctant and he never received one. So he may have felt unable to confirm the position either way. Nevertheless, it's difficult to explain now why such an important piece of evidence didn't emerge, one way or another. But I think it was almost certainly based on a misunderstanding, because Ron was an honest man and a very careful scientist, who took a balanced approach to all the work he did. And I thought it was very sad when he was arrested in 1994.

I think the implication was that he had written the report on the forensic investigation in such a way as to 'help' the police, some of whom, at least, were clearly convinced that Stefan Kiszko was guilty. But Ron was no slouch when it came to standing up to the police. In fact, he was known for doing so. So I think the position was much more subtle, and related to the fact that there had been considerable doubt – including, I believe, among medics, who would be the ones to know – as to whether or not Kiszko could have produced small amounts of sperm from time to time. Although people didn't understand about confirmation bias in those days, Ron simply didn't have any reason to try to pervert the course of justice, which is basically what he was accused of doing.

What may also have played a part was the fact that Ron's report on the evidence was written in the very sparse way that was typical forty years ago, and might have led to misunderstanding. I've always thought it's important – and much safer – to make sure people understand everything that has been done and found in the laboratory and why certain conclusions have been drawn. In fact, I had something of a reputation at the FSS for writing detailed reports that became known as 'Angela's essays', and attracted a certain amount of criticism from my managers.

Unfortunately for Ron, by the time the case got to court, the police and lawyers involved in the original trial had lost or burned all their papers. So, as his notes were the only ones available, he became the focus of the trial, and I don't know what the outcome would have been if it hadn't been halted in 1995 following the death of one of the police officers.

I'm sure there were people who still thought Kiszko

was guilty, and for a long time it looked as though the case would never be resolved. Then, in 2006, a routine swab was taken for DNA testing from a man called Ronald Castree, who was a suspect in a completely unrelated case.

In the strange 'circularity' of things in the forensic world, Forensic Access was called in to advise on the scientific evidence for Castree's defence, which included the results of some very sensitive DNA tests that hadn't been available during the original investigation. I was working at another company by that time and didn't find out about Forensic Access's involvement in the case until after the event. But I now know that quite a lot of time was spent looking to see whether there was any potential for the DNA result to be explained by some sort of unwitting contamination, and that nothing was found. A year later, Ronald Castree was convicted of the murder of Lesley Molseed and sentenced to life in prison.

The Kiszko case was very sad for many reasons. It was also a great pity that it cast a shadow over Ron Outteridge's career. The awful thing is that the outcome would have been very different for everyone if the defence had had their own forensic scientist to ask all the right questions, clear up any misunderstandings, and bring to light the weaknesses in the prosecution's case at the time of Kiszko's trial. As it was, a tragic death was followed by a miscarriage of justice and, ultimately, an ignominious end to someone's career.

What happened to Ron after the Kiszko case was just one example of why forensic scientists were wary of being blamed when things went wrong. It was a concern that was heightened when budgets were being cut and there was so much pressure on the scientists to get more work done for less money. Unfortunately, that's a situation that still exists today, albeit in a slightly different form.

By the mid-1990s, it was becoming increasingly easy to criticise some of the work being done by the FSS. That wasn't necessarily because of its intrinsic quality, but because of the gaps that existed in it and the potential for evidence to be missed or misinterpreted. It's what happens, of course, when you tell people to work quickly and they don't have enough time to think about what they're doing. Or when you tell them to summarise what they've found in their report and not to worry about taking circumstances or context into account. Or when you don't allow time for the creation of a culture in which people have the opportunity to discuss the work they're doing with their colleagues.

So I wasn't surprised by the fact that the scientists I talked to were becoming increasingly uneasy. I could also understand why some of my past colleagues had begun to ask me why I didn't get involved in doing some investigative work myself – and employ them to help me. It made sense, I suppose, in that I was already working independently. But it would have meant setting up a new company to deal with the issues that were being raised. And although that was an interesting idea, we decided it would probably be too difficult, and much too expensive.

While I absolutely agreed that the FSS needed to be leaner and fitter, I was apprehensive about the effects of their laboratory-closure plan. Of particular concern was the fact that it would leave some major police forces without local coverage when they needed someone to help urgently, at crime scenes for example. There was also a certain amount of corporate complacency and

arrogance within the FSS, which resulted in a tendency
to dictate terms. Which meant that when the police had
an urgent case and needed some results quickly, they
would simply be told what the lead time was, which could
be up to three months or more. At one point, it was actually taking eight months to get DNA work done even on
serious cases. The main reason for the delay was that
there had been insufficient planning and resourcing to
prepare the service for the tidal wave that was clearly
going to come with DNA, and that swamped it when it
did.

I had huge sympathy for the scientists, who were
completely overloaded with cases. But I've discovered
since running laboratories myself that there are always
ways to manage-down a backlog – by setting up special
teams to prioritise the work and focus it more, for
example. One of the problems the FSS had was that
they would sometimes do work on cases that had already
gone to court. It might happen because no one had made
any positive efforts to find out where a particular case
stood some months after they'd added it to their massive
backlog. Or it could occur because the police hadn't told
the scientists involved that, having got tired of waiting,
they'd got the work done elsewhere, or had simply not
bothered with forensics.

I'd realised quite quickly after setting up Forensic
Access that I was temperamentally well suited to working
for the defence. Not only did I find it very interesting, it
was also more varied, because you can get through more
work if you're checking what other people have done
rather than doing it all yourself. So I had never thought
about specialising in mainstream police work again.
In any case, we didn't have either the capability or the

capacity in our little lab to do all the different types of testing that would be involved.

Then, one day, I was approached by representatives from three police forces, who told me, 'We've been reading your reports for the defence, and in some cases it's the first time we've been able properly to understand our own crime scenes. That can't be right! So why don't you come and do our crime scenes for us?' When I explained that we didn't have the lab facilities to do the testing that would also be required, the solution they came up with was for us just to do their crime scenes, while they continued to use the FSS laboratories for the subsequent lab work. That might have made sense on the face of it. But I knew that if we did what they were suggesting, we'd lose control of the process and create the type of disconnect I'm always complaining about today.

What tipped the balance in the end was a joint study the police did with the FSS looking into the reasons behind some unexpectedly unsuccessful prosecutions. The conclusion they came to was that one of the primary common factors was the involvement of Forensic Access for the defence. Although that was obviously good from a commercial point of view, it was worrying in terms of justice. The whole reason for setting up Forensic Access had been to create a balance that hadn't previously existed, not to shift the advantage from the prosecution to the defence. What was also troubling was the fact that it seemed to be getting easier to expose flaws in prosecution cases. Although those flaws were often fairly minor, there were occasions when they were so significant that they would completely derail a case – for reasons that could have been avoided if they'd been addressed earlier.

What was becoming apparent, however, particularly

following the closure of the FSS lab at Aldermaston and the threatened closures of Chepstow and Huntingdon, was that the situation was only going to get worse. And eventually, after consultations with numerous police forces, we decided in 1996 that the moment was probably right to see if we could do something to redress the balance.

At the end of his time with the Home Office, Russell had transferred from the Central Research Laboratory at Aldermaston to work in London, and he used to travel on the train every day with a fantastic man called Tom Palmer. Tom lived in our road in Newbury and was the Financial Controller at AEAT. He became a good friend. But I had another reason to be particularly interested in him, because he belonged to a relatively rare PGM blood group. He used to joke that I had traumatised his children by turning up on his doorstep wanting samples of his blood every time I needed a control sample for my blood-grouping tests!

As luck would have it, Tom was about to retire at around the time that Russell and I started talking about the possibility of setting up another company to provide forensic services for the police. Although Tom wasn't a scientist, he had the financial knowledge and expertise that Russell and I lacked. So we were very lucky to be able to persuade him to join us in our new venture.

The first things we did were draw up a strategy and write a supporting business plan. Our aims, as outlined in the plan, were to provide a good range of services so we could tackle whatever was necessary; reduce costs and turn-around times so we could be properly competitive and the police had a better service; improve quality so that it was less easy to pick holes in forensic evidence the way we'd been increasingly able to do at Forensic Access; and extend innovation to include more ideas and technology from the wider scientific community than had happened hitherto.

To keep the costs down, we thought it would be a good idea to work with a partner. And the most obvious choice was a company with which we were already working closely called Cellmark. Having been set up as a DNA-fingerprinting laboratory in 1987 – the year after I started Forensic Access – Cellmark had trained quite a number of FSS scientists to do DNA testing. So having them as a partner would mean that we could avoid all the expense of setting up and running our own DNA facilities. Then, once we had Cellmark on board, we looked for a large, more general scientific company with lots of kit that might be interested in becoming our second partner.

Borrowing the equivalent to my last year's salary at the FSS from a friendly bank manager wasn't going to cover the set-up costs this time. And obtaining funding turned out to be the most hair-raising part of the whole enterprise. In fact, everything involved in establishing the new company was far more complicated than it had been with Forensic Access, which would continue to run alongside it. In the end, after having talks with various potential investors, including the merchant banking group Close Brothers, we actually had a choice between an investment house and Tom's old company, AEAT. The partner we chose was AEAT. With something like 40,000 scientists at that time working in forty countries around the world, AEAT had a nursery of start-up companies, some brilliant chemists, and all the latest state-of-the-art equipment that neither we nor any other forensic company could justify for forensic purposes or ever hope to be able to afford.

Finally, we had the alliance of scientific organisations we had been looking for, and Forensic Alliance became a reality – on paper, at least. It took us a while to think of the name. But it worked very well, and we went on to have various other forensic alliances, including with the police.

There were many potential concerns we had to consider and deal with. One of them was that because the practice manager at Forensic Access wasn't a scientist, we were going to need to keep an eye on the science side of things there ourselves – at the same time as setting up and running the new company. So it was a relief when we were offered premises at AEAT's site at Culham, which was just half an hour's drive from the Forensic Access offices at Thatcham.

In September 1996, when everything was still very much in the planning stages, we invited the scientific support managers (SSMs) from ten police forces to an event we held with Cellmark and AEAT. As well as telling them what the service was going to look like, we were able to show them where our labs and offices would be within the mass of buildings at Culham Science Centre. It was going to cost a huge amount of money to set up the new company. So it was really important that the police had confidence in us, and that we had confidence they would give us work.

We were very lucky to have some amazing support for our new venture. The former FSS lab directors Peter Cobb and Trevor Rothwell, Gill Rysiecki from Cellmark, and David Marson from AEAT all gave talks at the meeting. We even had support from the former FSS Controller

Margaret Pereira, who I'd gone to see all those years earlier when I was thinking about leaving the FSS, and who wrote the foreword to the introductory document we produced for the event. What made it all particularly encouraging was the fact that, having been a thorn in the side of the FSS for the last ten years, they clearly recognised and valued what we had been doing. Indeed, Peter Cobb always used to say that Forensic Access was 'the final layer of quality assurance for the FSS'. The feedback we received from the police forces was good too. And we were reassured to be told by all of them that, once we were up and running, they would be more than happy to use our services.

Four months later, we gave another presentation, this time to chief police officers at the police staff college at Bramshill in Hampshire. I'm generally very passionate about the work, and I felt strongly about what we were trying to do. So it would have been natural for me to give the talk at Bramshill, as I'd done at the inaugural meeting. But, after a lot of thought, we decided it would be better for Russell to do the speaking and for me just to come in for the questions. There had been some improvement in attitudes since I turned up at my first crime scene for Aldermaston and was met with misogynistic cynicism. But we knew the audience would be dyed-in-the-wool senior officers who wouldn't really want a (relatively) young woman telling them what might be good for them. It was clearly the right decision and, as things turned out, that meeting seemed to go pretty well too.

The lead time for setting up a DNA unit is much longer than it is for a standard forensic laboratory. So the three scientists from Cellmark who were going to be working with us moved into Culham first, in February 1997, to set up their equipment and validate their methods. Four months later, we were invited to an event to celebrate Cellmark's tenth anniversary. However much I might have wanted to, I clearly wasn't going to be able to avoid the managing director completely during the event. And when he did finally corner me and ask me the question I'd been dreading about how things were progressing financially, I adopted a suitably upbeat tone as I told him, 'Oh, everything's fine. It's all coming along really well.' Then I changed the subject swiftly. Because although it was true that it was going well, our two investors were actually still 'birds in the bush', and until we had a firm commitment, the huge amount of money that the people at Cellmark had already spent wasn't really secure.

Waking up in the night in a cold sweat isn't something I normally do. I had some sleepless nights during that period though, despite the fact that I was certain our confidence wasn't misplaced and that, one way or another, it would all work out the way we believed it would. Which, in the end, it did.

Shortly before we finally signed the deal and moved into some rooms off a ground-floor corridor in Culham Science Centre in November 1997, we started recruiting staff. As well as advertising in the *New Scientist*, we head-hunted some scientists from the recently closed FSS lab at Aldermaston and elsewhere, and ended up with really excellent teams covering biology, chemistry, toxicology and drugs. I think we recruited fifteen scientists to begin with, including three who we based within AEAT at Harwell, and the first arrivals started work in January 1998.

Although we had put together an excellent business plan, we had just been guessing about how much money we were going to make. So there were more anxious days ahead as our salaried scientists sat in the empty room we referred to, rather grandly, as the library, turning the pages of catalogues and writing long lists of all the very expensive lab equipment and consumables they were going to need.

After everything had been ordered and paid for, the same scientists measured out the labs themselves, drawing marks on the floor where the sinks, some very smart black-trimmed white benches and other furniture should go. Then they started collecting and analysing samples – of glass and paint, for example – as the foundation for their own sets of reference samples and databases, and did all the endless calibrating and testing of the equipment when it arrived. You didn't have to have the accreditation for all your processes in those days that you need today, but it was still necessary to do all the same sorts of things and it took a huge amount of time. Eventually though, in April 1998, the scientists were ready to start working on the first case that came in, as described in Chapter 21.

20

Lynette White

On the evening of 14 February 1988, the body of twenty-year-old Lynette White was found in the bedroom of a flat above a betting shop in Cardiff in Wales. She had been stabbed more than fifty times, and her throat and wrists had been slashed, in what had clearly been an incredibly brutal attack. Eleven months later, five black and mixed-race men were arrested by South Wales Police and charged with Lynette's murder. One of them was Lynette's boyfriend, Stephen Miller, who subsequently confessed to having killed her.

There was no scientific evidence to support the case against the five men. But Miller's confession was backed up by statements from two young women, Leanne Vilday and Angela Psaila. The flat where Lynette's body was found was actually rented, but not lived in, by Vilday, who had allowed Lynette to stay there following an apparent argument with Miller a few days before she was killed. The other witness, Psaila, was a friend of Leanne's who claimed to have been present during the attack.

The first trial of the five defendants began in October 1989, and ended four months later when the judge died. In November 1990, following a second trial, three of the five defendants – Tony Paris, Yusef Abdullahi and Stephen

Miller – were convicted of murder and sentenced to life in prison. Two years later, the convictions of the men who had become known as 'the Cardiff Three' were quashed by the Court of Appeal. The grounds for overturning the convictions were that they had been rendered unsafe by the fact that Miller's confession had been obtained as the result of a shocking level of bullying and intimidation by the police. By that time, however, everyone involved with the case was unhappy – Lynette's family because the convictions had been overturned, and the Cardiff Three and their families and supporters because of the fact that they had been prosecuted at all, let alone convicted of the crime. So when Forensic Alliance became involved in the case eleven years later, the investigation into Lynette's death was still a major cause of controversy.

What the police asked us to do initially was review the original scientific examination, which had been conducted mainly by scientists at the FSS laboratory in Chepstow. It was actually part of a general review of the original investigation by two retired police officers, William Hacking and John Thornley. And after talking to the scientists involved and examining many of the key items for myself, I produced an initial report in October 1999, in which I suggested some avenues for further investigation. Six months later, my full report concluded with the words: 'even at this late stage, with a different focus and one which is heavily dependent on context, and using new technologies now available, it is possible that a number of important issues may yet be resolved'. Not long afterwards, we were asked to re-investigate the case.

The scientist leading the original scientific work said

in his report that a small amount of semen had been found on a mid-vaginal swab taken from Lynette's body, with further traces on her knickers. It was his opinion, however, that the semen was unlikely to have been deposited during at least the last six hours before she died. The fact that the clothing on the lower part of her body had not been pulled down or removed also suggested that there hadn't been any directly sexual motive for the attack. (Lynette was working as a prostitute at the time of her death.) What the report also said was that Lynette had been on or very close to the floor by the bed when she received the first stab wound. Then, after her throat had been slit, she had been dragged to the position under the bedroom window where she was found.

Other than that, there was no real sense of the full sequence of events at the flat. So our brief was to try to ascertain what had taken place there on the night Lynette White was killed; to see if there was any evidence that might point to who had been responsible for her death; and to discover whether any of the 'foreign blood' found at the scene (i.e. blood that could not have come from Lynette herself, and that had been identified by blood grouping) still remained.

My main impression on reading the original forensic report was that a huge amount of effort had been put into the scientific investigation. Hundreds of items had been collected from the flat and from various suspects during the original investigation. Unfortunately, by the time most of the suspects' clothing had been seized, any evidence on it could have been lost, one way or another. And although there was interest in some blood that had been found on the jacket of one of the men who had been wrongly convicted, the stain had proved to be too small for blood-grouping purposes.

Among all the blood that could have come from Lynette herself, there was some foreign blood on her jeans and on one of her socks, as well as on the wall next to her body. Foreign blood is always interesting in a case that has involved repeated blows with a knife, as this one had done. As mentioned in reference to the case against Massimo Carlotto, if the assailant's hand slips in wet blood on the handle on to the cutting edge of the knife blade as they strike, their own blood starts to contaminate the scene.

What blood-grouping tests had shown was that the blood on the bottom of the legs of Lynette's jeans and on her right sock belonged to the same groups as Angela Psaila, but couldn't have come from any of the five original suspects. It was a result that police believed gave some validity to Psaila's claim that she had been present during the attack and had received an injury when she was forced to take a limited part in it. But the blood could alternatively and theoretically have come from any of the 1 in 3,800 of the rest of the population that shared that combination of blood groups. It was a statistic that was thought to be a reasonable 'match' for blood grouping at the time, although it wouldn't impress us today, when DNA-profiling techniques have accustomed us to links based on frequencies of occurrence of less than 1 in 1 billion between a blood sample and a particular individual.

Although DNA analysis was in its infancy in 1988, a new technique designed to distinguish between male and female DNA had been carried out at the FSS research laboratory at Aldermaston. And what struck me when I read the original forensic reports was that it had shown the presence of the Y chromosome in the foreign blood on Lynette's jeans and sock. So the blood must have come from a male – male sex chromosomes are designated XY, while females are XX. Which meant that unless Psaila's blood was somehow mixed with male blood, it couldn't be hers. It should have been a key discovery at the time. But it appeared to have been effectively ignored, perhaps because it wasn't what was expected, or because the scientists didn't quite trust the results from the new technique. Whatever the explanation, it's never a good idea effectively to ignore a loose end, because there is always a reason for it.

As well as being criticised for their role in the men's wrongful arrest and conviction, the police were also under fire for failing to find the real killer, or killers. But they *were* trying to solve the case, and had continued their investigation into the foreign blood each time a new DNA technique became available – although I think that was partly because they hoped to find something that would prove they'd been right about the original suspects. What was interesting in that respect was the way the case mirrored the early history of DNA profiling, which, at the time of the original investigation, required quite a lot of blood. In fact, the reason why the multi-locus probe (MLP) tests conducted by the FSS at Birmingham, and then the single-locus probe (SLP) tests carried out by Cellmark had proved unsuccessful was almost certainly partly because they required more blood than was available.

In 1992, the solicitor acting for one of the suspects had commissioned a new DNA test called polymerase chain reaction (PCR), to be done by the FSS in Aldermaston.

By multiplying up the amount of DNA extracted, results (in the HLA blood-group system) could be obtained from much smaller samples than was previously possible. But the test proved unsuccessful. In 1996, PCR was used for a second time – on that occasion as part of short tandem repeat (STR) profiling, which is the type of testing we still use today – particularly on blood that had been collected from the wallpaper near the body. Again, the test proved unsuccessful. In 1997, the same test applied to Lynette's jeans also failed to yield any useful results. And when STR profiling was used for her right sock and on wallpaper from the bedroom and hallway, the only successful result obtained showed that the blood on the sock was her own.

What had become clear as we looked at the reports was that the original investigation had been hampered by a number of things. One of them was a failure to think carefully enough about the blood patterns that had been observed in the flat and to work out what they might actually mean. The picture that emerged when we started to focus on the blood patterns was blindingly obvious, and gave us a useful framework on which to base our own investigation. And foreign blood was one of the first things we targeted.

Obviously, a DNA profile from the foreign blood could help to identify the person from whom it had come. If we were very lucky, we might even find a match for it on the National DNA Database, which could still theoretically contain relevant DNA, even though it hadn't been set up until 1995, which was some time after the murder. Also, the distribution of the foreign blood could help us to work out whether it had any real connection to the murder or was purely coincidental. For example, it might have come from someone who had simply been in the room at some point in the past.

Each time a new DNA test was carried out during the original investigation, more samples of the very limited amount of foreign blood had been cut out of Lynette's jeans and sock, always to no avail. So eventually – before we started working on the case – it was decided that if any more testing was going to be conducted on the blood samples from the crime scene, it had to be within strict guidelines. A lay panel of local people had been assembled to advise the investigating team, supported by two DNA experts – an FSS scientist called Peter Gill and a German professor, Bernd Brinkmann, or his assistant, Steve Rand – who drew up a strategy governing any further testing. Having to consult and obtain agreement from the lay panel and two DNA experts before we could do any testing on the small amount of potentially foreign blood that remained, particularly on Lynette's jeans and sock, made it a long, slow process. But, obviously, it was a good thing that they were all being kept up to date and were able to contribute.

Another major problem with the original investigation was that the police had focused on fingerprinting, almost to the exclusion of everything else. Obviously, there would have been lots of people going in and out of the flat after Lynette's body was discovered. But there was still a reasonably good chance that the police might have been able to find prints made in what would have been wet blood or from wet-blood-stained fingers, which would, of course, be highly significant. So their interest in looking for fingerprints was understandable. The problem was, they had sprayed everything with the chemical ninhydrin, which is used to bring up latent fingerprints

– i.e. fingerprints that can't easily be seen – but which also degrades DNA, rendering it useless for profiling.

One upside to their interest in fingerprints, however, was that the police had removed entire strips of wallpaper from the bedroom where the attack occurred, and from the passageway outside it. So, after I'd visited the crime scene and taken various measurements, we attached the wallpaper strips to boards of appropriate dimensions at our laboratory. Then we arranged the boards to reconstruct areas of the rooms we were particularly interested in. Being able to wander around the reconstructed scene and inspect the blood patterns in detail helped enormously as we tried to work out more precisely what had happened there.

When I went to the flat to take measurements for our reconstruction, it was being re-painted, apparently for the second time since Lynette's death. But it was still a great help to be able to see the actual rooms and get a sense of the relatively small space they represented and what might, and might not, have been possible in it. According to what the police still believed, Psaila and the five original suspects had all been in the bedroom while Lynette was being stabbed to death. And, of course, the more people you have in a small space, the more likely they are to leave signs of their presence behind them. So if that *was* what had happened, it would surely be possible for us to find at least some evidence that all those people had been there.

We knew from the original reports that there was no electricity in the flat at the time of Lynette's murder. Apparently, it had been cut off because the bill hadn't been paid. So the only light in the bedroom would have been from the streetlight outside, and the narrow hallway of the flat would have been almost completely dark. The light bulb that would have lit the communal stairway leading from the front door of the flat to the door that opened on to the street had also failed and had not been replaced, so that would have been dark too. With that in mind, when we started to think about how Lynette's killer, or killers, would have got from the bedroom to the pavement outside, the blood patterns on the walls in the hall of the flat began to make sense.

It was clear from the various reports and from numerous photographs of the crime scene that the police provided for us that there had been a great deal of blood in the bedroom, and that it comprised a number of different elements. The heaviest blood staining was on and around the end of the bed and on the adjacent wall and floor. The fact that some of it was in the form of classic arterial spray indicated that this was where the attack started and where Lynette received the injuries to her neck and/or wrists. Other blood in the same area was smudged and smeared, suggesting that there had been a struggle up against the wall there, or perhaps the assailant had leaned against it as the blows were struck.

Some blood stains in the form of spots and splashes on the adjacent wall close to where Lynette's body had been found had clearly been cast off something with wet blood on it. The knife, for example, and/or the assailant's hand if it had been bleeding at the time, as we suspected. If Lynette had been dragged from the corner of the room where the attack began to the position under the window where her body was found, that might also explain the presence of foreign blood on the bottom of the legs of her jeans and on her right sock, particularly if whoever was responsible had had an injury themselves and had held her by the ankles.

As you exited the bedroom, there was a wall directly in front of you, which meant you had to turn sharp left into the hall. Although there was very little in the way of written records of the blood staining in this part of the flat, there were a few photographs and, of course, the wallpaper strips we used for our reconstruction in the lab. Of particular interest was a very clear mark on the wall opposite the bedroom door that comprised a contact stain with splashes of blood forced out underneath it. What it indicated was that someone had smacked into the wall with the palm of a hand as they came out of the bedroom, before they realised they'd have to turn sharp left into the hall. Other smears between elbow and shoulder height on the walls in the hall could have been made by that same person touching them as they felt their way in the darkness, then down the stairs, before fumbling for the catch on the front door that opened on to the street.

Now that we had a viable explanation of what might have happened, we focused our attention on getting a DNA profile from the foreign blood and establishing just how extensive it was. By doing so, we would be able to confirm whether or not it was likely to have been directly associated with the attack. But because there was so little of it left after all the historic testing, we were going to have to find some more, which meant getting hold of as many of the items originally recovered from the scene as possible.

Some of these items had been returned to the police and were in police stores. Others, including all the samples taken from everything they'd looked at, had been stored by the FSS in their archive in Birmingham. So, during the three or four years it took to complete the various stages of our painstaking investigation, we often had to ask for the archive to be checked for particular items, and sometimes checked again when they couldn't be found. Fortunately though, things usually seemed to turn up in the end, thanks largely to the tenacity of the police, spurred on by our exhortations that the samples *must* exist somewhere, because the case notes said they did. Eventually, when we had retrieved a large number of the items seized during the original investigation, we started to go through them one by one.

One of the reasons you always start again from scratch, even if something has already been examined by a very well-qualified and experienced scientist, is because no one is infallible. Or you might take a slightly different approach from the one they did. Or use a different type of technique, or a more modern technique that wasn't previously available. Or you might notice something that you later see on something else, which might form an unexpected link in its own right. Besides, it's a good way of understanding some of the detail you're seeing in the photographs that were taken at the time of the incident, and of putting the likely significance, or otherwise, of something into proper perspective.

Some of the things we looked at – such as Lynette's jeans and socks – had already been examined countless times, but were so obviously critical that we had to see what else we could squeeze out of them. And, of course, there were challenges to be overcome. For example, the fact that the leg bottoms of the jeans were now just a latticework of fabric, with each hole representing where a sample of blood had been taken for testing years beforehand.

With the approval of the lay panel and its expert DNA advisors, and of our DNA colleagues Matt Greenhalgh and Andy McDonald of Cellmark, we had started trying to refine our DNA-profiling techniques. And to avoid using up any of the precious foreign blood until we felt we were ready to do so, we used blood that we were pretty sure had come from Lynette herself. But despite the improvements in our techniques, the indigo dye in the jeans still gave us problems by inhibiting our DNA reactions, rather like the ninhydrin on the wallpaper had done.

Among the items we looked at was a blood-stained key ring that had been found outside, at the back of the premises, which held what was apparently Lynette's key to the flat; two stacked cardboard boxes that had been on the bedroom floor close to her head; a box of condoms that was on the windowsill, and an unused condom discovered on the bare mattress on the bed; some cigarette ends; one or two swabs of blood stains that hadn't been looked at during the original investigation; and some apparently inconsequential debris from the floor near Lynette's body that included some biscuit packaging and a small piece of the cellophane sleeve from a pack of cigarettes. As any forensic scientist will tell you, it isn't always possible to predict which inconsequential items might turn out to be important. In this instance, our first break came from the cellophane.

In view of its close proximity to Lynette's body, we were pretty sure that the extensive smears of blood on the piece of cellophane would turn out to be hers. But there was also a single small, round stain that was potentially more interesting, because what it clearly represented was an airborne droplet of blood that had been projected off something with wet blood on it and intercepted by the cellophane.

The surface from which the droplet of blood had been projected might have been Lynette's body. Or it might have come from the murderer's injured hand. When we tested it, we got an almost complete DNA profile of a male. Shortly afterwards, we found some of the same blood on the outer of the two stacked cardboard boxes. That was the point at which we started to think we might be on to something. But we still needed more evidence to be able to make a direct connection between 'cellophane man' and Lynette's murder.

We knew from the blood-grouping tests that had been conducted originally that there had been some foreign blood on the wall underneath the window in the bedroom. So we looked again at the photographs that had been taken of the crime scene. What we were looking for this time were any spots or splashes of blood – like the spot on the cellophane – that could conceivably have been flicked off someone's hand on to something we could examine. It was a bit like 'It was there, but now it's gone.' Until, that is, we identified an area of the skirting board that might be of interest.

When the police went back to the flat to cut out a section of the skirting board for us to examine, they also brought us the front door that opened out on to the street at the bottom of the stairs. What we were particularly interested in as far as the door was concerned were any remains of the light smear of blood that had been swabbed and grouped during the original investigation without providing any useful results. And although the door and the skirting boards had been painted twice in the period since the murder, I still thought it was worth having a look at them. So I asked my very meticulous, instinctively observant colleague April Robson to scrape off the paint on the skirting boards, a tiny bit at a time and very cautiously, using a scalpel and a microscope. April is one of those people who can be looking at something and notice something else, *and* remember where she first saw it. It's a skill you can't teach – you either have it or you don't – and it can be very important when you're looking for connections between things but aren't sure what form they might take.

I could understand why April thought I was mad and wasn't particularly keen on the idea of trying to scrape off the paint. It would be a painstaking process. Also, there's a very fine line between going too deep so that you lose any traces of blood that might be present under the layers of paint, and not going deep enough to find anything. But you have to be careful about putting anything in the 'too difficult' box. And April did the job splendidly, managing to uncover some blood on the skirting board that hadn't been directly sprayed with ninhydrin for fingerprinting and had actually been protected by the paint, and some more blood down the back of the board, where there must have been a gap.

The DNA profile we got from the blood was a match for 'cellophane man'. So then April repeated the paint-scraping process on the front door. This time, she couldn't see any blood as she was scraping, because most of it had been swabbed off for testing during the original investigation. But she did obtain a positive chemical reaction for blood. Then a sample from the affected area was found to contain a mixture of the same male/'cellophane man' DNA and Lynette's own – which is exactly what you'd expect to find on the killer's hands as he fumbled with the catch in the darkness in his haste to get out of the building.

When we tested swabs from the wall outside the bedroom door, and one from the top of the stairs that no one had previously looked at, we again obtained the 'cellophane man' profile. Next, we turned our attention to Lynette's upper clothing, which was a bit more of a challenge. Not surprisingly, her clothes were completely covered in her own blood. So the chances of finding any of her attacker's blood felt a bit like looking for the proverbial needle in a haystack.

When Lynette's body was found, one of her arms had come out of a sleeve of the jacket she was wearing, and the back of the jacket lay across her front. It seemed odd at first. But when the long-suffering April dressed in similar clothing and lay on the floor, then allowed me to tug at her clothes to achieve the same arrangement as Lynette's, it became obvious how Lynette must have been held or manhandled. So then we were able to identify some critical points on her clothing. And when we tested samples of blood taken from those points, we once again got a profile that matched 'cellophane man' – mixed with some of Lynette's own blood, of course.

It was amazing. We had the same man's DNA on Lynette's sweatshirt and jacket, on both legs of her jeans, on her socks, on the cardboard box, on the cellophane wrapper from the cigarette packet, on the wall near where her body had been found, on the exit route between the bedroom and the front door to the street, and on the front door itself. Whoever he was, it seemed inevitable that he had been directly involved in her murder.

The police were still expecting Lynette's killer to be

one of the Cardiff Three. So we obtained DNA profiles from all five of the original suspects, including through the use of surrogate samples (i.e. from items of their clothing on which we had discovered body fluids that we were pretty sure would be theirs). But 'cellophane man' wasn't one of them. So who was he?

We didn't get any matches for his DNA when we looked on the National DNA Database, or from a mass screening that was done locally by the police. So we decided to do what would now be called a familial search of the database – in other words, a search for 'near misses' for our potential suspect that might lead us to his family. First, we selected the rarest component of his DNA profile, which was an allele (a form of a gene) known as FGA27 that occurs in about one in a hundred of the population. Then we requested a selective search of the database, which was restricted to include only men, only in the Cardiff area, and, I think, to some sort of age limit.

When the results of the search came back, there were 600 names on the list, which was far too many people for the police to investigate. Somehow, we needed to whittle it down – for which we owe a great debt to a very meticulous South Wales Police officer called DC Paul Williams. By looking at every single one of the 600 profiles to see which of them had at least seven alleles (out of a maximum of twenty) that matched those of the man we were looking for, Paul managed to reduce the number of profiles still in the frame to seventy. Then we looked at each of the matching alleles in those seventy profiles and at the frequency with which each of them occurred in the general population. And when we then multiplied all the matching frequencies in a profile together to get an overall frequency, we found one profile that stood out above all the others as being very close to that of 'cellophane man'.

The profile we identified belonged to a fourteen-year-old boy whose name was on the DNA database because he'd committed some (relatively) minor crime. He hadn't even been alive at the time of Lynette's murder. But the police looked at his family, and asked us first to check a sample taken from his mother. Obviously, being a woman, she wouldn't have been a match for 'cellophane man', but I think they just wanted to check that the FGA27 gene hadn't been inherited from her. When we were able to show that it hadn't been, they took a sample from the boy's father. And although his DNA profile was very close to that of 'cellophane man', he wasn't a match either. Nor was his brother. Then, just as it was beginning to look as though we were going to have to spread the net wider, the police discovered that the father had another brother, who had apparently been a recluse for some years.

My colleagues at the laboratory were desperately trying to get a profile from the sample taken from the second brother when I had to leave to go to a meeting in Birmingham. It was hugely frustrating, not least because the phone I had at the time always suffered from really poor reception around the Birmingham area. So when someone from the lab rang while I was still on the train, I heard him say, 'We've got some initial results, which seem to show . . .' and then the line went dead, leaving me in complete suspense. I got the news in the end though, when I arrived at my destination. By which time the police had picked up the fourteen-year-old boy's uncle, Jeffrey Gafoor, and taken him to hospital.

Fortunately, because they were pretty certain they had

the right family, the police had had the presence of mind to watch Gafoor after the sample had been taken from him for testing. So they'd seen him visit a few chemist shops, and had banged on his front door shortly after he got home. And although they didn't arrive soon enough to stop him taking some of the paracetamol tablets he'd just bought, they *were* in time to get him to hospital and prevent him from dying.

Perhaps it was because he thought he *was* going to die that Gafoor made a semi-confession to the police. We did a quick check of his blood groups to make sure they matched the original grouping results for the blood found at the scene and on Lynette's jeans and socks. And when he was faced with all the evidence when the case went to court in July 2003, Jeffrey Gafoor pleaded guilty and was sentenced to life in prison for the murder of Lynette White.

In most other circumstances, that would have been the end of the case. But as soon as Gafoor was convicted, the police started investigating the officers who had been involved in the original investigation that led to the wrongful conviction of the Cardiff Three. In 2008, Angela Psaila, Leanne Vilday and another witness in the original trial were found guilty of giving false evidence and received prison sentences. A year later, three serving police officers, ten retired police officers and two civilian members of police staff also faced charges related to the investigation. And when the case against 'Mouncher and others' went to court in 2011, I became involved again.

I knew the police officers were still insisting they had been right to arrest the Cardiff Three. What I didn't know until I was actually standing in the witness box was that they were claiming there was a relatively innocent explanation for Gafoor's blood being at the scene. Apparently, they believed he'd had some sort of inter- action with Lynette that had been followed by an argument and a bit of a struggle; then he had left the flat, and the Cardiff Three had come in and stabbed her. While I couldn't categorically say this couldn't have happened, there was no evidence to suggest anyone else had been there at the time of the attack. Which was a bit odd if at least five or six people had been present, as was being suggested, in what was quite a small flat. Because the more people there were, and the more active a role they took, the more likely it is that they'd have left some signs of their involvement.

It's always more difficult answering questions a long time after you did a piece of work. However meticu- lously you check all your case notes, it's impossible to remember all the details of everything you did and saw, and the results of all your tests. In a large case like this one, the case notes alone can fill a substantial number of ring binders. So you end up taking a lot of material with you into the courtroom, then irritating everyone while you search for specific answers. I remember I had some difficulty finding the relevant document among all the thousands of others when I was giving evidence in court and was asked a particular question. I think it was about whether I'd tested the blood around one of the stab holes in Lynette's clothing, presumably to see if it was more of the foreign blood. And, of course, the defence lawyer was quick to use the fact that I couldn't immedi- ately lay my hands on the appropriate document to suggest that it might indicate some level of bias or incompetence. I managed to rise above it though. And, fortunately, I did find what I needed while checking something in relation to another question, so I was able to redress the balance.

In the end, the trial collapsed because some critical documents had gone missing. When they resurfaced a few weeks later, they became the focus of another investigation that started in 2015. Meanwhile, eight former officers who had been among those formally found not guilty when their trial was abandoned launched a civil action in the High Court against South Wales Police for malicious prosecution. So then I had to write yet another statement, although I didn't have to give evidence on that occasion, because the case was dismissed by the judge.

There was still more to come, however, with the publication in 2017 of the Mouncher Investigation Report, which followed a comprehensive review of what had caused the trial against the original police investigators to collapse. The conclusion the report came to was that although many aspects of the work of police investigators and prosecutors had been poorly managed, 'bad faith' on their behalf had played no part and that the cause had actually been human failures.

After twenty-nine years, the case that began with the murder of Lynette White in a flat in Cardiff was finally over. But not before it had made history in three key areas. Legally, it was the first time the true murderer had been found and convicted after someone else had been convicted of the murder and then released. In terms of policing, it resulted in all interviews with people who have been arrested having to be recorded. And in relation to forensic science, it was the first time someone who had committed a murder was identified through a familial study of the National DNA Database and then convicted.

(Another murderer had been identified in a similar way the previous year, but he had already died.)

I hope that, for Lynette's family and for surviving members of the Cardiff Three, the identification and conviction of the real killer at least made them feel that justice had finally been done.

21

'Tell me how you're going to solve it'

The first case we did at Forensic Alliance was toxicological, and I can remember being very pleased that at last we were 'operational'. There was a trickle of cases after that, but it was generally very quiet. So it was a worrying period for many reasons, not least because of all the people who were relying on us, in effect, to feed their families and pay their mortgages. Although we'd expected to have to cover costs for a while, we obviously couldn't continue to do so forever. I just hoped I sounded more confident than I felt when I told our increasingly nervous scientists to relax and enjoy the quiet time we were having, because it wouldn't be long before they were all moaning at me about being too busy.

Unfortunately, despite the heartening responses of all the SSMs who had attended our inaugural meeting almost two years earlier, when it came to giving us actual work to do, all the police forces said more or less the same thing: 'We're very keen to use your services. But right now we have this [or that] problem to deal with.' The problems were usually to do with budgets or prior arrangements with other service providers. But I think the fear was that if anything went wrong, they could be criticised, whereas if they just continued to use the FSS, no one could say anything.

What we really needed was to get our first geographical area, which would provide us with some steady work. In October 1998, that finally happened when the cycle of caution was broken by the far-sighted SSM for Dorset Police, who was a wonderful man called Terry Marsden. The months between April and October had seemed agonisingly long. Soon, though, there was so much work coming in we had to employ more staff and buy more equipment.

Getting the balance right is a problem everyone must have when the new company they've set up starts to grow. And as the months passed, Tom, Russell and I seemed to spend an increasing amount of our time making sure we had enough of the right kind of scientists and all the equipment necessary to deal with the range of cases we were being asked to investigate. Eventually, however, as Forensic Alliance expanded and the peaks and troughs that matter hugely to a small firm began to smooth out, things got a bit easier in that respect too.

By the end of the 1990s, we were doing a significant proportion of all the cases that came up for Dorset Police, as well as for some other forces. One case I remember particularly as being a really good example of what can happen when all the different parts of a forensic investigation come together involved the brutal murder of the owner of a sex shop in Bournemouth. The case was investigated by Roy Green, who was a biologist and later to become one of the stars in the Forensic Alliance cold-case team at Culham, and Ray Jenkins, an excellent forensic chemist of the 'old school' who could turn his hand to almost anything chemistry related.

When Adam Shaw's body was discovered, there was blood everywhere in his shop. Unfortunately, as there was no match on the footwear database we used for the bloody shoe marks that were found at the scene, we weren't able to identify the sole pattern or make of the shoes that had created them. What we *were* able to ascertain was that someone had come into the shop, locked the door, stabbed the victim multiple times, searched for cash, washed blood off themselves, and then exited through a small, boarded-up window into the garden. Aside from the shoe marks, there was very little forensic evidence that might potentially identify the killer. What there *was* included some purple polyester fibres around the window through which it was assumed the assailant had escaped. Although, on the face of it, it didn't seem like much to go on, the fibres were actually to prove critical in the context of some CCTV footage of a section of the street near the shop.

When police examined all the comings and goings captured by the CCTV camera during the period when the attack was thought to have occurred, they saw a man walking down the street wearing a purple fleece under a jacket. The brand name on the uppers of his shoes was clearly visible, which was information that might not have been very useful if it hadn't been for the fact that that brand of shoes was only available through a specific mail-order catalogue.

We knew the killer's shoe size from the bloody footwear marks that had been found in the shop. So the police were able to identify the handful of people in the area who had ordered that brand of shoes in that size. Then it was a very easy matter for them to knock on the doors of those people, until one of them was opened by a man who bore a very close resemblance to the man in the CCTV footage.

Although the police didn't find a purple fleece when they searched the property, they took away various other items of the man's clothing. And when Roy examined a leather jacket, he found some blood on the right cuff which contained DNA that matched Adam Shaw's DNA; indeed, the probability that the blood had come from someone else, unrelated to Shaw, was 1 in 12 million. Then Roy also found some purple polyester fibres, which matched those that had been discovered around the boarded-up window at the crime scene.

Faced with the evidence when the case went to court in November 1999, nineteen-year-old Terry Gibbs pleaded guilty and was sentenced to life in prison for murdering Adam Shaw.

It was the success we had with that case and others that helped to establish Forensic Alliance's reputation as an independent provider of good-quality forensic services. But what really instigated the rapid growth of the company was an idea that was inspired by a couple of requests we had to look at some complex cold cases that the relevant police forces had been unable to solve. I've had a particular interest in cold cases ever since they became a recognised type of case, and the proposal we made to the police forces would have been difficult to refuse. Basically, what we told them was that if we didn't succeed, they wouldn't lose anything, because no one would know we'd been investigating them. If, on the other hand, we managed to solve any of the cases, they could claim all the credit. What made it an even more attractive proposition for the police was that we were offering to do the work very economically, in order to make the point that we *could* do it.

One SSM who had expressed an early interest in what we were doing at Forensic Alliance was an experienced senior investigating officer from Merseyside Police called Dave Smith. When he gave us the first case, I don't think anyone, including me, had any idea how successful we were going to be. At the meeting we had with him, I think he offered us a cup of coffee before putting us to the test almost immediately by saying, 'I'm not going to tell you anything about the case. I'll just show you a video of the scene. Then you tell me how you're going to solve it.'

All murder cases are obviously very distressing. Fortunately though, as I discovered very early on, you become so completely absorbed by what you're doing, and by the need to do it as quickly and diligently as possible, there isn't much time to dwell on 'man's inhumanity to man' or on questions about existence and the point of it all. Sometimes, however, the sheer horror of what has happened to someone does bring you up a bit short, as it did in the case of the brutal murder of Alice Rye.

Alice was in her mid-seventies when she was killed. When her body was found in her home in Merseyside in December 1996, her hands had been tied behind her back, a kitchen knife had been embedded in each of her eyes, she had been gagged, and as well as having been tortured and sexually assaulted, she had been stabbed in the chest. We weren't involved in the case at that time, and an extensive police investigation didn't yield any suspects. Then, about eighteen months later, a man called Kevin Morrison who was apparently a police informer, gave detectives from Merseyside Police details of the case that hadn't been made public and claimed that Alice's killer was a friend of his.

According to Morrison, on the day Alice was murdered,

his friend had asked him to look after a bag of stuff he said he'd acquired from a robbery. When Morrison opened the bag, he found various items that clearly belonged to Alice Rye, who his friend then admitted to having killed because she wouldn't give him the PIN number for her bank card. What Morrison's friend apparently also told him was that he had stabbed his victim in the eyes so that when police did a psychological profile of her killer, 'they'd be looking for a nut'.

What Morrison didn't seem to have taken into account when he related his story to the police was that he, too, might become a 'person of interest' in the investigation. Or perhaps, if he *had* considered the possibility, he had decided that if they were going to find any evidence to link him with the crime, they would already have done so. It was an assumption that might have proved reasonable if, before talking to the police, Morrison had disposed of the collection of ladies' knickers he kept in his lock-up garage.

When the garage was searched, the police found numerous pairs of knickers, including an old-fashioned pair they thought might be the ones that had been missing from the victim's half-naked body. But although Morrison's DNA was found on them when they were examined at the FSS laboratory at Chorley, there was nothing substantial to link them to Alice Rye – just a few textile fibres that could conceivably have come from her jumper. Therefore there was nothing to disprove Morrison's claim that, having bought them for his daughter in a flea market, he had ended up wearing them himself.

Recognising that if the knickers had been worn by Alice, they would be very likely to have traces of her

DNA on them, the scientists at the FSS had cut them up into twenty-two different pieces, all of which had then been tested. One of the things we were already learning about cold cases was never to make assumptions about previous testing, even if it has been done by well-qualified and experienced forensic scientists. So our team, led by the excellent Ros Hammond (who features elsewhere in this book), carefully selected just two or three of the pieces, cut from the crotch area, and re-analysed them.

After perfecting an extraction technique that enabled us to 'squeeze' the bits of fabric for everything we could get out of them in a chemical sense, we managed to obtain two full DNA profiles. One of the profiles matched Kevin Morrison, And one of them seemed almost certainly to have come from Alice Rye, with a 1 in 69 million chance that it had come from someone else, unrelated to her.

We found other evidence too, including some fibre and paint links with Morrison. And it also proved possible to establish that he owned a knife that had been found buried near his caravan, which he claimed was in the bag of items his friend had given him. When the case went to trial in July 1999, Kevin Morrison was convicted of what the judge called 'the wicked murder' of Alice Rye and sentenced to at least eighteen years in prison, which, at the time, was the minimum term before a prisoner became eligible for parole.

With their initially tentative confidence in us confirmed, Merseyside Police then started giving us more unsolved cold cases to work on. One of which involved the murder in October 1983 of a woman called Cynthia Bolshaw, who became known in the media as 'the beauty in the bath'. Cynthia was apparently well liked in the small town in the Wirral where she lived. According to her diaries, she also had many male friends around the world, some of whom had been interviewed by police after her death.

Following the initial investigations, it was thought that Cynthia had been strangled on her bed and transferred to the bath when she was already dead. But there was little potential evidence other than a semen stain on a nightie that was found on the bed, a sample of which had been cut out and used for blood grouping by the forensic scientists working on the case at the time. Blood grouping was the only test available in the mid-1980s, before the advent of DNA profiling, and it hadn't led to the identification of Cynthia's killer. Nor did any further evidence come to light when the FSS was asked to review the case eighteen months before we became involved in 1999.

With little to go on when we were presented with the case, we decided to examine the nightie more closely. The problem was, previous testing had apparently used up all the semen that might have been relevant. So we were going to have to think of another way of approaching it.

When you test for semen, you start by pressing a large piece of damp blotting paper on to the item to absorb the water-soluble components in any seminal staining on it, which then react with the chemical reagent you spray on to the paper. What often happens when you do this is that, although you can't see anything, traces of semen diffuse outwards into the fabric, enlarging the area of the original staining. So we decided to snip around the edges of the hole that had been cut in the nightie. Then we 'squeezed' the resulting long, thin strip of fabric to get as much as we could of any semen that might still be present. It was worth a try, but I don't think we even dared to hope that we might get the full DNA profile we managed to obtain.

During the years since Cynthia Bolshaw's murder, DNA profiling had added a whole new dimension to forensic science. However, the DNA database that had been set up four years earlier contained only a limited number of profiles, none of which matched the profile we'd obtained from the nightie. So the police put out all the usual requests in the media, reminding people about the case and asking for anyone with any information or any idea about who might have been involved to come forward.

I don't know how many responses they received, but it only takes one good lead to set you off on the right path. And the one that did it on that occasion came from a woman called Barbara Taft. During the sixteen years since Cynthia Bolshaw's murder, Barbara and her husband John had got divorced. But, despite what had happened, she had continued to keep the secret he had asked her to keep when he was interviewed by police during the original investigation. What she told the police now was that John Taft wasn't, as he'd claimed, at home with her on the day Cynthia Bolshaw was murdered. He had acted strangely throughout that day, she said, and when she woke up during the night and looked out of the window, she saw him burning something in the garden.

When John Taft was interviewed by police at the time of Cynthia Bolshaw's murder, he claimed he'd never met her. But he changed his story in the light of his ex-wife's statement and when faced with the evidence that DNA in a sample of his blood matched the DNA profile we'd managed to squeeze out of the semen stain on Cynthia's nightie. Apparently, he and Cynthia had become lovers after he went to her house to give her a quote for the glazing company he worked for. And he'd asked his wife to give him an alibi because he *was* there on the day Cynthia Bolshaw died, and had had sex with her, although he insisted she was still alive when he left.

As well as the DNA profile, there was other evidence that strengthened the case against John Taft, including a much weaker DNA link with some of Cynthia's jewellery that was found in a stocking in a telephone box near where he either lived or worked. And in November 1999, having been found guilty of murdering Cynthia Bolshaw, he was sentenced to life in prison.

We were lucky, both at Forensic Alliance and at Forensic Access, to have some brilliant scientists with specific skills that made it possible for us to undertake a wide range of cases. One of them was a very interesting scientist called Bob Mayes, who had previously led an RAF toxicology team. In fact, it was Bob's knowledge of a study of helicopter pilots in South America that was to prove critical to another cold case we were asked to look at for Merseyside Police.

In October 1998, a forty-three-year-old solicitor called Cheryl Lewis died in a hotel room while on holiday with her boyfriend in Luxor, in Egypt. Although small amounts of cyanide were found in Cheryl's body, interpreting the possible significance of this was difficult, because cyanide is unstable in blood and can be lost from samples of blood that are stored inappropriately. On rare occasions, it can also be produced as an artefact in the process of putrefaction. In the event, after a post-mortem examination, the cause of death was given as haemor-rhaging in the stomach due to a severe but unidentified irritant.

Cheryl had apparently made a will in which she had named her boyfriend – a forty-eight-year-old industrial chemist called John Allan – as her sole beneficiary. According to her family, it was an uncharacteristic thing for her to have done. So I think they already had their suspicions about Allan before his new girlfriend, Jennifer Hughes, was rushed to hospital with stomach pains a few months after Cheryl's death. Fortunately, Jennifer survived. And although tests proved inconclusive, Allan was immediately arrested.

One of the detectives who'd been involved in the case from the start remained deeply suspicious about John Allan, and it was apparently his dogged determination that eventually persuaded Dave Smith to ask us to take a look at it.

Our investigation was led by another brilliant toxicologist called Alex Allan, who has an absolutely encyclopaedic knowledge of anything and everything that can poison you. When we examined Cheryl's blood and a wider range of other body samples from her than had been looked at hitherto, we found levels of thiocyanate that simply couldn't be ignored. Thiocyanate is a breakdown product of cyanide, which can be attributed to smoking. Indeed, we also found nicotine and its metabolite conicotine in the samples. And as Cheryl was apparently a heavy smoker, the findings were dismissed by the defence, who suggested that what was more important was the presence in her body of quite a substantial amount of chloroquine.

It was the defence's claim that the true cause of Cheryl's

death had been an overdose of chloroquine, which is an active ingredient of the malaria pills she had been taking. And it was in relation to that claim that Bob Mayes' knowledge of the study of helicopter pilots in South America proved decisive. The focus of the study had been on pilots who were taking malaria tablets prior to being killed in helicopter crashes. What it showed was that all of them had high levels of chloroquine in their blood, which had been released from their livers and was actually a fact of death rather than a cause.

In media reports at the time of John Allan's trial, it was often stated that 'the death on the Nile' was the result of him having slipped cyanide into a gin and tonic Cheryl drank on the night she died. But we thought the more likely scenario might be rather different.

When John Allan was arrested, the police found four sodium cyanide brickettes in Cheryl's company car, which he had been driving since her death. What we discovered when we examined the cyanide brickettes was that a bit appeared to have been carved off one of them. If the missing piece had then been carved up further, it would have been sufficient to make several 'tablets' the size and shape of anti-malarial tablets, which Allan could have given to Cheryl in place of the anti-malarial tablets she was taking. That would certainly explain the small areas of marked thinning of her stomach lining that had been noted during the original post-mortem examination. It might also have been the reason why, as she lay dying on the bed in their hotel room, Allan had apparently refused to give her mouth-to-mouth resuscitation. If he knew it was cyanide that was killing her, he wouldn't have wanted to risk being poisoned himself by having direct contact with her.

Dr Eddie Tapp, the pathologist, said that the thinning of the stomach lining had been caused by contact with something corrosive. In the presence of moisture, sodium cyanide produces sodium hydroxide – drain cleaner! Alex had also found cyanide in the deep spleen tissues, from which he concluded that there were strong indications of cyanide having been the cause of Cheryl's death. And he had ruled out the alternative possibility that it could have come from the embalming fluids that had been used in Egypt and cyanogenic plants.

In March 2000, John Allan was found guilty of poisoning Cheryl Lewis and sentenced to life in prison. His arrest had probably come just in time for Jennifer Hughes, who was due to go on holiday to Egypt with him just a couple of weeks after she was admitted to hospital with stomach pains.

By 2000, we were doing so much work for Merseyside Police we decided to set up a second laboratory closer at hand, in Risley, near Warrington in Cheshire. Among the people who helped us set it up were two talented forensic biologists called Gerry and Andy Davidson. I'd actually head-hunted Gerry from the Strathclyde police lab in Glasgow after being very impressed by her work in a case I'd reviewed. And when she came to work for us, her husband Andy came too.

It was also Gerry who led the investigation into another cold case we were asked to look at by Dave Smith, which involved the murder of a pub landlord and was Dave's last outstanding case before he retired from the police force.

A year after Philip Lee's body was found in 1998 in what newspapers referred to as 'a notorious gay haunt' in south Liverpool, a man called Roy Jorgensen Kristensen was arrested for robbery in a completely unrelated case. While being questioned by police, Kristensen confessed, 'off the record', to having killed Philip Lee. It was a confession he refused to repeat on tape, however, and there was insufficient evidence to charge him. But the fact that he seemed to have detailed knowledge of the contents of the boot of Lee's Austin Maestro car, which was found abandoned some distance away from the crime scene, resulted in the police taking it seriously.

Two years after Lee's death, the police managed to track down Kristensen's Renault Megane at a car auction. And one of the focuses of Gerry's investigation was some potential evidence related to the secondary transfer of fibres between the two cars. During the original investigation, the police had collected tapings from Lee's Maestro, and when we looked at them, we found a small number of distinctive orange-red polyester fibres that looked very similar to some fibres on the tapings from Kristensen's Megane. Microspectrophotometry analysis provided detailed characteristics of the colour of the fibres, which, when we looked at the dye industry's database, we were able to identify as being similar to a dye supplied by a large pharmaceutical company for use in the automobile industry.

More detailed testing eventually confirmed that the fibres found in the two cars were from the same batch. And when we accessed Renault's quality-assurance archives, we were able to demonstrate through dye-batch variation that there was a very strong possibility they had originated from the seats in Kristensen's car. Which meant there was also a very strong possibility that the same person had been in both vehicles.

Although we appeared to be on the verge of producing

evidence that would implicate Kristensen in the murder of Philip Lee, we didn't manage to solve Dave Smith's final outstanding case before he retired after thirty-four years of service with Merseyside Police. Fortunately, however, he had taken on a new role as Business Development Manager at Forensic Alliance by the time the case *was* concluded. And in January 2004, after the evidence had been accepted by the court, Kristensen pleaded guilty to killing Philip Lee and was sentenced to twenty-two years in prison, to run concurrently with a life sentence he was already serving.

Forensic science had moved on since some of the cold-case crimes had been committed – particularly in terms of DNA-profiling techniques. But it was also looking at these cases from a different angle – using accumulating knowledge borne of our increasing experience – and dogged determination that helped solve them. Having proved what we were capable of doing, it wasn't long before my optimistic prophecy was fulfilled and we were taking on new staff, opening new laboratories and expanding Forensic Alliance as we tried to keep pace with the work that was coming in.

22
The next phase

Science is all about answering questions related to ourselves and the physical world around us in a thoroughly systematic way. Only by doing that will we be able to solve problems, expand our horizons, and better understand what makes us tick, where we came from, and what might be going to happen next. One of the ways in which forensic science differs from other types of applied science, however, is that it provides an almost constant reminder of the less admirable, sometimes downright evil, things human beings are capable of doing. Fortunately, although it can be a bit depressing to see the immediate results of someone's criminal activities, the feeling never stays with me for long. What helps to make it transient is the fact that there's usually something urgent, sometimes particularly interesting, and often very rewarding, that I should be doing.

As well as working on cases involving forensic biology, chemistry, toxicology and drug substances, we set up a small firearms unit at the Forensic Alliance facility in Risley. Purpose built and well equipped, the unit had a firearms inspection workshop, an examination room for clothing etc., a clean DNA laboratory, and a secure armoury with a high-tech acoustics room where firearms could be safely discharged. Headed by a firearms expert and chemist called Philip Boyce from Northern Ireland – whose wife Maggie, a very experienced forensic biologist, also joined us – the unit could take up to eight hundred cases a year. And when it was officially opened in September 2003, it added a whole new dimension to our services.

We were always doing something to try to improve both the quality and delivery of the services we were offering, and to find ways of controlling the environment in our labs. Transporting exhibits to and from forensic labs was something the police had previously been responsible for themselves, and it hadn't always been done under ideal conditions. So one of the ideas we had that proved very popular was to provide a free collection and delivery service for exhibits.

I also continued to give talks and write articles and letters to newspapers, as I've done for much of my career. Most of them were about the use and abuse of forensic science and about how careful we all have to be to ensure that it's properly understood and used appropriately. While it can be tremendously powerful for resolving things when there's disagreement, it can also potentially mislead and confuse, and thereby contribute to miscarriages of justice. So the purpose of all this extracurricular activity wasn't usually anything to do with advertising. It was mostly to air things I felt strongly about and thought people needed to be aware of – and when I was invited to, obviously!

One particular and persistent concern I shared with my colleagues was the fact that anyone with any sort of scientific background could stand up in court and claim to be a forensic scientist. The problem tended to be with scientists working for the defence who might have impressive scientific qualifications, but who often didn't even know how to operate the microscope they were supposed to be using to check the evidence. Or didn't appreciate what the likely significance might be in the specific circumstances of a case of, for example, finding six red nylon fibres on the inside front of someone's jumper. That lack of knowledge was inevitably reflected in their conclusions about the strengths and weaknesses of the evidence. And although, in other circumstances, that might just have raised a wry smile, the consequences in the arena of criminal justice were potentially extremely serious.

In an attempt to combat the problem, I'd been working throughout the 1990s with a number of *bona fide* organisations – latterly including the FSS – to try to introduce some system of practitioner accreditation for forensic scientists. (Here was something on which the FSS Director General Janet Thompson and I were in total agreement!) In 2000, I was one of the founders and then the first elected council member of the Council for the Registration of Forensic Practitioners (CRFP). For the first time, we had a certification system based on independent peer review of a selection of a scientist's work instead of, for example, simply what their clients said about them. Unfortunately, the CRFP was abandoned after just a few years, having proved too cumbersome and expensive ever to be able to support itself in what was a relatively small profession. But some things had changed by then. For instance, we had a Forensic Science Regulator – albeit one who still doesn't have the statutory power to enforce her own recommendations – and external suppliers of most forensic services for the police have to have achieved the International Organization for Standardization's ISO 17025 Standard.

ISO 17025 sets out requirements for competence, testing and calibration, and, it was argued, would adequately cover the main aspects of the CRFP system. But because its focus is on systems and processes in laboratories and not on individuals, it didn't quite fill the gap. And, of course, it didn't tackle the serious issue – that still exists today – of there being no requirement for defence experts' work to be accredited. So self-styled 'experts' continue to exaggerate their credentials, muddy the waters of forensic science, and have the potential to pose real risks to criminal justice. Because they are usually ineffective in spotting the real weaknesses in scientific evidence, they also fail to provide the critical safety net that forensic science and forensic scientists need, and that courts might assume exists because of their involvement.

In 2001, I was elected President of the Forensic Science Society. It was a result that was made doubly satisfying by the fact that the other candidate, who was a senior member of the FSS, had apparently run a campaign which included a tour of all the FSS laboratories to spread the word that, 'A vote for Gallop is a vote against the FSS.' I couldn't help smiling when I heard about it, and especially when the results were declared and it was clear that a lot of FSS scientists must have voted for me!

My time as president of the society was split between three main objectives. The first was to modernise and strengthen its administration. The second was to begin to lay some of the foundations that would turn it into a professional body for forensic scientists. And the third was to develop the then new university accreditation scheme that sought to improve the quality of what was being taught about forensic science in universities.

I had a particular bee in my bonnet about the third objective. What had been happening on some courses – especially at undergraduate level – was that a poor version of operational forensic science was being taught at the expense of the fundamentals of science. In fact, we'd been seeing the disappointing results in interviews for new staff at Forensic Alliance. The scheme had been set up by my presidential predecessor, Professor Brian Caddy from Strathclyde University's Centre for Forensic Science – of which I became Director of Strategy in 2016, and which is the oldest, and still one of the two best academic centres for forensic science in the country. I knew Brian felt as strongly about accreditation as I did. But I knew, too, that I wasn't going to be able to do all the things I'd have liked to have done. Maybe one never does.

Forensic science covers a very broad spectrum of sciences, and rather than employing specialists in all areas on the staff, we had a range of experts we could call on when the need arose. For example, anything to do with insects that was relevant to our cases was dealt with by wonderful people at the Natural History Museum in London – first Ken Smith, then Martin Hall – and occasionally by Zakaria Erzinçlioglu (known as Dr Zak) at Cambridge University. Eventually though, we decided it was time we had our own entomologist on the staff. And when we employed John Manlove, it was the first time an entomologist had worked in a mainstream forensic laboratory in the UK.

We soon realised that entomology was so closely connected with other areas of expertise that we ended up developing an entirely new area of forensic science, which we called forensic ecology, but which other people tended to refer to as 'the 'ologies'. Including anthropologists and archaeologists, soil experts (who could also analyse precious gems) and palynologists (experts in the study of pollen grains), as well as our entomologists, we could now provide comprehensive support for cases involving buried bodies and evidential traces from outdoors. Although forensic ecology isn't a large field, there are a surprising number of cases in which it's relevant. And it gave us another means of increasing the breadth of our investigations.

One example of the use of forensic entomology was in a case we did for Thames Valley Police involving a body that had been found face down in a ditch full of water. When John Manlove examined the body, he discovered some fly eggs and pupae on the front fastening of the dead man's shirt. Flies don't lay their eggs under water, so John was able to say that the man had been lying on his back for a specific length of time before being turned over and placed in the ditch. In other words, it looked as though his murderer(s) had returned to the scene and re-positioned the body. John's report was incredibly helpful to the police investigation, and when the killers were apprehended and admitted what they'd done, it turned out to be exactly what he said must have happened.

As technology continued to evolve, and lifestyles changed to reflect it, investigators began to recognise the value of all the information that was being stored on mobile phones and personal computers. So, in 2001, Forensic Alliance formed a partnership with a local computer analysis firm called Vogon. It was a collaboration that proved to be very valuable, as it enabled us to uncover all sorts of new kinds of information from digital devices, which we could combine with traditional forms of evidence such as fingerprints and DNA profiling. We could even interrogate digital devices built into things like washing machines to find out when they were last used and what programme had been selected.

Then, in 2002, AEAT suddenly announced their intention to acquire Forensic Alliance outright. It was a bit of a bombshell. But I think they could see us beginning to turn the corner financially and wanted more control over the company. Russell had retired a couple of years earlier. So it was Tom Palmer and I who made the very reasonable point that if AEAT could buy the company, we should also have the opportunity at least to make our own offer for it. We had borrowed in excess of £3 million to set up the business. So I suspect the reason they agreed was that they were confident we would never raise the necessary money in the very short, two-month timescale they stipulated. Suddenly, the race was on to find a financial backer.

The first thought Tom and I had was of Close Brothers Growth Capital (CBGC), the company that had given us such a warm reception when we were setting up Forensic Alliance. They weren't able to support us at that time, because we wanted funding for a start-up and, as their name implies, they only backed growth. But things were different now. And thanks to Bill Crossan and Garrett Curran, who were both absolutely brilliant, we had our money more or less within the agreed timescale. In fact, CBGC turned out to be excellent business partners, and over the next three years we were able to take the business in new and exciting directions.

In 2004, we were approached by a number of scientists from the FSS Birmingham laboratory who had heard what had been going on in Forensic Alliance on the professional front and wanted to join us. As a result, and optimistic that we could attract sufficient work to justify the decision, we set up a laboratory for them in Tamworth, Staffordshire. So then, among other benefits, we had an on-the-spot presence for West Midlands Police, which was the second largest police force in the country. It sounds so easy when I talk about it now. But Tom and I did a lot of nail biting at the time, because it didn't require much imagination to work out what would happen if we couldn't attract enough new work to balance all the extra costs.

One of the excellent things we were able to do after we teamed up with CBGC was establish a dedicated fire-arms laboratory within the Royal Armouries at Leeds. The new unit was opened in 2005 and included a full-length firing range, a firearms workshop, a ballistics comparison laboratory and other laboratories for recovering DNA and fingerprints from firearms and ballistics materials. As well as enabling us to do everything firearms related under one roof, it also meant that our customers had immediate access to the Armouries' experts and their collections of 25,000 firearms and ammunition, and an equal number of sharp-bladed weapons.

When the new laboratory opened, we closed down our firearms unit at Risley and turned it into a drugs laboratory, which went down well with our customers in the north of England. The unit at Leeds is still running today and is a huge asset for investigating really complicated cases for police forces all round the country. If the scientists there are trying to work out what sort of firearm or ammunition was used, for example, or want to do test fires with some rare ammunition, all they have to do is cross the corridor from the laboratory to work with the absolutely brilliant people at the Royal Armouries.

At around the same time as we were opening the laboratory in Leeds, we also got together with the largest group of forensic pathologists in the country – Forensic Pathology Services (FPS) – and started providing all their administrative services for them. One of the things we did at that time was help to trial a new Home Office IT system designed to professionalise delivery of their services. Another was to build them an in-house histopathology lab – which was the first one in a mainstream forensics laboratory – and a new, temperature-controlled archive for their samples. An archive like that is important because it ensures that samples are stored in the best possible conditions. So if, as sometimes happens, new questions arise, maybe years later, about the circumstances in which someone died, the samples can still be tested for drugs or DNA, for example.

23
Fact or cover-up?

Our success with cold cases, and our smooth delivery of 'routine' work, meant that we were being trusted with increasingly sensitive investigations. In some of the many high-profile cases we've worked on over the years, we've been responsible for the entire scientific investigation. In others, we've just been asked to look at specific aspects. And that was the basis on which we became involved in an investigation some time after the death of Princess Diana.

Princess Diana, her companion Dodi Al Fayed and their driver Henri Paul died in a car crash in Paris on 31 August 1997. The princess's bodyguard, Trevor Rees-Jones, was also seriously injured. Seven years later, in 2004, the Commissioner of the Metropolitan Police, Sir John Stevens, was asked by the Coroner of the Queen's Household and the County of Surrey to investigate a number of aspects surrounding the car crash. What the Coroner wanted to know specifically was whether there was any evidence to support an allegation made by Dodi's father, Mohamed Al-Fayed, and his legal team of a conspiracy to murder by the British Establishment.

The huge investigation that followed was known as Operation Paget. As well as interviewing more than three hundred witnesses and carrying out five hundred actions, the operation involved the collection of more than six hundred physical exhibits for potential examination and analysis. It also created one of the most thorough reconstructions of an accident scene there has ever been.

What we were asked to do was help clarify three different aspects. (1) Was Princess Diana pregnant at the time of her death? (2) Did the blood sample attributed to Henri Paul – which contained alcohol that was twice the UK's legal limit for driving – actually come from him? (3) Was there any justification for the elimination of a light-coloured Fiat Uno car belonging to the press photographer James Andanson from involvement in the collision with the Mercedes in which Princess Diana and her companions were travelling? James Andanson's wife claimed that her husband was with her some 170 miles (274 kilometres) away on the night in question. Three years later, he had committed suicide. And although there was a 'suspicious' break-in at his offices a month after his death, the only things that were taken were items of equipment.

The forensic investigation related to a possible pregnancy was led by Professor David Cowan, who was Head of the Department of Forensic Science and Drug Monitoring at King's College, London. There were two main strands to the work. The first was to see if the blood samples taken from Princess Diana contained any of the pregnancy hormone, human chorionic gonadotropin (hCG). The second was to look for any evidence that she might have been taking a contraceptive pill.

The blood transfusions Princess Diana had received after the accident might have complicated the pregnancy test. So the best sample for testing was some blood that had been recovered from the carpet in the footwell of her seat in the

Mercedes. And while David Cowan's team did some very impressive work developing a pregnancy test that would work on dried blood, we obtained a series of samples that had been taken from pregnant women in an earlier, unrelated study to act as controls for such a relatively old sample. We also extracted a sample of Princess Diana's stomach contents for testing for contraceptive residues.

In the end, the results of all the tests were negative. Which meant it was extremely likely that Princess Diana was not pregnant at the time of her death, and that she had not been taking contraceptive pills. According to Sir John Stevens, the results aligned with evidence from her family and friends that there had been nothing to suggest she was pregnant.

With regard to the blood sample attributed to Henri Paul, we confirmed through DNA testing that it was indeed his blood. So it had not been swapped with a sample from someone else, as had been alleged. And therefore he must have had the blood alcohol levels that had been reported.

Finally, we conducted tests on smears of light-coloured paint and bumper material transferred to the Mercedes from the vehicle with which it had evidently been in collision. What they showed was that this vehicle could have been a Fiat Uno, but there was nothing to suggest that it was the Fiat Uno that had belonged to Andanson. One of the problems was that the scene was not well preserved in respect of retaining evidence relating to collisions – both with another car and the walls of the tunnel.

The investigation also addressed a number of other claims, including the assertion that Dodi and Princess Diana were engaged to be married. Having looked into all of them, Lord John Stevens – as he was by that time

– and his team published a report in December 2006. The conclusion they came to was that there was no evidence to support any of the various allegations of wrong-doing or of a cover-up at the highest level.

Another sensitive case we worked on involved the death of a former weapons inspector with a UN Special Commission in Iraq.

Dr David Kelly was working for the British Ministry of Defence when he was thrust into the limelight in 2003 after having been named as the source for a controversial BBC report on Iraq. At the heart of the report was a challenge to the UK government's claim that Iraq had weapons of mass destruction that could be deployed at forty-five minutes' notice. After Dr Kelly's alleged comments made headline news in the wake of the joint UK–USA invasion of Iraq in March 2003, he was questioned by a Foreign Affairs Select Committee. Two days later, his body was discovered in woodland near his Oxfordshire home. Perhaps inevitably, in view of the sensitivity of the surrounding circumstances, his death gave rise to suspicions of unlawful activity and conspiracy at a high level, much like Princess Diana's had done.

The information we were given when we were asked to look at the case was that Dr Kelly had left his home on the afternoon of 17 July 2003 to go for a walk. He had apparently been suffering from depression. So his wife had good reason to be concerned when she reported him missing later that night.

When Dr Kelly's body was discovered the following morning in undergrowth of nettles and brambles, scenes-of-crime officers erected a tent over the body itself and the area around it to protect them from the elements. A knife was found next to the body, together with a bottle of water and a packet of powerful painkillers containing an old-fashioned formulation of dextropropoxyphene and paracetamol.

We became involved in the investigation at the request of Thames Valley Police. Roy Green inspected the crime scene, then examined blood patterns and damage etc. on clothing and various other items collected from it. And Alex Allan provided the toxicological analysis of samples that had been taken from the body by the Home Office pathologist Dr Nick Hunt.

When Nick examined the body at the scene, he noticed that the left hand and wrist were heavily stained with blood. At subsequent post mortem, he found no positive evidence to indicate that Dr Kelly had been subjected to a sustained, violent assault prior to death and/or that he had been dragged or transported by other means to the place where his body was discovered. What he did find was a number of deep cuts across the underside of the left wrist that had severed several blood vessels, including the ulnar artery. It was a pattern, Nick explained, that was typical of self-inflicted injury.

The conclusion from the pathology report was that the wrist wounds were the main cause of Dr Kelly's death, with the large quantity of painkillers he'd consumed and some undiagnosed underlying heart disease also playing a part.

Roy Green's findings supported the pathology report's conclusion in relation to the nature and distribution of blood staining on some of the key items. It was a pattern that was typical of arterial blood staining, and indicated that Dr Kelly's injuries had been sustained where his body was found.

Among the items received from the police for examination at our laboratory were some swabs from Dr Kelly's body and from his mobile phone, some nail clippings and hairs, and the watch, water bottle and knife that had been found at the scene. There was also, from his study, a camera and some shredded papers that were reconstructed by a company called Document Evidence Ltd.

Essentially, what Alex Allan found were relatively high levels of dextropropoxyphene in the samples that had been taken from the body, some undissolved pills in the stomach contents, and traces of paracetamol around the neck of the bottle. All of which one would expect to find if Dr Kelly had swallowed a number of the pills, washed down with water from the bottle.

Other things could also be deduced from the nature and distribution of the blood staining on the clothing and other items retrieved from the scene. For example, the blood-stained knife was probably the implement that had caused the eleven or so cuts on Dr Kelly's wrists. He had removed his wristwatch part of the way through the process. The blood had sprayed from his injured wrist on to surrounding surfaces and clothing. And, at some stage after he was injured, he had knelt in a pool of his own blood and had drunk from the water bottle.

There was no blood staining on the blister packs of the powerful painkiller, Co-proxamol, that had been found at the scene. But the presence on one of them of DNA that could have come from Dr Kelly indicated that he had handled the packs before he was injured.

After a series of exhaustive tests and investigations, it was concluded that there was extremely strong evidence to indicate that all the blood at the scene had originated from Dr Kelly and that only he had drunk from the water bottle. Also, although it couldn't categorically be refuted, the evidential findings provided no support for the suggestion that he had died at the hands of another person.

In view of the sensitivity of the case, the Prime Minister, Tony Blair, commissioned an inquiry into the death immediately after the body was found. In the report that was published in January 2004, Lord Hutton found that Dr Kelly had taken his own life by slashing his wrists. To protect the family from further distress, he requested that the pathology and toxicology reports should remain classified for seventy years. But because of the suspicion that continued to surround the death, those reports were eventually released in 2010. And when even that did little to allay people's suspicions, the Attorney General, Dominic Grieve, was petitioned to reopen inquiries.

After examining all the evidence, including checking our toxicological analyses and conclusions, Grieve concluded that there was overwhelmingly strong evidence that Dr Kelly took his own life. What his report also said was that Lord Hutton's inquiry had effectively acted as an inquest, and there was nothing to suggest Dr Kelly had been murdered or that there was any kind of conspiracy or cover-up.

As forensic scientists, we recognise the importance of being able to challenge the authorities and the experts they rely on when things don't appear to stack up. But we also appreciate how important it is to consider the whole picture rather than just looking at isolated aspects of it, which can end up being very misleading and creating unnecessary uncertainty. To a scientist, both of the cases described above seem pretty sound. I realise, however, that the scientific evidence may not allay the suspicions of conspiracy theorists, which are notoriously difficult to put to rest.

24

Rachel Nickell

Sometimes, an absence of evidence can be a clue in itself. In most cases, forensic scientists rely, in effect, on dogs barking and then have to work out why. Occasionally, however, what's important is why the dogs apparently didn't bark when you'd have expected them to. And that seemed to be the situation in the investigation into the death of Rachel Nickell.

While walking with her young son and their dog on Wimbledon Common in London on 15 July 1992, twenty-three-year-old Rachel Nickell died after suffering no fewer than forty-nine separate stab wounds in what appeared to be a sexually motivated attack.

Adhesive-tape samples were taken from parts of her body that had been exposed when her lower clothing was pulled down. When these were examined for DNA profiling by scientists at the MPFSL, the hope was that they would find some male DNA that didn't match either Rachel's husband or their two-year-old son. The scientists were undoubtedly competent, with all the right qualifications and experience. But sometimes people simply miss things; it's a fact of life. The problem in this case, however, was that not only did they fail to find any of the male DNA they were looking for; they didn't find any

DNA at all. And, apparently, they didn't stop to wonder why. If they had, they'd have realised something was wrong, because the tape should have been plastered with Rachel's own skin cells and DNA.

After interviewing several men as possible suspects, the attention of the Metropolitan Police focused on a local man called Colin Stagg. Convinced that Stagg was guilty, but with no evidence to implicate him, they organised a so-called 'honey-trap' operation. For several months, an undercover policewoman feigned a romantic interest in Stagg with the aim of trying to get him to confess to Rachel's murder. And although Colin Stagg didn't ever 'confess' to the murder, he was arrested in August 1993. A year later, at his trial at the Old Bailey, the judge excluded the entrapment evidence, the prosecution withdrew its case, and Stagg was acquitted.

In 2002, when Forensic Alliance became involved in the cold-case investigation into Rachel Nickell's murder – which was given the code name Operation Edzell – I put Roy Green on the job, assisted by several colleagues. Mike Gorn did the chemistry aspects of the case. Clare Lowrie was responsible for hairs and textile fibres. Andy McDonald took care of DNA analysis. And April Robson was appointed lead forensic examiner.

We prioritised our examinations based on what we thought was most likely to help identify the killer. As Rachel's clothing had been disturbed during the attack, there was a reasonable possibility that we might pick up some of her attacker's DNA on it. So the first thing we did was look at the items of clothing that had been retrieved from her and from her two-year-old son, Alex. Next, we examined the body samples – fingernail cuttings and scrapings – and the tapings taken from intimate parts of her body. Semen is a traditionally good source of DNA. But as the FSS scientists hadn't found any semen on Rachel's body, we anticipated that we'd be looking for smaller traces. Then, in phase three, we looked at various items that had been collected from the crime scene on Wimbledon Common and from some potential suspects. Later on, we added a fourth phase, which involved looking more closely at the debris the FSS had gathered from key items.

One of the things we were looking for was anything that might link the case with previous similar ones. But our investigation didn't focus on any one person. The law related to double jeopardy hadn't yet been changed in the UK, so having already been acquitted, Colin Stagg couldn't be tried again for Rachel's murder. However, the police still suspected him, and although we didn't focus on him, we didn't automatically eliminate him either.

To assist with the first phase of our investigation – our search for 'foreign DNA' that could have come from Rachel's attacker – Roy set up a reconstruction experiment in the laboratory. The aim was to try to identify the specific areas of Rachel's clothes that were most likely to have been handled by her attacker as he pushed her upper clothing up and pulled her lower clothing down. Another scientist put on clothes (over a scene suit) that were similar to the clothing Rachel had been wearing. Then Roy – acting as the attacker and with black powder applied to his hands – pulled and pushed them until they resembled the distribution of Rachel's clothing when her body was found. Residues of black powder indicated where contact had been greatest, and therefore where we should focus our attention and testing on her clothes.

We discovered some interesting things during the process, some of which we thought might be worth returning to if we found nothing else as a result of our initial strategy. Then we started work on phase two – which was when we found 'a way in' to the case.

When the FSS scientists had tested the tapings from Rachel's body, they'd used a DNA-profiling test called Low Copy Number (LCN). LCN is a variation on the standard DNA (STR) profiling that works by multiplying up (or amplifying) relevant bits in small amounts of DNA until there is enough there to analyse. With LCN, thirty-four cycles of amplification are used, as opposed to twenty-eight with the standard test.

You have to be really careful with DNA to get just the right amount for testing: too little and you get no result at all; too much and you'll swamp (or inhibit) the reaction. I think what happened in the original investigation was that because the scientists were expecting there to be only very small amounts of *male* DNA, if any, on Rachel's body, they used their most sensitive technique. It would have been a reasonable expectation in view of the fact that no DNA-containing body fluids had been detected that could have come from her attacker. The problem was, they didn't stop to think why they'd not only found no male DNA – which wasn't particularly surprising – but hadn't found any of Rachel's either.

We took a different approach. We always started with the standard (twenty-eight-cycle) test, so that we had a baseline of what our extracts contained in the way of DNA. Then we only moved on to LCN if we felt it was appropriate. We also always prepared dilutions of our DNA extracts, as these would warn us if our reactions were being inhibited by anything, including too high a concentration of DNA or some background chemical contaminant, for example.

When we looked at the tapings extract from the FSS, what we found using the standard method of twenty-eight cycles was a mixed profile. The major component looked as though it was from Rachel herself, while some minor components were from a male. When we then tested the same extract using a thirty-four-cycle LCN technique – the equivalent of the FSS test – it was clear that our reaction was over-amplified, leading to an excess of DNA and no result.

Intrigued by the tiny amount of male DNA, we went back to the original intimate tapings (vaginal and anal), and re-sampled them, creating our own extracts. Then we tested these as before. We always test samples in duplicate for DNA profiling, and only call a result confirmed if we obtain the same result from both of them. It's just another of the checks and balances that are needed in DNA profiling, which, in this instance, enables you to distinguish between a real result and an artefact introduced during the process and/or because of the particular nature of your samples. With the anal tapings, we got a full profile for Rachel, and although there *was* something else there, it wasn't confirmed by the duplicate test. With the vaginal tapings, however, even at twenty-eight cycles we were getting a major result from Rachel and a minor result from male DNA, but not enough to identify who it might have come from.

We'd never much liked the LCN technique. It was expensive and had been the subject of some really bad press. In the Omagh bombing case, for example, Mr Justice Weir concluded that it was 'unreliable' and that the test results were open to interpretation. And in the investigation into the disappearance of Madeleine McCann from a hotel in Portugal, it was used to suggest – unreliably – that there had been some of Madeleine's DNA in the boot of the car her parents had hired weeks after her disappearance. So we decided this was the ideal opportunity to take a different approach. Essentially, what that involved was cleaning up and concentrating our extracts: trying to get rid of as much extraneous material such as salts and impurities as possible, because they can inhibit DNA reactions; and tweaking the running conditions on our machines to optimise the process. It meant that we didn't have to resort to the extra amplification cycles needed for LCN, and suffer the associated complications. But it gave us just as good, if not better, results.

Our colleagues at Cellmark did the bulk of the work, with Roy making sure it was done as quickly as possible, because we needed to continue to make progress with this case in particular. In the end, it took the better part of two years. But it was worth it in view of the results, and the technique – known as 3100 Enhancement – quickly became a standard part of our DNA offering.

Andy McDonald then carried out some other DNA tests on our extracts from the intimate tapings in an effort to get as much information out of them as possible. Two of those tests (known as Powerplex Y and Y-Filer) were very handy for male/female mixtures of DNA, because they targeted just the male component (markers on the Y chromosome), in this case ignoring any contribution from Rachel herself. A third test (called Identifiler) looked at more areas of DNA than our STR tests, and was therefore more discriminating. By the end of it all, we had plenty of information with which to mount a search of the National DNA Database.

Roy had noticed at quite an early stage in the investig-ation that there were similarities between the MO of

Rachel's killer and that of a man called Robert Napper. Napper had been incarcerated in Broadmoor Hospital since 1995 for the murder of another young woman and her four-year-old daughter. And when the DNA extracted from the samples in our investigation into Rachel's murder was put on the National DNA Database, he came up as a match.

It's really important that DNA results are expressed in precisely the right way, as the statistics can easily be switched round and become misleading. The way they were described (by Andy) in this case was as follows: 'The probability of obtaining the confirmed STR components if the DNA came from someone unrelated to Robert Napper is approximately one in 1.4 million . . . In my opinion, these STR profiling test results provide *extremely strong scientific support* for the assertion that the minor components among the DNA recovered from the vaginal tapings (WL/4B) originated from Robert Napper rather than from another male who is unrelated to him.'

It was a good result. But for the purpose of corroboration – and on the basis that once you find one thing, you very often start finding others – we began to search for more links. One of the places we looked for them was on some of Napper's possessions that had remained untouched at Broadmoor since they'd been returned to him by the police a few years earlier. Police investigators had been particularly interested in a red-painted toolbox, which Napper would apparently get very twitchy about. It was of interest to us, too, after we found a tiny flake of red paint in some hair combings from Rachel's son. And when Mike Gorn compared the paint flake with the paint on the toolbox, he got a match. Also, a layer of metal on one side of the flake was shown to be steel – which was what the toolbox was made of.

As usual, we were still thinking about the crime scene and whether there was anything there that might conceivably provide a link with Napper. One of the things we considered was a couple of footwear marks that had been found in mud on a bridle path close to where Rachel had been attacked. Casts had been made of the marks at the time, one of which was of the heel of a shoe that was similar in style to the heels of a pair of Napper's shoes, but slightly smaller in size.

Normally in forensic science, if a mark – or, in fact, anything – is different from a suspected source, even in only one respect, it can't be associated with it unless there's a very good reason. In this case, the only way to find out if there *was* 'a very good reason' was to go back to the scene and, as my brother Jeremy might have said, 'do the experiment'. So, shortly afterwards, Mike and Roy found themselves on Wimbledon Common looking at what happened when a similar pair of shoes was worn in the same area of muddy ground. What they found was that as the wearer of the shoes lifted his foot to take another step, a partial vacuum was created that sucked the muddy soil in around the edges of the shoe. And when they then took plaster-type casts of the marks and compared them with the shoes themselves, they showed that what was left in the mud was a slightly smaller footprint than would normally have been made by a shoe of that size.

It was another example of how important experimentation is. Because what that particular experiment proved was that it was perfectly possible for Napper's shoes to have made the slightly smaller footwear mark that had been preserved in the casts made at the original crime scene.

In the face of what had turned out to be overwhelming evidence – including the DNA, the paint and the foot-wear mark – Robert Napper pleaded guilty when the case went to trial. In December 2008, he was convicted of the manslaughter of Rachel Nickell on the grounds of diminished responsibility and sentenced to indefinite incarceration in Broadmoor Hospital.

The ramifications of the case didn't end there though. The fact that evidence had been missed during the original forensic investigation, and that this had been due to a flaw in the DNA test used by the FSS, meant that they could have missed results in other cases too. So the police launched a huge operation, which they called Operation Cube, to identify the many other cases in which LCN had been used and no results had been obtained. The FSS then re-analysed samples in each of those cases, with the technical flaw corrected. As a result, several people who had originally dodged criminal charges for serious crimes suddenly found themselves facing prosecution, and maybe others were exonerated.

When questions were asked after the case concluded, the FSS claimed that the reasons the errors had been made were related to time and technology. In other words, if we'd done our investigation when they did theirs, we would have got the same results as they did; and if they'd done their investigation in 2004, as we did, their results would have been the same as ours. But that wasn't true, certainly in 2004. As I explained in the report I wrote about it all for the Metropolitan Police – and with which they agreed – there were actually three causes of the problem. The first was the FSS scientists' rush to use their most sensitive technique. They'd used that particular technique because they knew that when looking at tapings like those taken from Rachel's body, there might just be a tiny amount of male DNA. What they hadn't taken into account, however, was that they'd be amplifying *her* DNA too, which could swamp any other results. The second cause of the problem was the fact that they used the technique without some basic precautions. The third was their failure to stop and wonder why the dogs hadn't barked. In other words, why they hadn't even found any of Rachel's DNA in the samples.

Perhaps the advantage we had was that we were working on a lot of cold cases at the time. So we were creating and developing our own way of doing them. Maybe we thought about cases more holistically than the FSS scientists were able to do, particularly with all the increased pressures on them once the FSS no longer had a monopoly on forensic services and had to compete with companies like ours. They did get good results in a lot of cases. But you couldn't be sure that they would necessarily see the small things. And that's important, because it's often something small that leads to the break you need to be able to help solve a case. Sometimes, you get just a hint of something – like seeing an almost imperceptible flash of movement out of the corner of your eye. What had happened during the original FSS investigation into the murder of Rachel Nickell was that the flash was there, but their testing regime didn't pick it up. But you have to pursue these things, even if that involves developing new techniques, which was something we and our partners at Cellmark were good at, and part of what made us so successful.

In fact, the DNA Enhancement technique we developed for the investigation into the murder of Rachel Nickell was subsequently used to help solve several other cases. So it was a good outcome. Not only because it led to the conviction of Rachel's killer, but also because of all the other cases that were solved on the back of it. It was a sharp reminder, too, that you can't simply do tests and move on. You really have to think about what the results of each test are likely to mean in the particular context. Because as well as being absolutely critical to each investigation, the precise context is slightly different in every case.

25

The heart of the matter

One of the things that has helped me to keep a sense of perspective during the last forty-five years is the fact that I like people. It's a disposition that almost precluded me from having any kind of professional career at all when I was at school and paying more attention to my friends than to my studies. But there have been innumerable occasions since then when it has stood me in good stead.

Something that's probably true in any line of work is that it's absolutely critical to choose the right people for every job. I think I've made that into something of an art form over the years by moving some people around a series of jobs until finding the one they're just the right shape for. And I've been very fortunate, in all the companies I've set up and been involved with, to have employed some fantastic scientists and administrative staff, the vast majority of whom have been, and continue to be, brilliant.

Of course, not everyone is going to turn out to be a perfect fit. For example, there was one very nice woman who worked in an administrative post and used to talk all the time about her rather grand family and interesting boyfriend. She had already invited several colleagues to her wedding when she announced one day that it had been cancelled because her boyfriend had been tragically murdered. Fortunately – in terms of the heart-breaking aspects of it all – the boyfriend, wedding and murder all turned out to be figments of an overactive imagination. As did almost everything else she'd told her colleagues about herself. The poor woman obviously had a problem. But she was having an unsettling effect on the staff, some of whom had become very worried about her because of the terrible things that seemed to be happening in her life. So, in the end, we had to let her go. Perhaps if she learned anything from the experience, it was that it's a big mistake not to be straight with forensic scientists – who spend their entire working lives uncovering the truth!

For a good scientist to become a good forensic scientist requires very specific training. But even excellent forensic work can be rendered virtually useless if the person who reports it in court isn't able to express it in sufficiently lay terms, or buckles under aggressive cross-examination. So understanding what barristers really mean when they pose a question was one of the issues we addressed in the 'expert witness training course' we provided at Forensic Alliance. Among the training materials was a document entitled 'Courts and how to appear in them', which included the following list of 'Some coded messages from counsel'.

- *Thank you*, delivered in a clipped manner = 'I've scored a point.'
- *Grateful for that* = You haven't necessarily said what he wanted, and the score is 'fifteen all'.
- *I'll come back to that in a moment* = 'I've lost my train of thought, but I am sure I was on to something.'

- *I wonder if you can help me with this* = A fresh attack on a new front. Beware! He could go anywhere.
- *Yes,* with a long 'e' and often delivered while turning to the jury = He's got you on the run and you're heading in the direction he wants.
- *I understand your position, but I'd like to focus on just this one aspect of your evidence* = 'This is the only glimmer of light for me in the whole of your evidence and woe betide you if you stray from it.'
- *I'm just a simple barrister,* possibly as a prelude to *Perhaps you could explain in simple language* = 'I have a double first in analytical chemistry in addition to my legal qualifications, and I've just spotted a fundamental flaw in your technical argument which I am about to expose.'
- *This might not be a question for you, but would you just comment on this* = 'I know this is well outside your area of expertise, but a word from you would make my life a whole lot easier.'
- *Perhaps you are aware of [name], who is sitting behind me today* = 'I have the world expert advising me on your evidence, so it would be best for you if you simply agree with everything I put to you.'

After we'd trained them, we used to put potential reporters through their paces, to see if they were ready to start going to court. First, we'd give them a case to look at and write a report on. Then we'd get them to present their evidence and answer questions exactly as they would do in a courtroom. We wanted to make it as realistic as possible, to ensure that the interviewee was robust enough, emotionally as well as intellectually, to handle the pressures involved. So we would draft in colleagues, sometimes including lawyers, to act as the judge and barristers and to ask the sort of questions a reporter would be likely to be asked when giving evidence in court. Most people passed the test with flying colours. Some needed a bit more training. And, very occasionally, it would become apparent that someone wasn't cut out for that aspect of the job.

One of the interviews I remember particularly well involved a slightly self-effacing young woman called Clare Jarman, who just seemed to know instinctively which points were important and how to express them clearly and succinctly. In fact, she answered every question she was asked in exactly the same way I'd have answered them myself, with all the years of experience I'd had by that time. Both Clare and her husband Ed were in our first intake of trainees at Forensic Alliance in 2000, and both became exceptionally good forensic scientists. Clare now works in Forensic Access, as does another very gifted biologist, Caroline Crawford, who was from our second intake of trainees at Forensic Alliance. We were definitely doing something right! It was probably owing to the quality of our senior biologists, including Roy and Ros – who I've mentioned in connection with some of the specific cases they worked on – and Janet Manners, whose amazing blood-grouping expertise we'd all relied on in Aldermaston.

Of course, forensic science is a team enterprise, and we had many other wonderful scientists – too many to mention here. And when I think of all the scientists who have made a great impact on me and what I've been trying to achieve, my mind inevitably turns to those who helped us to start Forensic Alliance. Many of them left secure jobs in the hope that we would actually be able to achieve our ambitious aims. They must have been very nervous during those first few months of planning and set-up, before the commercial wheels began to turn, and I'll always be grateful to them for their courage, faith and sheer hard work.

It was a relief for many reasons when it became apparent that the company was going to be successful. I'd have hated to think I'd wasted a year of the lives of people like Heidi Halstead, for example, who'd been doing a research project in Forensic Access before I persuaded her to stay on while the idea of Forensic Alliance became a reality, and who turned out to be a really good forensic toxicologist.

I've mentioned some people in relation to various cases I've talked about in the book. Others include Roger Robson, for example, who was originally my assistant at the FSS lab in Wetherby and had developed into such a good textile-fibre expert that we offered him a job at Forensic Alliance. If he hadn't said that his wife, April, was a forensic examiner who was able to do chemistry *and* biology, and asked if we might have a job for her too, we might have missed out on employing someone else who turned out to be an utterly brilliant forensic examiner and trainer.

Ann Franc was another stand-out scientist I'd worked with at the FSS. As a drugs scientist at Aldermaston, Ann's vast knowledge of cannabis earned her the title 'the Cannabis Queen'. Knowing the yield of a cannabis plant is very important for distinguishing between personal use and intention to supply. And Ann seemed to be able to tell you what it was just by looking at the plant and sniffing – although her estimate was obviously always backed up by proper analysis! It was because of her skills and a certain indomitability that she was the obvious choice to put in charge of drugs at Forensic Alliance. She was supported by Cathy Frew, who was excellent at complex cases, and Kathy Clarke, who had an enormous knowledge of drugs intelligence. In fact, Kathy Clarke eventually took over our quality department, and played a vital role in ensuring we achieved and maintained those all-important ISO Standards.

Other stalwarts of the toxicology department working with Alex Allan – whose incredible knowledge of drugs and poisons I've mentioned earlier – included Allan Hiscutt, who I'd also known at the FSS. Then there was Denise Stanworth, who managed to identify the plant Indian aconite in a curry that was used to poison a woman's ex-lover and his new fiancée – he died, she didn't. And Pauline Lax, who identified heroin as the cause of death of victims of a serial killer in the Ipswich area, a task made technically difficult by the fact that some of the bodies had been lying in water.

We had brilliant chemists too. If we couldn't afford quantity, we were going to make sure we had quality. Pam Hamer, who is one of the UK's most distinguished forensic chemists, is probably the best forensic microscopist around and she was an inspiration to many of our young scientists. In one case she worked on, there was no evidence on the outside of a man's trousers to suggest that he had been stamped on, as suspected. But on the inside of the trousers Pam found footwear marks that were comprised of skin flakes from the surface of his legs, which had been driven into the fabric by the sheer force of the contact. Who else would have thought of looking for that? We used the same approach in another case to identify a footwear mark in skin on the inside of a white shirt, which we visualised using the fingerprint-enhancement chemical ninhydrin, since the detail on the outside had been obscured by blood.

Both Pam and Ray Jenkins – who I've mentioned earlier – were from my own era. So both of them could turn their hands to almost anything in their own line, including marks – from shoes, tools, tyres etc. – and chemical traces such as glass fragments and paint from break-ins. Ray was also very good at investigating arsons, in which he was supported by another chemist called Roger Berrett. Huge in stature and with a personality to match, Roger had been Head of Toxicology at the MPFSL before he transferred to the fire unit there, and then came to work with us. He was keen on reconstruction and was always setting fire to things in his back garden; and he had a particular interest in the concept of spontaneous human combustion, which was a subject that came up every now and then – and that he didn't believe in!

Of course, it wasn't only the scientists that we relied on. We had some excellent administrative staff too. People like Lorraine Williams, who has provided unstinting administrative support to me for many years now, and in no fewer than four companies. It was Lorraine who made my presentations look professional and ensured that I turned up at the right place and the right time for all my appointments. John Barrand, who was in charge of our facilities, could set up a new laboratory almost overnight. And our Head of Human Resources, John Cameron, helped to make sure we had the right people in the right places at the right time.

As anyone who has ever set up a company and employed other people will know, it requires a lot of work and energy. Quite apart from all the business and administrative aspects, you have to make sure that everyone is doing their own job to the best of their ability and has a sense of being an integral part of the corporate journey. Obviously, you have to have a leader to set the tone and keep everything on track, but it's really all about teams. With that in mind, starting in around 1999, Tom and I organised annual dinners at a big country hotel near the laboratory.

The idea behind the dinners was for everyone at Forensic Alliance to be able to get together with their colleagues to share a collective sense of achievement and pride in what they were doing, and to be generally entertained. Tom and I used to give a talk beforehand about what all the different sections were doing, picking out some high points and some of the interesting or bizarre cases we'd dealt with during the year. Then we'd summarise our financial performance and other achievements in terms of expanding our facilities and equipment, or our fleet of collection and delivery vehicles. Eventually though, as Forensic Alliance continued to grow and expand, I decided everyone had probably had enough of listening mainly to us and that it was time to get them involved in doing something themselves. So we started holding what turned out to be wonderful annual revues.

The company was big enough by that time for each department to put on its own brief show. It could be about anything they wanted, as long as it was both informative and entertaining. And they did the most brilliant things. To begin with though, realising that they'd be nervous about making fools of themselves, I decided it was only fair that the seven-strong executive team set an example by making idiots of ourselves first.

The first year we put the idea into action came at the

end of a difficult period when a new procurement system was being developed by the police and Home Office. One of the things they'd done was put a stop to the transfer of all work between suppliers. The idea behind it was to protect the FSS, which had been losing work – not least to us. And while one can understand the desire for stability, the interference with the market simply stored up problems for the future. What it also meant, in the short term, was that our smooth growth trajectory was abruptly cut short. So I wrote a sketch for the show in which a patient was being operated on in an operating theatre.

The patient – who was our company – was in a bad way and undergoing potentially life-saving surgery, which was being energetically administered by everyone on the executive team except me. Some rather odd activity took place during the operation, which included a lot of shrieking and people disappearing at intervals into cupboards. But it all worked out well in the end, and the patient made a full recovery. Meanwhile, I stood on the sidelines as narrator – because it certainly needed explanation – dressed as the Queen and clutching two inflatable corgis, to represent the *annus horribilis* we had suffered.

The following year, I re-wrote *Cinderella*, again with our company taking the starring role, while our main competitors – with some artistic licence – were the three ugly sisters. I'm sure you know the story, but I was able to 'forensicate' it with endless references to our work, such as Cinderella's dress being 'piped with mini-swabs and studded with a thousand glittering eppendorfs' [a type of laboratory tube].

Everyone entered whole-heartedly into the spirit of it all. And as well as it being great fun, I was incredibly impressed by how inventive they were, and by the amount of hidden talent we discovered, both as actors and script writers. One of the sketches that immediately comes to mind involved the drugs department singing a brilliant song about MDMA (Ecstasy) to the tune of the 1970s hit song 'YMCA'. The chemists did a wonderful radio show. The questions document department did a brilliant skit based on a real case about someone trying to pass off what he claimed was a million-dollar note. There was some live digital hacking into an audience member's phone (with their permission, of course). One of our toxicologists wore a bright-red wig, which he later presented to the ops director, whose hair was a rather less vibrant red colour, and who was very gracious and good-humoured about the whole thing. And some departments made videos instead of acting out their skits on the evening of the dinner. For example, a team from the laboratory at Tamworth showed a very funny film they'd made about how they solved the (fictitious!) murder of their head of biology after his body was found in a corridor at the lab.

Because everyone was doing such excellent work, which I felt should be recognised and rewarded, I decided we should also hand out awards for achievements such as the most innovative use of forensic science or the most interesting test result. The problem was that because almost everyone was so good, it was difficult to pick out just a few individuals to be recognised. So we selected people who had gone above and beyond in some way.

Everyone from all the different laboratories loved getting together for a good meal and a chat, and the dinners really were enjoyable events. But, as things turned out, the year the awards were instigated was the last year the dinner was held – in that format, at least – as I started to hand over control of forensics before leaving the company a year or so later, in 2010.

Of course, we organised professional events too. A lot of crimes take place outdoors, where circumstances can be challenging for numerous reasons. Exposure to weather and its unpredictability are just a couple of examples. Or you might not have easy access to light and power. Or the evidence might include vegetation, soil and other outdoor traces. So, in 2002, after we started getting involved with forensic entomology and palynology, we held the first of what turned out to be a very popular series of two-day outdoor-crime-scene workshops for police, senior crime-scene investigators and forensic scientists.

The workshops were organised by Pam Hamer, and their aim was to promote evidence awareness and collection techniques. So as well as including theory sessions on one-to-one taping – where each tape reflects a different part of the surface of an item – and the value of archaeology and anthropology, vegetation and soils, entomology and pathology on the first day, there were also some outdoor exercises on day two. Searching with specially trained dogs, for example; excavating buried bodies (of pigs); textile-fibre mapping on partially buried bodies (mannequins this time, which were lent to us by the police, who used them in training sessions); collecting insects from and around bodies (of pigs again); and the examination of surface bones. And to round off the whole event, there were unlimited servings of ice cream – an inspired ploy devised by Pam to ensure that absolutely everybody stayed to the end.

In 2003, we hosted the annual Coroners' Officers

Association conference at our lab at Culham Science Centre, which was based on the theme 'But is it evidence?' Attended by a hundred delegates from all over the UK, the conference involved a series of presentations from senior police officers, a forensic pathologist, and toxicology, entomology and DNA-profiling experts from Forensic Alliance.

That same year, we hosted a weekend traffic workshop in conjunction with the Forensic Science Society. The event was organised by Bill Westenbrink, who was a superb toxicologist we'd recruited from Canada together with his splendid forensic biologist wife Gail, in the 'two for one' arrangement we seemed to specialise in. In sessions delivered by Bill and other forensic experts from the UK, the USA and Germany, the focus was on drink and drugs driving, traffic collision reconstruction, and the various ways of detecting and quantifying impairment. One of the aspects demonstrated by the different groups was what happens with increasing alcohol intake when you try to walk along a straight white line. Another was related to whether or not eating a large meal affects the rate of alcohol absorption. And another was on whether using a mouthwash affects breathalyser results. In fact, they covered all the explanations and excuses people give, and all the questions the police officers had ever had about alcohol.

In 2004, we organised a one-day seminar on blood-pattern analysis, which was one of several similar seminars on different topics that formed part of an accredited course for the Royal College of Pathologists. The trainers we invited were world-class experts, including Bart Epstein, Terry Labor and the indomitable, profoundly deaf and profoundly talented Anita Wonder from the US.

The aim was to provide an opportunity for the eighty-nine crime-scene investigators and members of the legal profession who attended to get a better understanding of the evidential power of blood-stain analysis and its interpretation. Bart, Terry and Anita also assisted with the training of our own staff, which took place in a warehouse unit close to our labs on the Culham site, where we set up various crime-scene scenarios.

Fairly early on, we also started producing bulletins on the trends we were spotting in the drugs cases submitted by each of the police forces we were working with, and on DNA samples. The focus of the bulletins was on the numbers and types of samples submitted and the analytical success rates we were achieving. By analysing the data, it was possible to compare all those factors, then identify and adopt best practice in terms of, for example, the way to take samples at crime scenes and how to store them before submitting them to the lab.

Every year, the Association of Chief Police Officers (ACPO) – now the National Police Chiefs' Council – also held a conference. And in 2004, we took some space at their associated exhibition and set up an outdoor crime scene featuring a very lifelike 'dead body' lying on the ground beside a park bench. A gun and various other items were strewn around the scene, some of which were relevant to the case, while others were merely red herrings. We ran it as a competition for scenes-of-crime officers, and anyone else who wanted to take part, with questionnaires and a prize for the best answer. The idea was to get them to identify the items that should be collected for forensic examination, giving reasons for their choices and suggesting ways of establishing who had committed the crime. It elicited a lot of interest. In fact, one man, who was a model on another stand, was so fascinated by it that he came over during his lunch break, picked up the gun and sat on the park bench. He must have sat there, completely still, for at least half an hour, just holding the gun and staring at the body. It was very funny, and added a whole new dimension to our crime scene.

When that event turned out to be a success, we started doing it regularly, with a different crime scene each time. It was part of a house the following year, with an open window through which you could see some drug para-phernalia laid out on a table and one leg of a body that was lying on the floor round a corner. The year after that, it bore a striking resemblance to Tracey Emin's *My Bed*, except that there was a dead woman sitting up in the bed, wearing a nightie and surrounded by a half-eaten meal, a glass of wine and various other items, including some apparently used condoms.

The idea was to engage people's attention with the very serious purpose of making police officers think about what items might be relevant to the forensic inves-tigation in the context of the sorts of crime scenes they might attend. So I was taken aback to receive an angry letter about the body in the bed from a chief constable. The crux of the letter was how dreadful it was and how demeaning to women to encourage people to gawp at a scantily clad female mannequin. In answer, I explained that it had not in any way been a gratuitous exercise. In fact, I said, it was a very earnest competition to find out if police officers really understood how to get the most out of their crime scenes. In the very nice reply I received from the chief constable, she said she hadn't actually seen the exhibit herself and apologised for having misunder-stood. Perhaps it helped that I was a woman. Fortunately, everyone else seemed to realise what we were doing and to find the exercise useful.

I'd had some sleepless nights when we were setting up Forensic Alliance, wondering if we were going to be able to pay the salaries of the handful of scientists we'd initially employed. But, even then, I'd believed that the vision we had for the company would become a reality. Some brilliant people helped to make that reality possible, not only at Forensic Alliance, but at all the other companies I've worked with. I've mentioned some of them in this chapter and elsewhere in the book. I just wish I could mention them all. Because they really were the heart of the matter.

26

A force to be reckoned with

I think we started breaking even at Forensic Alliance in about 2001. It was a bit later than we'd originally thought it would happen, but at least at that point I was pretty sure we were going to make it.

By 2005, I had already dragged my inestimable business partner, Tom Palmer, back into work after he'd said he was going to retire. And that was *after* Russell and I had persuaded him to join us in setting up the company when he had just retired from his job at AEAT. So when he said it for the third time, I knew he meant it, and that maybe the moment had come for me to think about doing something different too. Forensic Alliance was employing about two hundred and thirty people at four laboratory sites around the country by that time. And although I was always thinking about doing bigger and better things, I was beginning to realise that I couldn't keep doing it indefinitely, and certainly not on my own.

We had been very imaginative about incorporating other people's technology into forensic science and doing as much research and development as we could possibly afford. But I knew that the best and most cost-effective way to expand and enrich Forensic Alliance further would be to join forces with a big science firm that was doing lots of other work and would have a much wider range of equipment we could use.

Although I hadn't actively been looking for a company to acquire us, I started thinking about it at around the time when LGC was trying to get into forensic science in a big way. The people at LGC were very good at the analytical side of things, and they were able to run a lot of tests simultaneously – and very cost effectively – to a high standard of quality. What they didn't have, however, was any track record of doing investigative forensic science, and certainly not the way we did it at Forensic Alliance. So when LGC approached us, both Tom and I thought it was definitely worth considering. I think their interest was at least partly prompted by the fact that they'd recently taken Lord John Stevens on to their board as a non-executive director. John had just retired as Commissioner of the Metropolitan Police, and because we'd been helping to solve some of the Met's cold cases, he knew the sorts of waves we were making in the forensic market.

LGC had been part of what used to be called the Department of Trade and Industry at the time when a 'market' was created in forensic services in 1991. Five years later, it became privately owned, and when it acquired Forensic Alliance in 2005, LGC Forensics was a real force to be reckoned with.

We were the most expensive acquisition LGC had made at that time, and as the head of their largest department, I was on their board. It was a position that was partly due to the prominence of forensics and partly, I suspect, so that they could keep an eye on me! I was sorry we had to lose the name Forensic Alliance. But it was a small price to pay for having access to such enormous analytical power and expertise, and to a laboratory site in London at their headquarters in Teddington.

I knew from experience with AEAT that you can make massive changes to your capability just by choosing slightly different instruments or tweaking attachments to those you already have. For example, by changing the type of electron microscope we were using at Forensic Alliance, we had been able to improve by about tenfold the discrimination of things like paint and glass samples. They did a range of forensic testing at LGC's Teddington laboratory, including toxicology, drugs, DNA and digital crime, and walking around the lab felt like being in the scientific equivalent of a sweet shop. I can remember thinking how brilliant it was going to be to be able to marry the skills and experience of the staff we had at Forensic Alliance with LGC's instrumentation and scientific expertise.

One thing I *had* been nervous about was not being my own boss any more. But LGC turned out to be an extremely nice company to work for. And as well as being always and unfailingly supportive, they were indulgent of some of my more idiosyncratic ways. For example, on one occasion, not very long after we'd joined the company, I was rather blunt in a news article about what I thought of the new forensics procurement system the police had devised. The aspect of the new system I was concerned about – and had criticised robustly in the article – was the way it had broken down forensic science into just a series of simple tests. For cost purposes, this made it easier for forces to commission work and use different suppliers for different aspects of it – 'I'll have six of those, and two of the other from your standard menu.' Which meant that no one would have an overall view of all the forensic evidence and could understand what it meant and present it properly. Also, there would be less opportunity to devise the sort of elegant and cost-effective strategies we'd been developing, or for evidential links to be made between one item or one case and another.

Perhaps inevitably, one of the people responsible for the new system, who also happened to be an important forensic cog in one of the largest forces we worked for, rang up to complain about what I'd said in the article, and was clearly very upset. Fearing there could be commercial repercussions after I'd spoken to them on the phone, I immediately suggested to LGC's CEO that perhaps I should resign. But he just laughed it off.

I know things weren't particularly easy for my colleagues to begin with though, both in the old Forensic Alliance and in LGC, not least because they came from different cultures. In Alliance, we had forged a new way of doing things that was very different from the way they were done in the FSS; while in LGC at that time, there were still strong echoes of the Civil Service to which the company had once belonged. So both sides of the business just wanted to be left alone to do things the way they'd always done them. But, of course, you can only have one culture and one way of doing things in an organisation, and it was clear to everyone that compromises would have to be made.

There were basically two ways of achieving the necessary merging of cultures: short, sharp shocks all round, or letting people find their own level, but with a fairly firm guiding hand. In the end, I chose the latter. It took a long time though. And I'm still not sure it was the best way, even though we did manage to avoid the thing I feared most, which was key staff leaving because they were unhappy. It was clear that the path was never going to be entirely smooth. But it all proved very worthwhile when we ended up being able to benefit from massive economies of scale, a wider range of services – with additional specialisms we could draw on when necessary – and the ability to do more research on a larger scale than we could ever have dreamed of as a small company hitherto.

After having had four laboratories in Forensic Alliance – at Culham (Oxford), Tamworth, Leeds and Risley (Warrington) – we moved to having six with LGC, including part of the company headquarters building at Teddington and another lab on the old ICI site at Runcorn. Staff numbers also rose, from about two hundred and thirty to what I think was around four hundred and fifty. And between them, they were able to do all aspects of mainstream forensics.

It had been extremely difficult to say goodbye to our old friends and staunch supporters, Cellmark. I think at Alliance we had all secretly hoped we would join Cellmark, which at the time belonged to an American company called Orchid Biosciences. But the offer the American company had made for Alliance was completely impossible to accept, and, more importantly, they had been aggressive and unpleasant while making it.

What really put an end to any discussions was what happened when Tom and I were invited to join them for dinner. It promised to be a great night. A car was sent to pick us up and deliver us to Raymond Blanc's restaurant Les Quatre Saisons at Great Milton, where they'd hired a private room. But it pretty soon became clear that they intended to bully us into submission. So the evening ended early, with Tom and me determined, regretfully, that we would never be part of Orchid Cellmark. Things have a funny way of working out for the best though, and LGC ultimately gave us much more than I expect Cellmark (or Orchid) ever could have done.

Once inside LGC, one of the first things we had to do was ensure that we had the necessary range of DNA tests to cope with some of the more difficult samples in our complex cases. Until then, the LGC DNA teams had been focused on the more routine side of the work, such as profiling reference samples (usually mouth swabs) and the simpler crime-scene stains. Their skill was doing it at speed and in quantity. Now, though, we needed tests that could handle very small amounts of DNA, degraded DNA, and mixtures of DNA, for example.

It obviously all took a bit of time. But before too long the LGC DNA team had created DNA SenCE (Sensitive Capillary Electrophoresis). Like Cellmark's enhancement technique, SenCE enabled us to obtain results from tiny amounts of material while avoiding some of the pitfalls of the FSS's LCN process that led, through the way it was used, to evidence being missed in the Rachel Nickell case. They also created a tool for searching the National DNA Database for family members of people who weren't on the database themselves and through whom they might be identified. One reason that it was an improvement on the familial search tool developed by the FSS was that it could rank people of potential interest in a hierarchy reflecting the closeness of their DNA to the DNA profile for which we were searching for a source. Having something like that a few years earlier would have made things a lot easier when we were trying to find the killer of Lynette White, for example.

Shortly after we'd joined LGC, I happened to mention that what we could really do with was a rapid DNA screening technique that could be deployed quickly and easily at crime scenes to give an initial result. Such was the breadth and depth of LGC's science that they thought it might be possible. One of their scientists was a marvellous man called Paul Debenham, whom I'd met some years earlier when he worked for Cellmark. Paul had developed what was known as HyBeacon technology for use in the medical diagnostics industry, which, with some minor adjustments, he thought might serve the purpose. On the back of confirmed interest from the police, LGC invested a lot of time and effort in the project over the next few years, and eventually produced a great piece of kit. Although less discriminating than normal profiling, it could produce results in a fraction of the time, could be taken out to scenes of crime, and was incredibly simple to operate. It was apparently a success in some other parts of the world – notably the US – and has potentially great application in some of the developing countries I now work in. But, like other rapid DNA techniques, it has failed to gain traction in the UK, which is a great shame and a missed opportunity.

Other techniques we looked at in LGC included forensic applications of radioactive isotopes in determining where in the world products and people might have originated and a new instrument for DNA analysis on hair. We also looked at how best to tackle the analytical side of drugs on money, the presence and amount of which on bank notes rises dramatically when they're involved in drug use or dealing.

It wasn't all smooth sailing though, and there were things happening elsewhere that had a knock-on effect on the growth of the new company.

Since it was first introduced into forensic science in

the latter half of the 1980s, DNA profiling has completely revolutionised forensic biology. Before everything changed during the 1990s, most of the money for tests and sophisticated instrumentation went into forensic chemistry. So biology was like the Cinderella of forensic science. The most significant factor influencing that change was the National DNA Database, which was set up by the government in 1995.

Established and run by the FSS, who at that time input all data into it, the database changed the face of forensic science and of criminal investigation generally. Later, after other companies started doing profiling, they were allowed to input their data too, provided they passed some specific proficiency tests. By the early 2000s, when it was realised just how powerful the database could be, the government began to inject serious money into it, under what was known as the DNA Expansion Plan. Then the police started taking DNA samples from anyone they arrested for an indictable (imprisonable) offence. And with the government providing matched funding to every police force, the database was able to grow very rapidly. A snapshot for one week in October 2005 showed that there were at that time 3.1 million people profiles on the database and 246,000 profiles from crime scenes. In that week, these had generated 6 'hits' (i.e. matches) in murders, 19 'hits' in sexual offences, and 1,080 'hits' in so-called volume crimes involving property and drugs offences. In the previous six-month period, the database had identified no fewer than 23,684 links between crime scenes and people.

Unfortunately, the database wasn't set up in such a way as to enable samples to be taken off it. So it later became a complete logistical and financial nightmare when the law eventually caught up with the technology and it was decided that the profile of anyone who ended up not being convicted of a crime must be removed. Meanwhile, by 2005, the government decided it had spent enough on expanding the database and withdrew the extra funding. So the DNA Expansion Plan was halted, which was always going to happen, because there's a finite criminal population and therefore a limit to the size the database needs to be.

As that coincided with the development of the new 'menu-style' forensic procurement systems, we effectively suffered a double whammy. The first effect was that we were no longer able to continue on our natural growth trajectory because police were stopped from being allowed to switch their work to us. The second was that, like other suppliers of forensic services, we had obviously built capacity and come to rely on the DNA expansion funding that the government had now withdrawn.

So there were uncertainties in the market that caused some anxiety for us in the early days of LGC Forensics. I suppose it's the same in any area of business: there are forces striking you all the time that can be good or bad and that you simply have to deal with. Looking back on it now, our journey seems remarkably smooth, although it certainly didn't feel like it at the time – as evidenced by some photographs I have of myself at the time in which I look pretty stressed. Eventually though, and despite all the teething problems with the new procurement system, things settled down a bit and we started growing again. Then it wasn't long before we were giving the FSS a real run for its money.

Inevitably, I suppose, I seemed to be spending a lot of time on the managerial side of the business. But we were working on many fascinating cases too, some of which were started in Forensic Alliance and continued to completion in LGC Forensics – a few of them are mentioned elsewhere in this book. Among them were several of the most high-profile and complex cases in recent criminal history, and the lessons we learned from them have been absolutely invaluable.

One very interesting case we were involved with during that period was a programme instigated by the Commonwealth War Graves Commission. During the Battle of Fromelles, which took place during the First World War, on 19 July 1916, soldiers of the British 61st Infantry Division and 5th Australian Division launched what turned out to be a disastrous attack. Intended to draw German troops away from the Somme offensive, it ended with hundreds of the allied soldiers being buried behind German lines. The aim of the programme was to identify and recover the remains of the British and Australian soldiers who fell during the battle.

After several years of painstaking research and investigation, a number of burial pits were identified in 2006 in Pheasant Wood near Fromelles. Three years later, in May 2009, our specialist DNA team found themselves working with archaeologists from Oxford Archaeology to excavate the pits and take DNA samples from the remains of the soldiers. By early September, they had removed 250 soldiers. Our specialist team of DNA scientists then attempted to extract some viable DNA samples, while we collated the details of potential relatives in the hope of gaining some positive identifications. In January and February 2010, many of the soldiers were re-interred at a new military cemetery at Fromelles.

I prefer to work in smaller companies where I can have a bigger, more immediate impact, and get things done more quickly than is possible in the large company we'd created. So I had only intended to stay with LGC Forensics for a couple of years after they'd acquired us. By which time, in my naivety, I thought everything would be nicely stitched together and working like a single – if not entirely well-oiled – machine. But because it proved to be hard work trying to integrate the different cultures and approaches that were inherent in the two companies, and as the result of a bit of understandable carrot-and-stick encouragement from LGC, I ended up staying for five years.

I did enjoy working with LGC though, not least because of the things it enabled us to do. One of those things was being able to make more acquisitions to build the strength and diversity of our forensic offering. As well as acquiring two German DNA firms, we also made small acquisitions in the UK in the form of two digital forensic companies, which would extend our capability in that area too. A new robotic system we installed at Runcorn improved our capacity to process DNA in reference samples and enabled us to analyse up to two hundred thousand samples per year. And we took on two animal DNA experts, Rob Ogden and Ross Ewing. Just as it was with humans, DNA was fast becoming the main way of identifying and comparing animal traces, in cases of poaching and animal cruelty for example, and as another kind of evidential link between people and places.

One of my personal interests had always been the investigation of the most complex cases – which were often cold cases – and we had been making very good headway with a number of them. For example, by 2008, we had presented critical evidence in the Lynette White case, leading to the conviction of Jeffrey Gafoor and the exoneration of the Cardiff Three. The Preddie brothers were in jail for the manslaughter of Damilola Taylor, with the four youngsters originally charged with the crime definitively in the clear. And Robert Napper had been convicted of Rachel Nickell's murder, for which Colin Stagg had been exonerated. But we were always looking for ways to improve our understanding of things from the point of view of the police, so that we could be more imaginative in the use of our services to support them. To that end, I had taken on a few former officers over the years as police advisors, each of whom had brought something really useful to the role. And when the former Head of CID for West Yorkshire, Chris Gregg, got in touch to say that he was leaving the force and would welcome a chat, I was interested to hear what he would say.

Chris had started work as a constable for West Yorkshire Police in 1974 – the same year I began my career as a forensic scientist with the FSS. Indeed, unbeknown to both of us, we had attended two of the same Yorkshire Ripper scenes. By the time Chris retired as a Detective Chief Superintendent in 2008, he had established the ground-breaking West Yorkshire Police Homicide and Major Enquiry Team, and had been awarded the Queen's Police Medal (QPM) in recognition of his outstanding services to policing. After retiring from the police, he joined us at LGC. And what quickly became apparent when I started working with him was that he thought about investigations in precisely the same way forensic scientists do, and had been using forensic science precisely as it should be used. He also had an unerring ability to 'read' people, which comes in handy in business as well as in the job of policing itself. And he found the same things funny that I did. So he was extremely helpful and very popular with everyone at LGC, and the obvious choice to go into business with when I finally left the company in 2010.

27

Damilola Taylor

In November 2000, just three months after his family had come to England from Nigeria, ten-year-old Damilola Taylor was found bleeding to death in the stairwell of a block of flats in south-east London. The artery in Damilola's left thigh had been severed by a shard of glass.

After various experts had given their opinions about what might have happened, the Metropolitan Police concluded that the little boy had fallen on a broken bottle after being attacked. The investigation that followed, which was known as Operation Seale, involved more than a hundred and twenty police officers and resulted in four suspects being arrested and charged with murder.

The position of the defence was that Damilola hadn't been attacked at all, but had simply fallen on a broken bottle. And there was certainly no forensic evidence to incriminate the suspects. So when the four youths went on trial at the Old Bailey in January 2002, the prosecution relied heavily on the evidence of a girl – known as Witness Bromley – who claimed to have witnessed an attack. But when the girl was exposed as lying, the case collapsed and two of the accused were acquitted on the direction of the judge, while the other two were found 'not guilty' by the jury.

A year later, the police announced a review of all the evidence using new forensic techniques. In fact, although the techniques are constantly evolving and improving, it was the approach rather than the techniques themselves that was new and different.

There had been other suspects apart from the four who had gone on trial. So one of the first things we decided to do when we were asked to look at the case was examine all the suspects' clothing, just in case something had been missed. After all, no one's infallible, and even well-trained scientists sometimes miss things.

I had chosen Ros Hammond to lead the re-investigation, as she was really starting to distinguish herself in the more complex sorts of cases. Ros was supported by April Robson and other examiners, and by Tiernan Coyle, who was one of our textile-fibre experts at the time. What we found almost immediately was a nine-millimetre blood stain on a trainer belonging to Danny Preddie, who, with his brother Ricky, was quite near the top of the police's list of potential suspects. Nine millimetres is quite a large stain in forensic terms. What made it even more interesting was the discovery of a textile fibre embedded in it. Testing proved that the fibre matched the fibres from the jumper Damilola had been wearing at the time of his death. And the fact that it was embedded in the blood on the trainer meant that it must have been transferred when the blood was wet.

There were also traces of blood in the ribbing on the cuff of Ricky Preddie's sweatshirt that were so small they weren't visible to the naked eye against the dark background of the sweatshirt fabric, but were discovered using the Kastle-Meyer (KM) test. We found other textile-fibre links too, although we couldn't use them in the end, because, when we looked into it, we discovered there was at least the theoretical potential for fibres to have been transferred between the Preddie brothers' and Damilola's clothing, as they had been transported in the same police car. So even though the risk of contamination would have been minimal, it was still a possibility, and therefore that evidence would have been unreliable.

The textile fibre in the blood stain on the trainer and the blood on the cuff of the sweatshirt *were* evidence that could be used, however. And when we did DNA profiling on both blood samples, we found they matched Damilola's DNA.

In 2005, nineteen-year-old Hassan Jihad and the two Preddie brothers – who couldn't be named at the time because they were minors when the incident occurred – were charged with manslaughter and assault.

The position of the defence was the same as it had been during the first trial, and a trauma expert gave evidence to the effect that he thought Damilola hadn't been attacked but had fallen on the shard of glass that had severed the artery in his leg. In the end, the jury found Jihad not guilty of the charges, but was unable to reach a verdict in relation to the two brothers. A few days later, the CPS announced their intention to retry Danny and Ricky Preddie, who were apparently already well known to the police for their involvement in numerous robberies. In August 2006, both brothers were found guilty of manslaughter and were subsequently sentenced to eight years in youth custody. It was a strange trial, with the FSS scientists ultimately advising both prosecution and defence, which was unusual, to say the least.

The judge explained at the time that the boys hadn't had any plan to kill Damilola and hadn't taken a weapon with them to the scene – the broken bottle was already there. One of the unfortunate things about the case was that even though the police had had their suspicions in relation to the Preddie brothers and had seized their clothing only five days after the attack, the critical evidence had been missed. As a result, four other people were put on trial and Damilola's family had to endure a lot of additional heartache.

Once again, the Metropolitan Police were criticised for being institutionally racist and for not having learned the lessons from the Stephen Lawrence case. But the criticism was undeserved, as they had actually done a very good job following the death of Damilola Taylor. This time, the delay in finding those responsible wasn't due to any lack of interest or effort because the victim was black, which is what they were accused of. It was actually forensic science that had let everyone down.

The Home Office was clearly very concerned that the evidence could have been missed, and was so worried about the work the FSS was doing, they commissioned an independent inquiry. The inquiry was led by Alan Rawley QC, assisted by Professor Brian Caddy, who, as mentioned earlier, was the former Head of the Centre for Forensic Sciences at Strathclyde University. Brian had been involved in other government inquiries, including into the explosives evidence that led to the conviction of the Birmingham Six, contamination of the Forensic Explosives Laboratory in relation to the Maguire Seven, and the DNA LCN technique following criticism of it during the trial of Sean Hoey for the Omagh bombing. So he was a good choice to help Alan Rawley.

I met with Rawley prior to the hearing to make sure I understood the terms of reference for the inquiry

– especially since the FSS had legal representation – and to assure him that we were keen to be as helpful and constructive as possible. There was going to be no crowing over our 'success' in the case. When an error has been made in a forensic investigation, the only thing that matters is finding out why things went wrong, then ensuring that safeguards are put in place so the same thing can't happen again.

Unfortunately, however, the subsequent hearing was a nightmare. As well as Alan Rawley and Brian Caddy sitting around a large table, there was a senior QC assisted by a junior acting for the FSS, and a senior manager from the FSS who was there to advise them. And what very quickly became apparent was that the people from the FSS had no intention of being constructive.

The most significant evidence to have been missed by the FSS was blood on two items of clothing, including the nine-millimetre stain on Danny Preddie's trainer. What's more, there had been a textile fibre embedded in the blood that helped to confirm its significance to the case.

We didn't meet the original scientists at the inquiry, but being a forensic scientist myself, I had great sympathy for them, and was keen that they shouldn't be left to take all the blame, which is what usually happened in those sorts of circumstances. No forensic scientist works on their own; they are always part of a team. And it seemed clear to me that the failure was likely to be related to training, or checking, or management of work going through the lab, or all three. So it was important to discover what it was before other cases were damaged in the same way.

The proceedings ended up being completely dominated by the FSS's QC, who was particularly aggressive towards one of our examiners when she was explaining how we'd done certain things. I couldn't do anything about it, particularly because the QC suggested that I had told her precisely what to say. So if I *had* interrupted, I'd have proved his point.

I had taken the precaution of bringing our in-house company lawyer with us, but she was unused to this sort of thing and didn't open her mouth. And although Ros and April were very good, neither of them was put under the same sort of pressure. Unsurprisingly, the examiner was in floods of tears afterwards, and periodically over the next few months thought about leaving the profession altogether, which would have been a huge shame.

When Rawley's report came out, it found that there had been no systemic failure by the FSS, and congratulated them on the 'excellent' standards they set. There were recommendations, but I think they just needed to ensure that their staff stuck to their procedures and didn't invent a whole load more. There were also some recommendations relating to the role of the Forensic Regulator, which were relevant. But I was glad, at least, that the individual scientists weren't made to shoulder the blame, although I did vow afterwards to be much more careful about agreeing to take part in any future independent Home Office inquiries!

Ultimately, the only thing that really mattered was that Damilola's family finally had some answers to the questions they must have had about his death, and that those responsible for it had been brought to justice.

28

New challenges

Around the time I left LGC Forensics, it was announced that the FSS would be closing down. There was *no one* in the forensics industry who thought it was a good idea – even competitors like us. Because as well as being by far the largest supplier of forensic services at the time, the FSS was obviously a strong and reliable organisation. It could, and should, have been modernised and made properly commercial several years earlier, in the same way LGC had been under its chief executive Richard Worswick. I'd thought the FSS had finally found someone who was capable of doing that in its last CEO, Simon Bennett. But the Home Office had clearly run out of patience with the £2 million losses it was reported to be making every month.

The irony is that it was partly the 'extracurricular' demands placed on the service by the Home Office, in terms of doing research and sitting on advisory panels etc., that contributed to its dire financial straits. The FSS had been happy to go along with those demands, because they gave them a substantial commercial advantage over other suppliers and enabled them to dip their hands into the government's back pockets from time to time – £50 million had apparently been injected into it as recently as

2009. But the writing had been on the wall for a long time, and they should have read it.

I knew when I left LGC Forensics that the company was doing well and had proved it could handle anything, including the most high-profile and complex criminal cases. In some instances, it had succeeded where the FSS had been shown to be lacking. So when the FSS finally closed its doors in 2012, it was no surprise that LGC became the lead supplier of forensic services in England and Wales, and the largest independent supplier of forensics in Europe.

Part of the agreement that was made when I left LGC Forensics was that I would be locked out of the UK forensic-science market for a year. Chris Gregg and I had recently been working on an opportunity to train some Libyan scientists, which I think LGC had always been a bit doubtful about. So they were probably quite glad to hand it over to us when we suggested it might form the basis of our new company, Axiom International. Also, it gave LGC the opportunity to make a new deal with me, and as well as being locked out of the UK market for a second year, I was forbidden to have any contact with six named UK forensic companies. One of those six companies was 'my own', Forensic Access. But we reckoned it would be worth it. So, despite the fact that it had never been part of any master plan, our sights were then firmly set on the overseas market.

We were extremely lucky to be able to persuade Lord John Stevens to become our chairman. And what we particularly focused on was seeing if we could help other authorities with their law enforcement and forensic-science challenges, using all the lessons we had learned in the UK over the past few decades. We didn't have any premises when we set up the new company. All we had was a large barn near Abingdon, part of which we quickly converted to accommodate a very small core of administrative and scientific staff.

I'd forgotten how difficult it is to set up a company from scratch. Don't they say that you tend to remember more of the good bits of your life than the bad, and that the older you get, the better you are at it? Whatever the reason for it was, I found myself having to learn all over again some of the excruciating lessons I'd learned when setting up Forensic Access and then Forensic Alliance.

The contract Chris and I had brought with us from LGC involved designing and running a massive training course to turn 107 Libyan scientists into forensic scientists. Having lost our intimate connection with LGC, we had to find another large partner to enable us to deliver it. Huddersfield is Chris's home town. And during his previous life with West Yorkshire Police, he had become very well acquainted with the University of Huddersfield, which provides quite a lot of police training for the West Yorkshire force. So he approached them to see if they would be interested in supporting us, and was introduced to the Professor of Diagnostic Engineering and Pro-Vice-Chancellor for Research and Enterprise, Andrew Ball.

With the full support of the Vice-Chancellor, Professor Bob Cryan, and of Professor of Enterprise and Entrepreneurship Graham Leslie, Andrew turned out to be absolutely brilliant, and effectively ensured that we had everything we could possibly need from the university. As well as labs and equipment, we had access to academic teachers and all the infrastructure required to look after 107 people, and their families, for the eighteen-month period we reckoned would be necessary.

Meanwhile, we would provide a wide range of operational trainers and organise specialist facilities for the students to gain first-hand experience of 'live forensics'. As a result of the collaboration, we were able to create a unique training course combining academic teaching and operational training. The academic teaching would ensure that the scientists understood the science behind forensic testing, while the operational training would enable them to deliver high-quality forensic services to their local police and courts. It was a plan that clearly impressed the Libyan authorities, and in what turned out to be a cold and snowy December in 2010, our first students began to arrive.

Before the course itself started, we gave the students six months of English-language training to get them all to the right level and ensure they could understand what they were being taught. Then we introduced them to the idea of forensic awareness, which covered the whole range of the forensic sciences and is something I'm very keen on. Although it's important for people to specialise in specific areas of forensic science – crime scenes, for example, or toxicology – they have to have some knowledge and understanding of the other areas. If they don't, they don't know how their part fits in, and they can't interface properly with all the forensic scientists working on other facets of a complex investigation. For the next part of the course, we split them up into thirteen different specialist groups and provided them with in-depth training in operational forensics. Finally, we gave them some multi-disciplinary, collaborative exercises and then individual research projects to do.

The course was a great success, with eighty-five of the one hundred and seven students achieving an MSc, forty-five with Merit, and twelve with Distinction. As I write, thirteen of those original students are just completing their PhDs with the university. So they turned out to be really great students. In fact, some of them were positively outstanding by any standards.

Our work with them didn't end there, however. The construction and development of a large new and permanent laboratory in Tripoli had been abandoned during the civil war of 2011. So, at the end of the course, we went with the students to Libya, where we spent the next five months helping them set up a temporary forensic laboratory and start using their new-found expertise to assist local police in solving real cases. I say 'we', but I didn't spend the whole five months there; I just dropped in and out as appropriate.

It was gratifying to see some of the immediate successes the Libyan teams had after they returned to Tripoli. In 2013, for example, they solved a case involving something of the order of sixty deaths and seven hundred instances of poisoning, which their toxicologists discovered were caused by methanol overdose from drinking some locally made alcohol. In another case, they demonstrated that some fires which had been put down to electrical faults were actually due to arson.

Over the months and years since then, we've been involved in an enormous number of projects related to strategic capacity and capability building, institutional reform and development of national security around the world. We've worked with overseas policing, national security and criminal justice authorities – both through their own governments and on behalf of the UK government, including in other parts of Europe, Africa, the Middle East, the Caribbean and Asia.

Some of our work has obviously involved forensic science, which has provided excellent new challenges for me to think about it in terms of what local police need and, just as importantly, what they can cope with. The experience I'd had about thirty years earlier when I went with Russell to advise on the lab in Nigeria was useful too, as it helped us to translate all those local requirements into the sort of laboratories that it would be best for people to build and the equipment they should order.

I wasn't someone who was easily shocked even before I'd spent forty-five years working as a forensic scientist. But something that has truly shocked me has been the waste of money I've seen in laboratories around the world. One of the main reasons for it is the procurement of equipment by people who know nothing about what it's going to be used for. As well as just wanting to make a quick sale and pocket the profit, there's often a tendency to think that the larger the kit and the more flashing lights there are on it, the better it is. As a consequence, I've seen instances of very expensive equipment being used as 'coffee tables' or gathering dust in some little-used parts of the building, simply because it isn't the sort of thing a forensic scientist would ever need, and even if it was, the local power supply wouldn't support it!

Other challenges relate to what sort of scientists the authorities need to employ. Not being forensic scientists, they need specific training and mentoring tailored to the local conditions, the types of crimes that are prevalent in the particular territory, policing and government priorities, and cultural values. They also need to be able to provide safe, reliable services, rather than some meaningless gloss that can actually promote and sustain miscarriages of justice. I mentioned earlier that forensic science is a very powerful tool. But it's also very dangerous if it isn't used properly. And that's true in all jurisdictions, however basic or advanced their forensic science might be.

In terms of casework, we have helped solve cases or address miscarriages of justice while working variously with the police, families and lawyers in many parts of the world. It's fascinating work, and it brings a whole new dimension to what we are able to do. Of course, some forensic scientists refuse to work in countries that have the death penalty, and you can understand why. But I take a different view, which is that if forensic science is going to be used at all, it had better be right, and if I can do anything to make that more likely, I should do it. And what I *can* do to that end is introduce approaches or types of testing that aren't available locally, or highlight shortcomings in technical performance or the interpretation of results.

One example of a case that illustrates the potentially critical, literally life-and-death effect of accurate forensic evidence involved the alleged murder of a Kuwaiti coastguard by an Iraqi fisherman. It was claimed that the fisherman – who was one of several in a boat that had apparently been fishing illegally off the coast of Kuwait – had shot a coastguard who boarded the vessel to apprehend them. The case against the fisherman included some ballistics evidence, which was said to show that the shot had been fired by someone on the fishing boat, and DNA evidence that allegedly proved the gun had been handled by the fisherman himself.

We were asked by the Iraqi Embassy in Kuwait to check the evidence and confirm, or question, its reliability. So the Axiom team spent some time in Kuwait examining relevant items, inspecting the local laboratory's records, and talking to the lawyers. The conclusion they came to was that the trajectory of the fatal shot showed that it could not have been fired from the fishing boat, but had originated from the water to one side of it. In other words, the shot must have come from the coastguard's own boat, thereby representing a 'friendly fire' incident. As far as the DNA was concerned, and taking into account the details of the case, it could simply have been transferred to the gun secondarily. Those explanations were apparently appreciated by the court, and the automatic death sentence that hung over the fisherman was commuted to life imprisonment. Sometimes, you have to accept that the best you can do isn't necessarily the ideal outcome. But it was an important case, in terms of a life being saved, and because it demonstrated the potential fallibility of forensic evidence and the danger of automatically accepting it at face value.

Among the many and varied cases Axiom has been involved with are several drug-trafficking cases in another country that has the death penalty, where we have been approached on each occasion by lawyers representing defendants. Every case has involved prosecution evidence from the official forensic-science laboratory, which is an agency of the government of that country. In every instance, we have been able to show that, because the laboratory hasn't been working to acceptable standards, there is considerable doubt about their findings and conclusions. And after our evidence has been accepted by the courts, the death penalty the crimes would have attracted has been commuted. I hope that, one day, we will be able to help the laboratory directly to produce more reliable results.

Examples of some of the other cases we've worked on at Axiom include being asked by a Dutch prosecutor to re-examine a house in the Netherlands for any evidence to suggest that it might have been one of a series of locations relevant to a violent crime that was being investigated. In another country, we've examined a range of historic documents and signatures in an attempt to establish the rightful heir to a venerable religious order. And we've worked on high-profile cold cases from Europe, Africa, the Caribbean and Mauritius on behalf of private industry, families and their lawyers, who are not satisfied that the police have got to the bottom of suspicious deaths or obvious murders.

Specialising in security and justice services in many parts of the world, particularly in fragile, post-conflict areas, Axiom is very unusual in having such a powerful forensic-science capability. We've been able to use it to very good effect to help not just with casework, but also with underpinning aspects such as assisting with the design, construction and equipping of local facilities, establishing intelligence databases and electronic case management systems, and training to international standards across a wide range of forensic disciplines. So I've been very pleased by the way things have turned out, and by the symmetry of it all – initially training in forensic science, support for the defence, support for the police, innovation and complex cases, and now providing services overseas.

All those years ago when I was happily collecting sea slugs on a beach on the Isle of Wight, I couldn't ever have imagined that, one day, I'd be a forensic scientist. Or that, in a way that's very unlike what's portrayed on TV and in films, I'd be fighting crime and injustice, not just in the UK, but in other parts of the world too. Let alone that I'd still be doing it when I was in my late sixties!

You might have thought that after forty-five years as a forensic scientist I'd have seen everything. But, of course, I haven't, because there is no end to the variety of individual cases. Besides, while there will always be a need for the sorts of things I've specialised in, because people will go on behaving in generally the same way, a new frontier is opening up – in cybercrime – and we need a new outlook, different skills and cutting-edge tools to fight it.

29

Looking ahead

Ever since my early days at the FSS, I have been passionate about forensic science. Every case is different and, at the time you're doing it, it's the most fascinating case you've ever worked on. Every complicated puzzle solved is a source of immense satisfaction. And every innovative approach you decide to take or new technique you develop or use is a reminder of the phenomenal power of science.

Forensic science has evolved considerably during the last forty-five years. So much so, in fact, that if someone does get away with committing a crime today, it's most likely to be as an indirect result of budget restrictions, rather than because they left no trace at the crime scene. Because if the police are able to put as much effort into each of their investigations as they'd like to, and if the forensic scientists have been properly trained and can get hold of enough contextually relevant evidential items, there's now a very good chance of solving most crimes.

Without doubt, DNA profiling has been the most significant development in forensic science during my career. The other big change has been the emergence of digital forensics, reflecting the universal and extensive use of digital devices of one sort or another, particularly mobile phones, personal computers and laptops, which have transformed our daily life, and CCTV, which records us living it.

Digital devices can provide incredibly useful evidence about who has been talking to whom, where they were at the time, where they've been recently, what they're interested in, what they've been buying, and so on. It's possible to watch CCTV recordings of people actually committing crimes, or coming and going to and from them. Sometimes this provides direct evidence of identity, and sometimes it tells you the best places to take samples for traditional analysis. But, like DNA profiling, it's not without its own challenges. In the context of digital forensics, those challenges relate to the mass of data that often has to be checked, and the time and costs associated with doing so. Pressures on police budgets, and the need to have enough suitably qualified people to do the work, inevitably place limits on those checks, and we've seen the impact on several individual court cases of gaps in the digital record. They are gaps that exist either because information wasn't searched for, or because it wasn't disclosed. And they have the potential to turn a case on its head and damage public confidence, both in forensic science and in the police/prosecution.

What also doesn't help matters these days are the streamlined forensic reports that were introduced a few years ago. SFRs were intended to be short, factual reports that would be produced early to assist investigators and prosecutors to identify and explore the potential for guilty pleas. The idea was that by providing a more proportionate approach to forensic evidence, they would reduce costs, bureaucracy and delays in the criminal justice system. Divided into two types, SFR1 reports present the bare bones of a case and are often compiled by non-scientists, while SFR2 reports do involve scientists but still only provide the facts of the evidence, with nothing about context.

When there is no challenge to an SFR1, it can be tendered as evidence. When there is such a challenge, an SFR2 has to be prepared. And this is where the problem arises, because it can be difficult, particularly for non-scientists, to identify what grounds there might be for a potential challenge. As a barrister told me recently, if lawyers aren't able to understand the specific grounds for challenging the evidence in an SFR1, they can't apply for the necessary funding. So what often happens is that the prosecution is content to rely on an SFR1 that contains scientific evidence – which might relate to a DNA sample, for example – that really needs to be looked at and considered in the particular context of the case. As a result, what was intended to be an efficient system has often turned out to be poorly understood and incorrectly applied, giving rise to general confusion and real risks to criminal justice.

Even more worrying over the past few years have been the substantial reduction in the number of items sent for examination, price erosion of 30-40%, and increasing reliance by the police on in-sourcing of forensic services – all as a result of budget cuts. During a similar period, the external market has shrunk from just under £200 million to around £60 million. Those factors, combined with having to pay service credits (fines) for missing what are often incredibly tight timescales, the rising costs of accreditation, and higher salaries to retain staff, have resulted in traditional suppliers of forensic services running at a loss or on the thinnest of margins. Also, with many forensic scientists now being recruited by academic institutions, we may end up being able to teach forensics but not practise it. All of which, together with an uneven tendering timetable – 75% of police work was tendered last year – and the large swings of work between suppliers under the 'winner takes all' model, has affected the stability and ultimate viability of the forensic market as a whole. Consequently, some suppliers have closed down altogether, while others have turned their backs on police work. In fact, one of the three main suppliers recently went into administration and had to be rescued by its police customers while it found a new backer. One wonders what the next chapter in this particular story holds.

What's forgotten about in all this is the fact that forensic science is a very cost-effective tool for helping to solve crime. You've only got to look at some of the big cases and compare the cost of endless re-investigations and public and other inquiries with the cost of the forensic science that finally helped solve them. Added to that is the human cost of enduring unnecessary extra years of misery before closure could be gained.

But one *really* important question that needs to be answered is whether it's appropriate for the police to be both hunting criminals and, at the same time, deciding what items from the crime scene, victim and suspect are going to be examined and for what; conducting all the necessary tests; then producing what is supposed to be impartial scientific evidence at court. Even if it doesn't actually matter in a particular case, there's always the risk, and therefore the perception, that it might. And in the minds of many people, 'perception is reality'.

Just the selection of which items to examine can influence the evidence that emerges. If you only look for certain things, you will only find certain things, and then cases are at risk of becoming self-fulfilling prophecies. One of the activities that is particularly popular with police – because it sounds fairly straightforward and tends not to need any very expensive equipment – is 'searching', i.e. examining items for evidence. But search-ing is actually one of the most critical aspects of the scientist's job, not least because it's the process during which evidence can be found or lost – or even, heaven forbid, 'created' if contamination risks are not kept strictly under control. Those dangers are further exacerbated if you also ignore context and report just the facts of your results without taking into account the individual context-ual circumstances of the case.

We now understand much more about cognitive bias, thanks chiefly to the work of Dr Itiel Dror and his colleagues at the Institute of Cognitive Neuroscience at University College, London. Put simply, cognitive bias usually occurs when aspects of prior knowledge subconsciously influence someone's judgements and conclusions. Its effects have been demonstrated in a series of experiments in which fingerprint examiners were presented with fingerprints from a crime scene and asked if they matched the prints of a suspect. What was consistently found was that the judgements of qualified and experienced examiners were influenced by whether or not the suspect had confessed to the crime. Even the same examiner could reach different opinions about the same mark when provided with different contextual information. We have certainly seen this in practice. In the Madrid bomb-ings, for example, the FBI positively identified Brandon Mayfield as having left a fingerprint that was found on a bag containing detonating devices. Not long afterwards, the Spanish authorities matched the print to the real bomber, who was an Algerian national. Confirmation bias – which is a type of cognitive bias – was listed as a contributing factor to the original misidentification. There have been cases closer to home too, and other experiments have found that cognitive bias applies equally well to DNA.

Another risk in the current forensic set-up is the fact that, despite a lot of progress, not all police scientific facilities are internationally accredited, and it may be difficult for those that *do* get accreditation to keep it. That isn't particularly surprising, because such accreditation is complex and expensive, both to achieve and to maintain. However, it does put external suppliers of forensic services at a commercial disadvantage compared with the police's own internal arrangements, as external suppliers are *obliged* to have accreditation, and therefore to bear the expense of it, before they can bid for police work.

The government-appointed Forensic Science Regulator, Dr Gillian Tully, has set deadlines for police facilities to gain their own accreditation. But some of those deadlines have come and gone, and because her role still lacks statutory teeth, there isn't a lot she can do about it. Obviously, accreditation isn't the answer to everything, but it does provide a necessary firm base on which to build. It also ensures that staff are trained, and that their systems and processes are up to the job and subject to continuous improvement.

Something that's of great relevance in the context of accreditation is a study of forensic science that was commissioned by the US Government from the National Academy of Sciences (NAS) in the wake of concerns that faulty science was leading to wrongful convictions. In its report in 2009, the NAS summarised its conclusions in a series of thirteen recommendations. Interestingly, these included the recommendation that forensic science should be removed from the administrative control of the police/prosecution. Also, support should be provided for research into the accuracy, reliability and validity of forensic sciences, and into human observer bias and sources of error. And there should be mandatory accreditation of all forensic laboratories and certification of all forensic practitioners.

With forensic effort in the UK divided between in-force facilities and external suppliers, and with a procurement system that splits activities down to their lowest common denominator for ease of commissioning and control, two things are happening. One of them is that work is often fragmented between different laboratories, which risks losing overall direction and coherency and makes it difficult to be sure that results have been interpreted properly. Sometimes, lawyers don't know which scientist should be answering the questions in court. Should it be the police scientist who saw the item in its original state? Or should it be the scientist who conducted some sophisticated testing on a sample from it? The fact is that neither of them will have the full picture. Ultimately, it's obviously up to the court to decide whether someone is guilty or innocent. But the task can be made more difficult than it should be if the evidence is fragmented.

The second effect is that testing is increasingly being focused on just a few types of analysis. So the range of choice one used to have for developing imaginative investigative strategies is progressively narrowing. And scientists are complaining of becoming 'de-skilled', as they term it, and of how the skills and expertise simply won't be there in the future when they're needed.

A really good example of one area that is disappearing before our eyes is textile fibres. Everyone wears clothes, and when one set of clothes comes into contact – especially forceful contact – with another, or with furnishings or car seats etc., tiny fragments of these fibres tend to be transferred between them. We would almost certainly never have found the blood (and DNA) evidence in the Stephen Lawrence and Pembrokeshire Coastal Path murders, for example, if we hadn't been looking for fibres.

Even when you've got a huge number of items, fibres can tell you which of them might be relevant to focus your attention on. They can also provide very good evidence in their own right. The problem is that because we still have to search, recover, analyse and compare fibres by hand, the work takes a long time and is therefore relatively expensive. Ironically, perhaps, we now have the technology to automate the whole process; we just need a bit of research money to adapt it for our specific purposes. But no supplier enjoys the necessary margins, or is going to risk the investment required in the current environment, to 'take a punt' themselves. And you can't blame them. Look what's happened so far with the lack of take-up of ParaDNA in the UK, for example. Although some research money *is* being provided by the government, most of it seems to be required by the police for forensics transformation programmes, which will enable them to in-source more forensic work. And so the downward spiral continues.

When I talk to police officers about the lessons I've learned during the many years I've worked as a forensic scientist, they always become animated and want advice about their specific cases. It's advice I'm very happy to provide, of course. But it's clear that as soon as they return to their day jobs, they become overwhelmed by the quantity of work they are expected to do and the cases go back into their pending trays. It's a situation with which anyone who ever worked at the FSS must be able to empathise!

One major concern about all of this is that, when re-investigating old cases, one of the types of samples that is most fruitful to search for in the archives is tapings. Yet fewer and fewer of them are being taken, even though it doesn't take long in the greater scheme of things. What that means is that when all else fails in our current cases – and it will – there won't always be a conveniently placed CCTV camera, or an offender arrested sufficiently soon for his mobile phone to be seized and examined. So we'll have nothing much to fall back on for re-investigation. That will obviously reduce our effectiveness in the future, and make it more likely that some miscarriages of justice will remain uncorrected. Then what will happen when the police are absolutely convinced of someone's guilt – as in the case of the Cardiff Three, or Colin Stagg, or, more recently, the retired Bristol school teacher Christopher Jefferies, who was wrongly suspected of having killed Joanna Yeates? Are we going to return to the bad old days of hunches, but – despite all our knowledge and skill – without the insurance policy of sufficient samples to test to expose those hunches for what they are?

Of course, many would argue that what's happening now, with more forensics being conducted by police, is simply a return to the status quo. But that isn't true. With the notable exception of fingerprints – which the police still deal with, for historical reasons – forensic science has always been an independent activity. Indeed, I remember how fiercely we guarded that independence in the FSS if ever it was questioned in court, as in, 'Of course, you would say that because you work for the police.'

The vast majority of forensic science in England and Wales was originally provided by the Home Office, and then it was all privatised. So it has never before been a police activity to the extent it is today. Interestingly, in Scotland, the reverse has happened, with the Scottish forensic laboratories now removed from the direct control of individual forces and placed instead under the Scottish Police Authority. In Northern Ireland, forensic services are administered by Forensic Science Northern Ireland (FSNI), which is an agency within the Department of Justice.

I should probably clarify my comments about the police by saying that they only relate to this one specific aspect of their activities. I have huge respect for the police service generally, for the work it does, and for many individual officers, like Steve Wilkins, who was responsible for the Pembrokeshire Coastal Path murder investigation, Brent Parry of the South Wales Police, who led the successful investigation into Lynette White's murder, and, of course, my partner in Axiom, Chris Gregg. Naturally, as with any other organisation, there are some members of the different police forces who leave a lot to be desired. And that matters, because they are in powerful positions. But, in my experience, the vast majority do a really good job, often in very difficult circumstances.

I've given a lot of lectures to various audiences, including senior police investigators, judges, lawyers, medics and university students. And when I spoke a year or so ago at an annual conference that's attended by senior investigators from every police force in the country, it was amazing how many people came up to me afterwards to describe a case they were working on and ask me what I'd do with it forensically – and there's always something. So there are clearly a lot of people who are very keen for there to be a much more imaginative and holistic approach to forensic science. But that's difficult to achieve when there's a wall of procurement standing between investigators and forensic scientists, as there is now. That's why the minds of academics are currently occupied with aspects such as the way the system works, cognitive bias, and the risks of miscarriages of justice. And it's one of the reasons why I believe we shouldn't simply sleepwalk into what amounts to a police take-over, albeit because of the systems now in place and through no fault of their own.

I am definitely an optimist by nature, and I do believe that forensic science will find its way out of its current difficulties. But that won't happen – or certainly not as fast as it should – if we all sit back and just hope that things will look after themselves. Everyone needs to take an active interest in criminal justice. You never know when you might come up against it in an immediate and personal way – I don't mean by anything necessarily as dramatic as having murdered someone! But if you're in the wrong place at the wrong time, who knows what you might be suspected of. And suspicions and their after-math are quite enough on their own to wreck lives. So we all need to make our voices heard by those we have elected to represent us in the management of this most important aspect of our safety and freedom.

What would be ideal is a system that provides police with 'instant' forensics at the crime scene, but that is organised and managed independently, and doesn't cost too much. Such a system would not only be able to support them in their day-to-day work, it would also provide the capacity for them to be advised and/or challenged when things could and should be approached differently. Those services should include fingerprints, which are just another, specific kind of mark to a forensic scientist that is an integral part of mainstream forensic work and should be joined seamlessly with it. The Scottish system is apparently showing great benefits of this sort of joined-up approach.

Innovation needs some attention too, because over-competitive behaviour encouraged by police forces dealing with budget cuts has pushed prices too low for firms to be able to fund sufficient research and development on their own to enable them to keep pace with developments in the rest of the scientific world. So either an element for this will need to be included in prices, or separate funding for research and development will need to be made available, or more accessible, to suppliers, especially in areas with fast-changing technology such as digital forensics. Collaborative partnerships with academia should become the norm for this.

I appreciate that all of this is going in the opposite direction from recent trends, but something certainly needs to happen – and soon. There is a lot of 'rose-tinted thinking' about forensics, especially following the demise of the FSS. But I favour the market approach generally, because of the state the FSS got into and the dramatic positive impact competition had on the cost of services and innovation when it was introduced. What I dread is some superficial research which suggests that things started to go wrong in about 2012, then assumes it was because of the closure of the FSS, and concludes that we need to re-create it. We should be in no doubt that, splendid though the FSS was in many ways – remember that I'm a product of it myself – it became arrogant and complacent, dictating to police what they were going to get and when. Until, eventually, it was far easier than it should have been for a new supplier that knew what it was doing to show a better way.

Before we leave the subject, let's just think about profits. There's a widespread belief that any commercial organisation is only interested in making massive profits it can share with its shareholders. Never in all my time in the forensic business have there been any profits to share in this way: they have all been ploughed back into the businesses. And we don't expect to make much in the way of profit anyway, from what is, essentially, a privately run public service.

The public has a lot to worry about, and it's understandable that forensic science is probably quite low on most people's list of concerns. But I do wonder if they wouldn't be a little more anxious about it if they realised the police are increasingly responsible for providing the 'impartial' forensic-science evidence that supports their prosecutions. There will always be risks of cognitive and other forms of bias. My concern is that we're currently taking more of those risks than we need to.

By and large – with the exception of some horrible miscarriages of justice – our system has worked reasonably well. But we can't rest on our laurels. Things are changing, and as the American philosopher George Santayana said, 'Those who cannot remember the past are condemned to repeat it.' So don't let's sleepwalk into what we can predict now will be further miscarriages of justice, for which individual forensic scientists caught up in the system will inevitably shoulder all the blame. Let's make sure our forensic science remains robust, transparent, logical and balanced, as the Association of Forensic Science Providers recommends. Let's ensure that it's checked by a properly qualified independent forensic scientist on behalf of the defence if it's critical to the case. And let's also make sure that we don't lose any of the essential skills we've spent years acquiring – in relation both to specific types of evidence and to how to knit them together to create effective investigation strategies, which have been so successful in solving so many of our most complex cases in recent times.

30

The Pembrokeshire Coastal Path murders

Between the ages of seventeen and twenty-one, John Cooper had been charged with carrying an offensive weapon, TWOC (taking without consent) of a motor vehicle, assaulting a police officer, being drunk and disorderly, and ABH (assault occasioning actual bodily harm). Then he got married, had children, and seemed to settle down.

Cooper must have been in his thirties in 1978, when he won £90,000 in a Spot the Ball competition. Although it was a huge amount of money at the time, it apparently wasn't long before it had all been spent and gambled away. Then, in 1983, there was a burglary not far from his home in Wales, followed by two robberies in 1985, another burglary in 1986, another in 1988 ... By the time he went to prison in 1998, Cooper had committed thirty burglaries and a violent armed robbery.

During the years when he was burgling and robbing his neighbours in Pembrokeshire, some even more serious crimes were committed in the area. Eight years into his prison sentence, LGC Forensics – which was the company I was working with at the time – was asked by Detective Chief Superintendent Steve Wilkins to participate in Operation Ottawa. Newly arrived at Dyfed Powys

Police from Merseyside Police, and suspecting Cooper might be linked to some of the serious crimes, Steve had set up the operation to look into them. The ones we were asked to review were two cold-case double murders and a multiple sex assault at gunpoint that had taken place in Milford Haven.

The first murder involved the deaths just before Christmas in 1985 of brother and sister Richard and Helen Thomas, both of whom were in their fifties. It was a fire that brought emergency services to their isolated farmhouse, Scoveston Park. Helen's badly burned body was found on the ground floor among debris that had fallen with it from the bedroom above as a result of the fire. Richard's was discovered on a half-landing on the first floor.

Because they both had gunshot wounds, it was thought at first that they'd died as a result of murder/suicide. Then a mud-stained blanket near Richard's body and a pool of blood with three cartridge pellets in an outhouse raised the possibility that he had been shot in or near the outhouse, then wrapped in the blanket and dragged back to the main house through the dirt. But despite a concerted effort by police to catch the killer, the case hadn't been solved.

Four years later, husband and wife Peter and Gwenda Dixon were murdered just a few miles away on the Pembrokeshire Coastal Path. The Dixons, who were also both in their fifties, had arrived for their usual camping holiday in Little Haven on Monday 19 June 1989. Ten days later, on Thursday the 29th, they left their tent to dry out at the campsite while they set off for a last walk along the coastal path. They apparently intended to drive back to their home near Oxford later that day. But when they didn't return to work as expected on the Monday, their son rang the owner of the campsite, who reported them missing to the police. Almost a week after they'd last been seen, their bodies were found, partially concealed by broken branches and vegetation, in undergrowth on a flat strip of land at the edge of a precipitous cliff next to the coastal path.

Gwenda had been shot twice at close range. The disturbance to her clothing immediately suggested that she had also been sexually assaulted. Peter's body – fully clothed – was discovered nearby, very close to the edge of the cliff. His hands were tied behind his back with a length of grey polyethylene rope and he had been shot three times, also at close range.

Robbery seemed to have been the main motive for the attack, and whoever had killed the Dixons had obviously searched their rucksacks and stolen Peter's wallet. The killer must also have obtained the PIN number for at least one of Peter's bank cards, because money was taken out of his account at four different cash machines in three towns after the couple were last seen alive on 29 June.

A police appeal for information resulted in a witness giving a detailed description of a man he'd noticed acting strangely while withdrawing money from one of the cash machines. The resulting artist's impression was of a man with collar-length hair, carrying a rucksack and wearing walking boots and knee-length, khaki-coloured shorts. In fact, he was a man who bore a close resemblance to someone who had been seen by other witnesses using a bank card at other locations during the same period.

By the time the bodies were discovered, hot weather had hastened the process of decomposition, making

DNA evidence very difficult to find. And despite a huge police effort, no suspect was identified.

The third unsolved case that had baffled Dyfed Powys Police involved an attack seven years later on five young people in Milford Haven. The teenagers were walking through a field when they were approached by a man who demanded money, then held them at gunpoint while he sexually assaulted one of the girls and raped another. The attack left all five of them deeply traumatised. But because their assailant had been wearing a balaclava, they were unable to describe him. One thing they did mention, however, was that his gun seemed to be covered in black paint, which was a detail that probably had no apparent significance at the time.

After reviewing the three cases, Steve Wilkins was convinced John Cooper was a prime suspect. And it was because Cooper would soon be eligible for release from prison that Steve asked us, in 2006, to look particularly at the murders of Peter and Gwenda Dixon.

'We've got a lot of circumstantial evidence that implicates Cooper,' Steve told me. 'We just need one golden nugget of independent, impartial scientific evidence.'

'Which you may or may not get,' I can remember thinking. 'Because you may or may not be right about him.'

It was only DNA Steve wanted us to look at, because it can provide such statistically strong evidence. So I set a really good team of scientists in our lab at Risley on the case, who looked in all the obvious places: the rope that had been used to tie Peter Dixon's hands behind his back; his belt; items of Gwenda's clothing that had been pulled down or pushed up; and swabs that had been taken from their bodies. The task was made more difficult than usual because of the state of decomposition of the bodies. And when we weren't getting anywhere with our investigation, we decided we needed to begin to look for other types of evidence.

As mentioned in relation to several other cases described in this book, we had learned from experience that textile fibres from clothing, for example, which are usually transferred when people come into contact with one another, can sometimes lead you to DNA, as well as providing useful evidence of the contact in their own right. But perhaps we didn't explain that well enough when we told the police about our concerns. Or maybe we weren't sufficiently convincing. Because they continued to be adamant that they were only interested in DNA.

The first indication I had that there was any problem with our side of the investigation was when Steve phoned me one day and said, in effect, 'You've had this case for eighteen months and you haven't found anything. I'm going to take it off LGC Forensics and give it to someone else.'

We'd had so many successes by that time – both with cold and current cases – that I knew there must be a reason why we apparently hadn't made any progress. So, having talked to my colleagues at Risley about precisely what had been going on, I arranged to meet with Steve.

I have to say that it was one of the most difficult meetings I'd ever had with police. There was a whole bunch of them, and they were all uniformly hostile. But after I'd explained that we were in a DNA straitjacket, which we clearly needed to break out of if we were going to find a way into the case, Steve eventually agreed that we could have a bit more latitude and a bit more time.

I could understand why he was so fed up with us. If Cooper *had* committed the four murders and the sexual assaults, as the police strongly suspected he had, a violent killer was about to be released back into their community. So, with Steve's agreement, we widened our forensic investigation, starting specifically with textile fibres. I selected Roger Robson for the job – as I knew he wouldn't leave any stones unturned – and his inestimable wife, April, to lead on the searching.

As usual, we looked to the crime scene to help us prioritise our search. And almost immediately we started to find blue acrylic fibres on the branches used to hide the bodies and on Peter Dixon's belt. As we knew the offender must have handled those branches extensively, it looked as though he had been wearing gloves, which might be another reason why we'd been having so much trouble finding any 'foreign DNA'.

All the burglaries that had been linked to Cooper had taken place within a radius of a couple of miles or so from where he lived. And part of his MO had been to discard in the hedgerows along the fields as he walked home any jewellery he didn't think was worth selling, items of his own clothing – his offending gear – and, presumably, anything else he didn't want. Among the clothing that had been found were a black balaclava, a brightly coloured fleece jacket, and a large number of gloves, several of which had been knitted from blue acrylic fibres. One of the gloves was made of fibres that matched some of the fibres on the branches and on Peter's belt, and other fibres were so similar we thought they were probably from its missing pair. It was the breakthrough we'd been waiting for. I don't know how impressed the police were, but we knew at that point that we ought to be able to open up the case.

It's funny how one remembers the unique numbers given to identify individual items that become really important in a case. The number for the glove was BB109. I'm sure some of my colleagues still remember it too. In the end, we also found BB109-type fibres on Peter's shorts, jumper and leg tapings, as well as on exposed parts of Gwenda's body and her sweatshirt.

The brilliant thing about adhesive tapings is that they can pull off anything and everything from the surface of an item – textile fibres, glass, paint, hairs, blood and semen. And it was while we were examining the tapings from a pair of shorts that had been found on top of a cupboard in the kitchen of Cooper's house for textile fibres that we noticed a tiny flake of blood.

DNA profiling of the flake of blood on the taping produced a full profile, which matched Peter Dixon's. The probability of obtaining a matching profile had the blood come from someone other than or unrelated to Peter Dixon was less than 1 in 1 billion. But before we told anyone what we'd found, we had another look at the shorts – this time painstakingly with a microscope – and discovered the stain from which the flake must have come, which we also profiled. The result we got from the tiny blood stain on the back of the left leg of John Cooper's shorts was similar but slightly less complete. Even so, the chance that it had come from someone other than Peter Dixon was 1 in 480 million.

When the results came in from DNA profiling of the blood, I phoned Steve Wilkins.

'I'm in the car,' Steve said. 'How are things going?'

'Why don't you pull over and call me back,' I suggested. 'Then I can tell you where we've got to.'

He was obviously just expecting an update of what we'd been doing. So it was very satisfying when he phoned back a few minutes later to hear the elation in his voice and the sound of his fists thumping the steering wheel as I told him, 'I think we may have found your golden nugget.'

When Cooper was arrested in 2009 and questioned about the shorts, he apparently claimed that his son would often wear his clothes. But further forensic testing revealed only his DNA on a handkerchief that was submitted with the shorts and had presumably been in a pocket, and his own and his wife's DNA in a mix of semen and vaginal secretions in the fly area of the shorts. So it was a fair assumption that he was the wearer, not his son.

Another piece of evidence Cooper disputed was that he bore any resemblance to the artist's impression of the man using the bank card at various locations shortly after the Dixons' bodies were found. His main point of contention was that he had never had shoulder-length hair like the man in the drawing. But it turned out that Cooper had appeared on a national TV programme called *Bullseye* just a month before the Dixons were killed. And when a journalist managed to track down the footage, Cooper's hair was almost exactly the same length as it was in the sketch.

Another item we were very interested in was a sawn-off shotgun that had been found in a hedgerow during the burglary investigations. A tiny screw was missing from the gun, and one of precisely the right type had apparently been discovered in sweepings from a shed at Cooper's house, and had formed part of the evidence that had secured his previous conviction. Also, the barrel of the gun was painted black.

The police had stored the gun in a bag. And when we looked under a microscope at some flakes of paint that had been retrieved from the bottom of the bag, some of them appeared to have a reddish cast to them, which tested positively for blood. When we scraped some more of the black paint off the gun, we found blood on the surface that produced a partial DNA profile with less than a 1 in 1 billion chance of being from someone other than or unrelated to Peter Dixon.

Meanwhile, we had amassed a large number of textile-fibre links, variously connecting BB109 and other gloves, the balaclava and fleece jacket found in the hedgerows with gloves found at Cooper's home address and with sweepings from his shed floor. Pockets are good places to look when you're examining items of clothing some time after an event, because they pick up fibres from hands and retain them when most surface fibres could be expected to have fallen off. What we found in the pocket of Cooper's shorts were two types of polyester fibres.

Most of the clothing Richard Thomas was wearing at the time of his death had been consumed or irretrievably damaged by the fire at Scoveston Park in 1985. But part of one of his socks had escaped the flames, and the fibres in Cooper's pocket turned out to match two types of fibre that had been collected from the sock.

There were also strong textile-fibre links with the two girls who had been sexually assaulted in Milford Haven. These included fibres found on the inside of the girls' clothing that could have come from a pair of gloves discovered in a hedgerow, and other fibres transferred in the reverse direction, from the clothing to the gloves. There was even a single fibre that could have come from BB109, which dropped off one of the girls on to the sheet of paper on which she stood during her subsequent medical examination. There were also links between the gloves and the armed robbery for which Cooper had already been convicted – including with the gun found in a hedgerow that was used in it.

We had extremely strong scientific evidence that it was Peter Dixon's blood on the shorts. But this was slightly clouded by the fact that, although similar, the shorts worn by the man in the artist's impression appeared to be longer. So we looked at Cooper's shorts again. And when we examined them more closely, we realised they had been re-hemmed since manufacture. It was a very neat job, but it had clearly been done domestically – perhaps by Cooper's wife, who had worked as a seamstress.

When we unpicked the hems of the shorts, we found a small, rather odd-looking stain that contained blood and something else, possibly some sort of mucus or nasal secretion. We tested the stain using our most sensitive DNA techniques, DNA SenCE – LGC's version of the enhancement technique we had first developed with Cellmark – and thirty-four-cycle STR as an additional check. What we found was that the DNA in the stain inside the hem of Cooper's shorts was mixed, but contained all the elements of DNA from the Dixons' daughter, Julie.

As well as having regular meetings with the police, we were keeping them updated with written reports, and they were clearly pleased with the progress we were making. However, when we explained to them and, particularly, the prosecution lawyers what we had found in the upturned hem of the shorts, we were told angrily, 'That's completely preposterous. We suggest you go away and do the tests and calculations again.'

But although the new evidence might have seemed unlikely, science doesn't lie – and truth really can be stranger than fiction. So we knew that what we actually had to do was find an answer to the question, '*Why* would Julie Dixon's DNA be on John Cooper's shorts when she hadn't been anywhere near him or near the coastal path where her parents' bodies were found?'

Our tests had shown that some components of the stain in the turned-up hem of the shorts were from a 'person unknown'. In view of the criticism that was levelled at us, we'd enlisted the help of one of the best-known statisticians to specialise in forensic DNA, David Balding, to give a second opinion. And having confirmed that our conclusion was correct, he stated that, 'The DNA profiling results for the SenCE profiling system . . . are 990 million times more likely if Julie Dixon and one unknown female unrelated to her are the sources of the DNA . . . than if the sources are two unknown females unrelated both to each other and to Julie Dixon.' So we looked again at the evidence related to the crime scene, to make sure we hadn't missed anything there.

We already knew that the Dixons had been shot at close range and that their killer would have had to manhandle their bodies to get them into the positions in which they were found. And that would have been difficult to do without getting some of their blood on his own clothing. The photographs that had been taken at the crime scene showed the bodies in the undergrowth, the couple's open rucksacks, and various items that had been taken out of them. Some of the items that were scattered on the ground near the bodies appeared to be spare clothing they must have been carrying with them. So, what if the shorts had belonged to one of the victims, and when Cooper found them while he was searching through their rucksacks looking for money and bank cards, he decided to swap them for his own blood-stained shorts? That would certainly be a plausible explanation for the traces of DNA from their daughter, who lived with her parents at their home near Oxford. Then, if Cooper had taken the shorts back to *his* home and at some point his wife had re-hemmed them, he wouldn't even have known about the blood stain that had been concealed inside the new hem and was too small to have been at all obvious.

I'd chosen a DNA scientist called Phil Avenell to look after those aspects of the case. Phil is one of those people who isn't fazed by anything out of the ordinary. And not only did he do a really great job, he also withstood some severe criticism while the police and lawyers worked out that, far from undermining the critical evidence, what he'd found actually supported it.

One of the principles underlying any scientific investigation, forensic or otherwise, is not to be put off if things don't stack up, or if you find something you weren't expecting. Having checked and re-checked the results of the DNA tests, we knew the science wasn't wrong. Once the jury had been presented with all the evidence and possible explanations for it, it would be up to them to make up their own minds about it. Which is what they did at John Cooper's trial in 2011. After being found guilty of murdering Richard and Helen Thomas and Peter and Gwenda Dixon, of a serious sexual assault and five attempted robberies of the young people who had the misfortune to encounter him in the field, he was sentenced to life in prison.

31

On reflection

Looking back through many hundreds of case files while writing this book, I was struck by the fact that all the bits of hole-punched paper held together by green, metal-ended tags or in bulging blue-ring binders represent a large part of my life. When I was in my twenties, I always imagined I'd struggle to stay at work when I was 'old'. (Being old wasn't something I could imagine then. And I'm not sure now whether it's even 'a thing'!) I was quite convinced I'd retire by the time I was fifty-seven, as some of my colleagues did when the FSS hit a demographic and financial crisis. But now, here I am in my late sixties, still at it. I suppose it's because I continue to enjoy the challenges, no two of which are ever quite the same. I love the fact that, however old and complicated a murder case might be, I will have a whole raft of ideas about how to get to the heart of it. I love knowing that I'm surrounded by people who will have more, and probably better, ideas and who will know precisely what to do. And I like being able to walk into any failing forensic laboratory, anywhere in the world, and know instinctively what's wrong and how to put it right – like the Gordon Ramsay of Laboratory Nightmares, but a bit nicer about it, I hope, and without the swearing!

One of the things I enjoy most these days is seeing my younger colleagues develop their own professional personalities. I work with some extremely talented people, several of whom understand completely the holistic approach to forensic science that we've been developing all these years and that has proved to be so successful. After all, what can be more satisfying than helping to bring the guilty to account and sometimes, at the same time, exonerating the innocent?

The combination of that holistic approach and new technology can be truly amazing. One of my hopes for the future is for that to be properly recognised and nurtured. Because the alternative is that everything we've learned might be thrown on to the scrapheap of history in favour of much more mundane, less effective ways of doing things. Then the quality of investigations, and of justice, would be poorer – all for the sake of short-term financial targets that are focused on cost rather than value.

What worries me today – apart from all the things I've mentioned in Chapter 29 – is the thought that forensic scientists are no longer being trained to look and think more broadly, beyond their own increasingly narrow specialisms, and that the skills that made good holistic training possible are being lost. This makes it much harder to tackle new trends in crime – like the current wave of knife crime associated with drugs gangs, or the increasing sophistications of cybercrime – in the most imaginative and effective way.

I realise that one can usually pass on no more than about 10 per cent of what one's learned. Things are always changing, and new generations will inevitably want to try out their own ideas in their own ways. And, obviously, they must be encouraged to do that. What it means, however, is that an unnecessary amount of time is spent re-inventing the same old wheels. If only we could recognise when we have actually managed to build a first-class racer, we could then try to incorporate some of its essential elements into whatever we design next.

It was extremely difficult trying to choose just a few cases to write about from the thousands I've worked on over the years. Then someone asked me recently if there are any cases I'd like to have worked on but didn't. The answer is that one of them would definitely be the Madeleine McCann case. I don't know if we'd be able to find anything. But I haven't been impressed by what's been reported in the papers. It feels as though there's been too much focus on standard scenes of crime, and not enough on what one might be able to do with what remains – however little – in the laboratory.

Another crime scene I'd like to go back to is a remote farmhouse in Wales where Megan and Harry Tooze were shot and murdered in 1993. I went there some time later, after their daughter's boyfriend had been tried, found guilty of their murder, sentenced to life in prison, and subsequently had his conviction quashed by the Court of Appeal. I think the FSS at Chepstow did the original investigation, and I can't remember now why the police asked me to go there with them. Nothing apparently useful was found at the time in the way of evidence. But with all the experience and success we've had with cold cases since then, who knows now?

Maybe this book will help to highlight the fact that forensic science is not just about scenes of crime and scientists crouching in ditches, imagining things, which is the impression I think most people get from the TV.

Obviously that's where it all starts, and we do crouch in ditches, but it's usually to look at something more closely. Crime scenes are critical for informing what you might do next, and what you make of the detail of the results. But that's where most of the real skill comes in. That's the bit that's hard work, and the bit that's going to find the answers if the right questions have been asked. And it's the bit that gets left out of the crime dramas on television, in which the role played by forensic scientists becomes slightly distorted, for understandable, but ultimately misleading, reasons. Because the reality is that what happens in the laboratory involves days, weeks, months, sometimes even years of meticulous observation, intricate testing, looking down microscopes, refining strategies, writing reports, and discussing and agreeing next steps with police, with each stage designed to use as little of the precious budget as possible. But it's usually worth it, and, as I've already mentioned, always cost effective compared with the alternative of endless re-investigations of one sort or another, and the occasional public inquiry if things have gone badly astray.

The following are just some of the many lessons I've learned, specifically in relation to how to solve cold or complex cases, during all the years I've been involved with investigating them.

- Never assume that just because a good, experienced scientist worked on a case, any evidence that's there will have been found.
- Challenge historic expectations about what you might or might not find. Some of them are wrong.
- Always start with the crime scene, however long ago the crime occurred and however much the crime scene

might have changed in the intervening period. You need to understand it, and it's quite likely that no one else ever quite got to the bottom of it in the detail that's required.

- Remember that every contact really does leave a trace – it might just be difficult to find it. What has tended to complicate the issue historically is that we seem to have alternated between finding things that are too small for us to test, and being able to test things that are too small for us to find.

- Be imaginative about things to test and be tenacious in your search for them. (We had to return many times to the FSS archive when we were working on the cold-case murder of Lynette White, for example.)

- Invent new techniques if you need to. Even if it takes a bit of time, it will be worth it in the long run.

- Recognise when you may be on to something, however small and however unlikely, and make sure you investigate it thoroughly. This is hugely important.

- If you find one type of evidence, there are likely to be others.

- Beware of the 'too difficult' box – scrape the paint if you have to.

- Accept that truth is often stranger than fiction, and don't be put off when it looks like it is.

- Look outwards to the wider scientific community to get the full benefit of specialist knowledge and experience. But make sure this is presented in the right way – courts can't cope with boffins at close quarters!

- Take investigators on the journey with you – otherwise they'll probably try to stop you just a bit too soon.

- Maintain your independence, and don't get sucked into traditional or biased ways of thinking.

- When things don't stack up and the dogs aren't barking, find out why. There will be a reason, and it could be very important.

After forty-five years as a forensic scientist, I think the best career advice I could give anyone is to find something you really like doing. Once you've done that, your work automatically becomes your pleasure, and then your passion. And when that happens, you cease to notice the long hours and all the scary moments when you *have* to deliver what you've promised, by tomorrow, and it has to be totally accurate and *really* good, because someone's life might, quite literally, depend on it.

Acknowledgements

Throughout my career, I have been lucky enough to work with many of the UK's most talented forensic scientists. Some of them are mentioned in this book, but there are also many more to whom I owe a huge debt of gratitude for enriching my life in a whole host of ways – both personal and professional – and for providing me with the greatest possible level of job satisfaction.

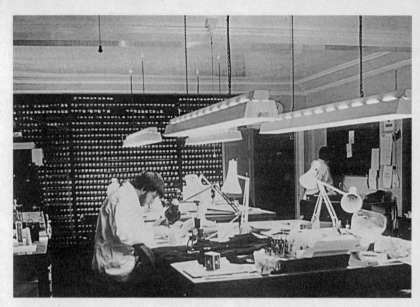

The biology search laboratory at the Forensic Science Service facility in Harrogate in the late 1970s. The wall at the back of the lab is lined with small, black-lidded glass jars that contained our reference collection of botanical samples such as seeds etc.

The crime scene in a park in Halifax, West Yorkshire, where Josephine Whittaker was murdered in June 1979. It was my second Yorkshire Ripper crime scene, and I was working as an assistant to the lead scientist, Alf Faragher.

The scaffolding under Blackfriars Bridge in London from which the body of the Italian banker Roberto Calvi was found hanging in 1982.

Four scientists doing what was referred to in the Home Office's Chepstow Report as 'just standing around' at a crime scene. What they're actually doing is making important observations about which areas to examine in detail, and what items to take back to the lab for examination.

Footwear marks in blood on a dark-coloured carpet that only became visible after treatment with luminol.

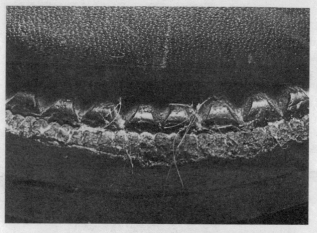

Hairs and flakes of skin embedded in the welt on the toe of a shoe that was collected as an evidence item from someone who was suspected of having kicked the victim of an assault.

A 'crime scene' set up by Forensic Alliance, for a competition at the Association of Chief Police Officers' annual conference in 2005.

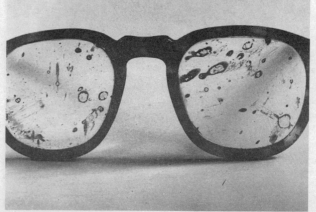

When police officers visited the house of a man they suspected of having been involved in a murder, he opened the door wearing these blood-spattered glasses.